JEWISH POLAND REVISITED

NEW ANTHROPOLOGIES OF EUROPE

MATTI BUNZL AND MICHAEL HERZFELD,
EDITORS

FOUNDING EDITORS
DAPHNE BERDAHL, MATTI BUNZL, AND MICHAEL HERZFELD,

JEWISH POLAND REVISITED

Heritage
Tourism in
Unquiet
Places

Erica T. Lehrer

INDIANA UNIVERSITY PRESS
BLOOMINGTON & INDIANAPOLIS

This book is a publication of

Indiana University Press
Office of Scholarly Publishing
Herman B Wells Library 350
1320 East 10th Street
Bloomington, Indiana 47405 USA

iupress.indiana.edu

Telephone orders   800-842-6796
Fax orders   812-855-7931

Manufactured in the United States of America

Cataloging information is available from the Library of Congress.
ISBN 978-0-253-00880-0 (cloth)
ISBN 978-0-253-00886-2 (pbk)
ISBN 978-0-253-00893-0 (eb)

1 2 3 4 5   18 17 16 15 14 13

FOR MY PARENTS—AND THEIR *NACHES*.
AND FOR ERYKA—
MAY SHE GROW TO KNOW THE BEST OF
POLISHNESS AND JEWISHNESS ALIKE.

Is it only the blood and ashes of the victims that will become the true bond joining Poland and the Jewish people? My impression is that this will not be the only bond but that, with the passing of time, the evidence of other bonds will become increasingly visible. Willingly or unwillingly, Poland will never be able to forget the Jews.

—Aleksander Hertz, *The Jews in Polish Culture*

CONTENTS

PROLOGUE: SCENE OF ARRIVAL

December 1, 1998
Kraków, Poland
8:45 PM

I climb the stairs in Mateusz's (temporarily my) shiny, as-yet-ungraffitied apartment block and step through the steel-reinforced, triple-bar winding-bolt door ("Israeli," Mateusz told me later, an almost prurient glint in his eye). On a nearby cabinet sits a lace doily on which two knitted *yarmulkes* (skull-caps) are decorously propped. They lean against a fragment of black granite tombstone in which Hebrew letters are chiseled; he has gilded them since my last visit. An old wooden packing box from a Jewish margarine concern sits on top of the refrigerator, emblazoned with a menorah and product informa-tion in Polish and Hebrew. Among antique Jewish books on the bookshelf are nestled a *yorzeit* (memorial) candle in a mass-produced Israeli tin can and a Hebrew-language Coke bottle. It's a mindfully atavistic aesthetic. It is elegant and cozy. It is also a bit strange.

Mateusz is not Jewish. But there was a time he wished he were. I am. I spent a lot of my life wishing I weren't, trying to escape a darkness and dis-comfort that were the principal inheritance of my line of Jewish descent. We met each other following a path of shards from the broken vessel of Euro-pean Jewishness, shattered in this part of the world in our parents' and grand-parents' generations. The tangible debris was strewn in fields with new own-ers; less concrete fragments were embedded in unlikely bodies.

I chuckle at the surrounding décor (after many trips to Poland, I can fi-nally laugh), flip up the glowing screen of my laptop, click to the fresh folder I had prepared entitled "Fieldnotes," and begin my scene of arrival in the field. I think of Malinowski—from Krakow, no less—father of modern anthropo-logical fieldwork methodology. Yet my "native informants," the Poles whose *imponderabilia* I am here to investigate, have assembled such displays of Jew-ish culture as part of their own cross-cultural expeditions.[1] As it turns out, I am equally their native. I am reminded of my very first trip to Poland in early 1990. For an American Jew—abruptly confronting her nationally and culturally cultivated blind spots—it was astounding in every way. First of all, it existed in color. There were young people, happy people. Flowers grew. But most of all, I recall discovering a menorah—one of the few Jewish ritual objects my family still used—on display in a Polish Catholic home. I ask its owner what it was and why he had it, and received a one-word response: "Artifact."

This word, uttered in this place at this time by this person, brought up a host of questions, none of them comfortable. Where did he get it? What does it mean to him? Is he really not Jewish? Does he deserve to have it? And, more quietly, but perhaps the real root of my discomfort, I felt the fineness of the line that separated his relationship to the menorah from mine. For me it was only barely alive, as my post-Holocaust, assimilationist American upbringing left me without the universe of ritual, meaning, and social ties that would animate it. But surely (my gut prodded me) a cultural world emanating however shallow a breath is still a world away from one in which the menorah would be an "artifact" (isn't it?). Surely I had a claim to that menorah, even if only as a relic, that this Polish Catholic man, however hospitable and generous, did not possess—didn't I?

My journey to Poland would put me in the company of tens of thousands of (mostly) American and Israeli Jews who would make similar trips that decade, unbeknownst to me at the time. The question of the Jewish "artifact," and larger ones of cultural ownership and sharing, destruction and recovery, memory and desire that it provoked, kept me coming back to Poland. While my renewed and inquisitive relationship to this place made me something of an anomaly among the masses of Jewish visitors, for whom visiting Poland is generally a one-time, pre-scripted, and self-consciously negative ritual, I also found that I was not completely alone. There were a few other Jews who lingered, a few for whom Poland felt like a truncated limb they couldn't go on without. But wherever I went in Poland in search of Jewishness, I also found Poles on their own searches. This overlap of searches, of losses, of longings for a Polish-Jewish place, is at the center of this story.

ACKNOWLEDGMENTS

I am indebted to many people for their support over my many years of anthropological education, field research, and the writing of this book.

First, my teachers and mentors: Jon Andelson at Grinnell College in Iowa inspired me to become an anthropologist with his enthusiasm, kindness, and nurturing instruction in the joys of theoretical thinking. His own teacher (and later mine) at the University of Michigan, the late Skip Rappaport, remains another role model for anthropology as a humane and humanistic discipline; he suggested to me the provocative if unpopular idea that if one ethnic group imagines itself to have cohabitated amicably with another in the past, perhaps they will be better equipped to do so in the future. Also at Michigan, Crisca Bierwert, Tom Fricke, Conrad Kottak, Bruce Mannheim, and Jennifer Robertson each opened my eyes to new ways of thinking about culture.

Janet Hart responded to my fraught e-mails from the field with equal parts reassurance that my feelings of chaos and confusion meant that I was a "real anthropologist" doing exactly as I should, and admonition (after graciously reading some of my field notes) to please not get into cars with any more crazy drivers. During the writing process, Andrew Shryock was a wry, sage, and welcoming voice, with an unusually open office door and a refreshing honesty about academia. His ability to do both fieldwork and public cultural work, and write brilliantly about both, remains an inspiration. Don Seeman, friend, mentor, and colleague, is a rare model of expertise in two different analytical worlds—anthropology and Judaism—and he infuses each with the other in rich and courageous ways. He looked on my project with particular engagement, stressing the importance of being true to one's vision and reminding me that he would be applying his own to mine when he would review this book. Barbara Kirshenblatt-Gimblett, whose work I had long admired, graciously agreed to serve as an external committee member. She is a force of nature, a one-woman institution, a connecter of people, and a generous mentor as I continue to follow paths of cultural inquiry and practice she has blazed. Ruth Behar, my main graduate advisor, gave me—and a cohort of other aspiring ethnographers—permission to examine the vast, generally unspoken sea of emotions that much ethnography traverses in its creation. She provided an example of professional possibility, blurring boundaries, exploring creative collaborations, and writing beautifully. If not for her, I never could have imagined the career I now have.

The University of Michigan, I realize more than ever in hindsight, was an incredible place to become an anthropologist. I was challenged in profound ways, vastly enriched by the intellectual offerings, and learned perhaps most of all from my amazingly dedicated, interesting, and energetic fellow students. My fellow travelers in the "Live Anthropologists' Society," Luke Bergman, Summerson Carr, Severin Fowles, and Karl Steyaert, were my first mentors in the art of possibility. The writing group "The Termites," including Meghan Callaghan, Doug Rogers, and Genese Sodikoff, offset anxiety with good food and cheer and was essential for getting the dissertation done. Ray Silverman welcomed me to the Museum Studies Program, offering a new context for thinking about public heritage, and Julie Ellison, Kristen Hass, and David Scobey provided models of publicly engaged scholarship; Julie continues to inspire me with her championing of hope as a political sentiment. At Michigan I also benefitted immensely from the vast array of resources the university provided for creative and professional development. These included a luxurious year as a graduate fellow at the University of Michigan Institute for the Humanities in 2001–02, and one more at the Gayle Morris Sweetland Writing Center in 2003–04. Stefan Senders at Sweetland was a true gem, smart in just the ways I needed.

My graduate training and research were also supported by a USIA Fulbright Dissertation Research Scholarship, an IREX Individual Advanced Research Grant, a Kosciuszko Foundation Tuition Scholarship, an American Council of Learned Societies Summer Language Study Grant, an American Academy for Jewish Research Graduate Seminar, and a Junior Scholars' Training Seminar in East European Studies sponsored by the Woodrow Wilson International Center for Scholars and the American Council of Learned Societies.

Generous postdoctoral fellowships in 2005–06 at the Illinois Program for Research in the Humanities at the University of Illinois at Urbana-Champaign and in 2006–07 when I was the Hazel D. Cole Fellow at the Jackson School for International studies at the University of Washington in Seattle allowed me time to research, write, discuss, think, and grow, surrounded by gifted and generous scholars such as (at UIUC) Edward Bruner, Matti Bunzl, Alma Gottlieb, Brett Kaplan, Martin Manalansan, Ellen Moodie, Bruce Rosenstock, Michael Rothberg, and Helaine Silverman, and (at UW) Laada Bilaniuk, Susan Glenn, Noam Pianko, Sarah Stein, and Janelle Taylor.

A number of people took precious time to read parts or drafts of my developing manuscript. These include members of the Jewish Identities reading group at Concordia University's Centre for the Interdisciplinary Study of Society and Culture (especially Norman Ravvin); Concordia's Centre for Ethnographic Research and Exhibition in the aftermath of Violence Post-Conflict Studies reading group (especially Mark Beauchamp, Shelley Butler, Cynthia Milton, Monica Patterson, Matthew Penney, Joseph Rosen, Margo Shea, Anna Sheftel, and Stacey Zembrycki). Other sympathetic readers include Claire Rosenson at the United States Holocaust Memorial Museum, Mark Kramer at Boston University, Michele LaFrance at the University of Washington, and Carol Berger at McGill University. Michael Meng at Clemson University has turned into a particularly enthusiastic colleague, whom I thank for being an exceptional critical reader and co-organizer in 2010 of a United States Holocaust Memorial Museum Center for Advanced Holocaust Studies summer workshop, "The Politics of Jewish Spaces: Interdisciplinary Perspectives on Preservation, Memory, and Renewal in Post-Holocaust Poland." Monica Patterson merits a category all her own, for her brilliant interventions, tireless word-smithing, and gently ribbing commentary on my prose.

It is hard in fieldwork to distinguish among research interlocutors, friends, and even kin, especially as individuals often change categories over the years these projects may take. Many people were integral as helpful, kind, patient sources of information, opportunity, and good company. In Krakow: Joachim Russek at the Center for Jewish Culture, Robert Gądek there and later at the Festival of Jewish Culture (with its director, Janusz Makuch), Wojciech Ornat at Klezmer-Hois, Marek at Noah's Ark café, Artur Modziejewski at the (former) Brother Albert House, Jonathan Orenstein at the Jewish Cultural Center (JCC), Allen Haberberg at Hotel Eden, and the late Henryk Halkowski, everywhere. In Warsaw: Andrzej Folwarczny of the Center for Dialogue Among Nations, Kostek Gebert, Staszek and Monika Krajewski, and Rabbi Michael Shudrich. In Israel: Jacek Olejnik at the Polish Embassy in Tel Aviv. In Canada: Elie Rubenstein of the March of the Living.

A few people watched me "grow up" in Poland; as I wended my way from an awed college student to a professor, they turned from patient cultural shepherds to cherished colleagues: Sławomir Kapralski, Michał and Janina Galas, Jonathan and Connie Webber. Some of us grew into our professional roles together, turning from fellow students (or ethnographic subjects) to professional scholars: Ania Cichopek, Magdalena Waligórska, Monika Murzyn-Kupisz. Other people I am happy to have intersected with both in and out of Poland over the years include Jonah and Rachel Bookstein, Dorota Głowacka, John Hartmann, Jack Kugelmass, Jessie Labov, Ewa Malachowska-Pasek, Anna-Maria Orla-Bukowska, Shana Penn, Antony Polonsky, Michael Steinlauf, Michael Traison, and Josh Zimmerman. In this category are also Faye and Julian Bussgang, parents of a childhood friend; I reconverged with them in adulthood around our shared fascination with Jewish-Polish issues. Friends have also made me feel at home *w Polsce:* in Krakow, they include Norman Jacobs, Sebastian Molski, Basia Pasek, Bartek/Natanel Radziemski-Migura, Karen Underhill, and especially Wiola Szczepocka, whom I admire deeply. In Warsaw, I am glad to know Michał Bilewicz and Kasia Zarnecka. Steven and Niki Rousso-Schindler came to Poland with me during my fieldwork to film, and Hannah Smotrich and Stephanie Rowden accompanied me there to create an experimental exhibit. Their fresh eyes, eagerness for adventurous collaboration, and willingness to be infected by my personal obsessions and translate these into unique forms brought me new energy and insights that have sustained and enlarged this ever-unfolding project.

Montreal and Canada have provided the final context in which this book was completed. I am grateful to the Canada Research Chairs program for an extraordinary faculty position, to my colleagues in Concordia University's History Department for embracing an anthropologist, and particularly to former Associate Dean Graham Carr and department chair Shannon McSheffrey for doing the necessary administrative acrobatics to secure me a semester free from teaching to get this book out the door. Current chair Norman Ingram has been a truly stalwart support. The late Roger Simon at the University of Toronto became an important influence and supportive new colleague and mentor.

Books pass through many invisible hands, which do essential work of shepherding, editing, formatting, and more. Kirsten Bohl and Kimberly Moore were instrumental, as was my editor Rebecca Tolen at Indiana University Press.

Other friends, fellow travelers, and family (professional and otherwise) who deserve special thanks not only for their generous and critical intellects, but also for their willingness to be leaned on in countless ways, include Matti

Bunzl, Laura Citrin, Jenny Gaynor, Lourdes Gutierrez-Najera, Carol Kidron, Ellen Moodie, Patty Mullally, Abdessalem Daghbouche, Yofi Tirosh, Sarah Womack, and Martin Zabron. Laura Landman, Eric Stein, Meredith Levy, Naomi Meyer, and especially Kristen McLean and Russell Mofsky (the Mc-Mofskys) provided soft places on which to land during my periodic returns to Boston. My brother, Damon, who took that first trip to Poland with me in April 1990, also belongs here (as, more recently, does my ever-ebullient sister-in-law Aimee LeBrun). My extended family—my late uncle Ron Goldstein and my aunt Sally, along with my uncle Fred Reif and my aunt Laura—has shown me love disproportionate to their small ranks. I have dedicated the book to my parents, Sherwin/Sam Lehrer and Liane Reif-Lehrer, for everything.

My colleague Magdalena Waligórska warned me that I am probably not going to agree with the politics of some people who will like my book and use some of its arguments for very different ends from those I intend. Her work on Poland's Klezmer music revival has pushed me to reflect anew on the very situated quality of ethnographic scholarship. I hope her book *Klezmer's After Life* will be read together with this one, for a fuller picture of the highly divisive topics we share.

I will inevitably fall short of doing justice in words to what the Jarden Jewish Bookshop, and its owners, Zdzisław and Lucyna Leś, have meant to me. The bookshop has been, over a period of years, the place I went first upon arriving in Krakow (often with baggage in tow), and the last place I visited before leaving for the airport to fly home. During countless hours spent there (often in the company of their dedicated, helpful, and convivial employees, including Ania, Ewa, Krzysiek, Magda, Małgosia, Marta, Paulina, and others), I have laughed, cried, ate, drank, worked, studied, napped, waited, planned, and talked and talked and talked. Zdzisław and Lucyna have seen me through birthdays and breakups—and now a book. They also conceived and are raising a beautiful daughter, whom to my great joy and honor they named Eryka. For me, she is proof of their recurring exhortation to me, "*będą z ciebie ludzie.*"

*   *   *

The issue of personal naming practices in ethnography is a difficult one. It has long been standard practice to employ pseudonyms to protect fieldwork subjects. Yet some now see these as flimsy, symbolic protection for authors, while disempowering subjects who may want their own personal and intellectual contributions to ethnographic works to be known. Kazimierz is also a unique site, as integral to my analysis as it is impossible to make anonymous, and many of its culture brokers are inevitably "public figures," at least locally, and thus their identities are difficult to obscure. Further, networks of texts today circulate among different publics under different circumstances with different potential consequences for those described—yet these networks increasingly overlap. Some of the people in this book also appeared in (and signed consent forms to be pictured and named in) video footage I recorded for a related film. Many of the individuals I describe have been written about publicly by other anthropologists or journalists—or have written about themselves—in relation to the issues I describe. It is possible they have also written about me, or may do so. The approach I have settled on involves erring on the side of providing a thin veil of privacy for all but the most public local figures, changing both names and occasionally personal details that might make someone more easily recognizable locally. I have weighed various factors—including the fact that much of my goal with this book has been to honor individuals who have done important work in public. I thus want to emphasize that without all of the individuals—both named and unnamed—who shared their experiences and aspirations with me, this book would not exist. I am, nonetheless, solely responsibility for its shortcomings.

* * *

An earlier version of chapter 4 was published as "Bearing False Witness? Vicarious Jewish Identity and the Politics of Affinity," in *Imaginary Neighbors: Mediating Polish-Jewish Relations after the Holocaust,* edited by Dorota Głowacka and Joanna Żylińska (Lincoln: University of Nebraska Press, 2007), 84–19; and chapter 5 as "Repopulating Jewish Poland—In Wood," *Polin: Studies in Polish Jewry* 16 (2003): 335–55.

JEWISH POLAND REVISITED

POLES AND JEWS: SIGNIFICANT OTHERS

With one culture, we cannot feel!

—SŁAWOMIR SIERAKOWSKI IN YAEL BARTANA'S 2009 FILM *MARY KOSZMARY (NIGHTMARES)*

Kazimierz, Krakow's historically Jewish quarter, is one among a number of iconically Jewish spaces that have been "put back on the map" across the new Europe, in places where Jews lived in concentration before World War II and sometimes long before: Berlin's Scheunenviertel, Paris's Le Marais, Bologna's "Il Ghetto," Prague's Židovské město (Josefov), and other pockets in Vilna, Lvov, Czernowitz, and elsewhere. Despite Poland's minuscule contemporary Jewish population (estimates from the decade ending in 2009 vary from about 5,000 to 20,000 among 40 million Poles), in the past fifteen years the country has seen a profusion of Jewish-themed events, venues, and sites.[1] Significant efforts at the state level to remake Poland's Jewish heritage through museums, monuments, and commemorations have emerged. Jewish conferences, ceremonies, memorials, performances, festivals, and other events in Poland outstrip public programming in countries with much larger Jewish communities.[2]

While new interest in and cultural activity around Jewish themes began in the 1970s and 1980s among non-Jewish Polish priests, scholars, writers, and other elites, often working expressly to resist the communist state, since 1989 engagements with Jewish heritage have been increasingly entwined with tourism and other forms of commercial culture brokering in this newly capitalist society. For the first twenty years after communism, it has been the accidental custodians of orphaned Jewishness in Poland—the keepers of cemetery keys, collectors of scavenged ritual items, singers of Yiddish songs, taxi drivers and tour guides and history buffs (who occasionally have grown into archivists, scholars, educators, and activists)—who have formed the most common points of contact for the many thousands of Jews the world over who have visited Poland annually. Such heritage brokers were among my first and most important guides, and their work predated recent, larger-scale government or NGO efforts.

Despite its often-commercial contexts, the growing engagement with Jewish cultural heritage is not only a source of entertainment, or even artistic or spiritual enrichment, but continues to represent political and moral concerns as well. Among Jewish heritage tourism sites, Kazimierz has become a unique urban crucible in which new kinds of Jewish memory, multifaceted dialogue, and productive engagements with the difficult past are being forged among people of different nationalities, ethnicities, generations, and perspectives. Derelict only a few years ago, the neighborhood is today thick with emotion, encounter, and burning questions.

In making sense of this place, I draw on Diana Pinto's notion of "Jewish space" as more than just a physical site of Jewish heritage. As Pinto defines it, Jewish space is "an open cultural and even political agora where Jews intermingle with others qua Jews, and not just as citizens. It is . . . present anywhere Jews and non-Jews interact on Jewish themes or where a Jewish voice can make itself felt."[3] While Jews are essential to Jewish space, unlike a Jewish community it cannot exist with their presence alone. Yet while many observers have noted the significance of Europe's newly emerging Jewish spaces, we know little about their inner workings. How are these spaces made manifest? What social, cultural, and identificatory practices are developing among those who populate them? What forms of memory work give rise to them, and what new forms do they enable? What is it like to be Jewish—and non-Jewish—in relation to such Jewish spaces today? As physical manifestations, heritage spaces form social catchments that are useful frames for research. Self-conscious and public Jewish spaces in Eastern Europe in particular have drawn a variety of forms of hidden Jewishness into the light, offering an opportunity to consider them. As social fields, Jewish spaces link Jews and non-Jews in generative cultural engagements and interactions that rework notions of Jewish (and majority) culture and identity, making these newly available to Jews and more accessible to others. This study, the product of an immersion in a key Jewish space, thus opens a window onto a broader phenomenon of great significance that has been extremely challenging to broach: the attempt to re-envision a Jewish Europe.

The Unseeable Poland

On the postwar map of Jewish culture, Poland has been a site of abjection and repudiation, a void punctuated only by "the camps." The country has been treated by the Jewish establishment as ritually desecrated; it has become a symbol of condensed evil that overrides meanings or histories other than "the Holocaust." Jews today do not cast the same kind of aspersions on France (whose Vichy regime officially collaborated with the Nazis), Lithuania (where local institutions and populations participated zealously in murdering Jews), or even Germany itself, the architect of the destruction.

Disputes over the role of Polish citizens in antisemitic violence both during and after the Holocaust, the conflicts around memorialization at the Nazi death camp Auschwitz, and the question of Jewish property restitution remain unresolved, and these are certainly contributing factors in Jewish perception. Yet the contemporary issues are in a way secondary. They do not significantly determine collective Jewish sentiment about Poland. Rather, they fit into an overarching framework of taboo; as historian David Engel has described, despite the lack of present-day political struggle between the two groups, "the *terms* of contention [between Poles and Jews] have survived the disappearance of actual physical friction."[4] While Eastern Europe more generally looms ominously in post-Holocaust Jewish symbolic geographies (and places like Ukraine are also obscured in popular memory), Poland has become at once distinct and iconic. This is a somewhat paradoxical function of the presence in Poland of all the Nazi death camps, the relative ease and luxury of travel to the country during the first decades after communism, and the vague knowledge many Jews have about their ancestral roots.[5]

The image of Poland is shaped and reinforced by a web spun of anecdote and hyperbole, both private and public, which connects many disparate sectors of the Jewish world. Former Israeli prime minister Yitzhak Shamir's widely circulated statement that Poles drink antisemitism with their mother's milk finds a parallel in the popular anecdote about the former Lubavitcher rebbe Menachem Schneerson's to his followers to establish Chabad Jewish outreach missions to aid in the flowering of Jewish life in every country in the world—except Poland, because it is no place for Jews. This quasi-official stance reigned even when Chabad had missions in all of Poland's neighboring countries, including multiple venues in Germany, where its website proudly proclaimed that "Judaism is flourishing in the very country where Nazis thought to annihilate the Jewish people."[6]

If Poland became uniquely relevant for Jews as a symbol of evil in the late- and post-communist eras, it is because the beliefs that many Jews hold about Poland "serve as supporting pillars of a collective consciousness, identity, and purpose."[7] Ethnographic research offers insight into how this symbolic power is generated and sustained: by a combination of distance and very particular kinds of closeness and contact. A half century after the war the fall of communism returned the mythical Poland to the actual map, as a real place one could visit. A piece of the "old country" and the epicenter of Holocaust abomination were suddenly available for picking and prodding, open to popular exploration and inquiry. An accessible Poland has proven magnetic and powerful. By the late 1990s tens of thousands of Jews were visiting Poland each year; it is second only to Israel as a destination that garners communal resources, and many Jews travel there in organized missions like the March of the Living or with Israeli school groups. For most, the trip is a once-in-a-lifetime ritual undertaken with a sense of obligation and foreboding; it offers a chance to enter the tragic past, for the sole purpose of witnessing. For a few, it is more multifaceted: an opportunity to explore one's roots, to untangle and refashion snarls of memory, to try out another possible homeland to anchor one's ethnic self.

Geographical and logistical accessibility are not necessarily edifying; they also provide fodder to reinforce familiar views, or indeed to create new myths. Who we are—as defined by our membership in a social group—structures in deep ways what we see and feel as we move through space and interact with people. Powerful forces can combine to produce a template—what anthropologist Rebecca Stein has called "national intelligibility"—that constrains our field of vision and yokes even our emotions.[8] There is a seemingly infinite Jewish capacity for bad news about Poland, for projects both popular and scholarly that—important as they may be—slide seamlessly into this predetermined structure of feeling. The configuration of much Jewish memory culture has seemed unable to assimilate any other news.

A potent combination of the predispositions of critical scholarship and the demands of institutionalized Holocaust memory have made it difficult to tell other Polish stories, whether these be stories of the centuries-long, vibrant former life of Jews in Poland or its striking recent reemergence.[9] Descriptions of European Jewish life have tended to reflect the concerns and identity categories of American or Israeli Jewry rather than the lived realities of local Jews. And the opening of Eastern Europe to historical scrutiny has led Holocaust scholars to unearth new depths of horror.[10] There is a sense of impossibility—even undesirability—surrounding Jewish life in post-Holocaust Europe. European Jews are envisioned by many Jews from afar as a "vanishing diaspora," living on a cemetery, under constant siege by hostile neighbors.[11] This depiction has led to feelings among European Jews, and Polish Jews in particular, of rejection or erasure from the global Jewish community. "Poland is not some half-real remnant bound to the dead," wrote Stanisław Krajewski, a leader in Poland's Jewish community who has written critically about the "cult of the Holocaust." "We are as real and as future-oriented as other Jewish communities around the world."[12]

More important, the burdens of the past are being grappled with anew, and Poland is a key staging ground for these struggles. New voices among foreign Jews are no longer content with a Poland reduced to the Holocaust, and a growing minority of ethnic Poles is challenging the idea that Poland is essentially Catholic. Polish Jews themselves—a tiny, motley group—are reinventing themselves amidst a variety of impassioned opinions about their very existence. These alternative voices are not merely critics, but active agents working to build new cultural realities and reframing accepted distinctions between "us" and "them." Poland—the epicenter of the destruction of European Jewry—is now a key site for the regeneration, rearticulation, and redefinition not only of a local Jewish community, but of inventive, hybrid ideas of post-Holocaust Jewishness itself.

An Intersection of Gazes

A generation of Poles grew up in official quasi-silence regarding the ubiquitous prewar presence of Poland's Jewish citizenry. Along with the Holocaust's extermination of Jews and Roma, the shifting of Poland's borders 300 miles to the west as a result of postwar negotiations at Yalta (and the forced re-settlement of Germans after Potsdam) left an overwhelmingly homogeneous Polish-Catholic population where there had once been a great deal of heterogeneity. In the early postwar years things Jewish and particularly Holocaust-related, while not yet politically taboo (and indeed present on a modest scale in some museums and memorials), were perceived by most as an undesirable component of Polish heritage, and silence around them was the norm in the public domain. The few discussions that occurred were at the pleasure of and to the extent desired by the national authorities, and government policies toward Jews (and by extension their former property) "oscillated between benign neglect and outright hostility."[13] While signs of grassroots interest emerged in the early 1970s (after most of Poland's remaining Jews had been forced out by the antisemitic campaign of March 1968), it was only in 1983—spurred by the fortieth anniversary of the Warsaw Ghetto uprising—that the first general text on Polish Jewish history was made available, followed by the first museum exhibitions of Jewish artifacts, translations of Yiddish literature and poetry, and the television premiere of Claude Lanzmann's film *Shoah*.[14] For postwar generations, the prewar world of their parents and grandparents—populated by Jewish next-door neighbors, schools, shops, rituals, and languages—seemed like a fairytale. As Mateusz, the twenty-something Catholic Pole whose apartment I rented, described it, his introduction to Jews was through figures in the Polish literature he read as a child in the 1970s; with no real-world reference points, they existed for him not as an ethnic or cultural group, but as just another character, "like Maria, John, and Jew."

If, for young Poles, encountering real Jews (an increasing possibility since 1989) was akin to having these characters step off the pages of a book, for older Poles it must have been more like seeing a ghost. Elderly people approached me in train stations, shops, and village squares, drawn, it seems, by my face.[15] Some spoke of healing wounds, filling blank spots, plumbing deeply sensed amnesias. Others seemed to long for absolution for crimes they did not themselves commit, but for which they nevertheless felt remorse. At a retreat center attached to Auschwitz, over lunch at a long table, a former Polish prisoner broke his long stare only to comment that I reminded him of all the young Jewish women he saw murdered. I am not alone in having this kind of experience. The desire on the part of some Poles to return memories and other lost things to "a Jew" has emerged as a new cultural contact zone. The transactions are at turns noble, charitable, guilt-laden, or commercial, but always fraught.

Local Jews, too, flocked to me, assuming I could provide an experience of and information about the "real Jewishness" they yearned for. I disappointed them. Many foreign Jews—myself included—came to Poland from a similar place of lack. The choices made over generations that unwittingly formed points along the line of assimilation—plus the quantum leap of the Holocaust—had left many of us with fragments of form but little coherent content. As ethnographic endeavors so often do, my story thus accrued layers of intersubjectivity. It grew to encompass more than a Jewish anthropologist observing Poles objectifying Jews, or watching Jews act out their traumatic memory in Poland. The crux of the encounter for me as both ethnographer and Jew was not simply how Poles (both Jewish and Christian) looked at me, but *how they looked at me looking at them*. The limits of a unidirectional gaze were brought home to me through a growing density of disconcerting confrontations with unfamiliar perspectives. My sojourn in Poland, and specifically the social opening provided by Kazimierz, provided a window onto what my own quest looked like—and meant—to those whose fate was to live on what for me was only desecrated ground—ground that I had the luxury of visiting occasionally and otherwise avoiding. It is what transformed this project from a consideration of tourism to a reflection on the role of heritage in intergroup dialogue and reconciliation. The experience triggered—and troubled—my thinking about the politics and economics of memory in enduring ways.

*   *   *

Ethnographers today acknowledge the global milieu in which we function, where "there" is no longer so separate from "here," nor "us" cleanly distinct from "them." By the late 1990s Kazimierz was already a quintessentially postmodern field site: transnational, increasingly cyber-mediated, tangled up with the flows of tourism.[16] Less has been said about another key characteristic of much contemporary field experience: the confrontation, dialogue, or at times blurring among ethnography and other practices of cultural representation, translation, and brokering.[17] I went to Poland to learn, write, and depict something unique about Jewishness, but I arrived to find a crowded field of endeavor, already "full of texts."[18] I crossed paths with tourists, filmmakers, journalists, and other seekers—Jews and non-Jews alike. Multidirectional currents of people—*zamlers* of sorts, the term for amateur collectors of Yiddish culture and folklore—crisscrossed the neighborhood's narrow streets and open squares and eddied in its multiplying public venues, in search of cultural fragments or on quests to make sense of "the other" in a way formerly regarded as the unique purview of ethnographers: through observation, contact, and representation.[19] No matter how much Poland changed over the years, each of us arrived seeing ourselves as Christopher Columbus, the first to discover the lost, last Jews of Poland. Yet the tiny community of Polish Jews had already been busy since the mid-1970s with their own underground cultural revival project, and they had long viewed visiting Jews as potential contributors to their task. Poland's de-assimilating Jews yearned for an energizing connection with their foreign counterparts, who were bearers of Jewish knowledge and a cultural vibrancy from which Poland had been po-

litically and socially isolated. Yet Poland's few Jews were generally either unnoticed or uncomprehended in Western Jewish circles, among whom Polish Jewry registered as moribund or extinct. While this image has begun to
show cracks in recent years, a crucial effect of the overall disinterest of Western Jewry in Poland's Jewish life meant that during my fieldwork in the early
2000s, the local Jews' most energetic partners in the generation of Jewish
spaces were still non-Jewish Poles.

Much new Jewish heritage in Poland has been dismissed in popular and
even scholarly discourse as "virtual," "kitsch," or "necro-nostalgia," not least
because of the disconcerting role of Polish non-Jews in its propagation.[20]
There are blond Polish singers who perform pitch-perfect Yiddish klezmer
tunes; a village ice-cream vendor who carves wooden figurines of Hasidic
Jews with gaunt faces; young people who gather every Friday for Shabbat
(Jewish sabbath) dinner but who also attend Catholic Mass on Sunday. Some
of the strongest advocates and even producers of Jewish culture and knowledge are indeed not Jewish by a range of norms. Yet much of Poland's critical
new memory work emerges from deep forms of Jewish/non-Jewish collaboration and dialogue that blurs group boundaries and complicates claims to cultural ownership.

Kazimierz's urban landscape was rich with assertions—verbal, visual,
aural, material—of Jewishness and Polishness, self and other, past and present. A visiting Israeli professor circulated unpublished personal memoirs of
his visit. A local Jew published critical considerations of *Schindler's List* tourism and local history. His non-Jewish partner filled local shop shelves with
exquisite Jewish papercuts, reviving a forgotten craft. An American Jewish
educator wrote a tourist guide booklet (as did Poles hoping to attract foreign visitors). And an ethnographer (me) wrote PR copy for souvenir book-
marks and brochures and hung signage advertising "Schindler's List tours"
for a Jewish bookshop. One kind of representation quickly became another
as the context changed. Jewish cultural fragments were given new meaning
as they were introduced to new publics in new ways. For Jews, the opening
up of a Jewish space in Poland provided a new signifying framework, an opportunity for cultural reanimation and renegotiation. But the particular mechanisms of the Jewish heritage industry developing in Kazimierz also extended
the reach of this new cultural domain, making it a bridge for dialogue and
(re)connection among Jewish and Polish people, places, and ideas. Rabbinical
lectures became key attractions at the annual Jewish festival. A grandfather's
Yiddish letter was transformed into a map navigating the neighborhood's

winding streets for both an American granddaughter and her Polish guide. Jewish grandmothers' memories recounted to local restaurateurs live on as recipes in the quarter's klezmer cafés.

This kind of feedback loop is not new. Versions of the joke about the anthropologist being handed her predecessor's ethnography by the native villager abound. But the speed of the process has increased. One quickly feels one's own impact. I have continued to return to Kazimierz during my writing and related projects, walking around from this to that shop, café, and museum, offering the people who shared their stories with me evidence of what I have been making of it all. Even if I hadn't managed the trips, my popular and academic articles are online. More fascinating is the dialogue generated by, and inherent in, these representations. The Jarden Jewish Bookshop owners—my adoptive parents in the field—shared their reflections with me about my work, solicited mine about theirs, identified additional individuals for me to interview (and so shaped my project), and constantly reminded me that they are saving space on their shelves to sell the text you are reading, as they rightly see it as part of their own creation and a contribution to their own cultural project.

I wondered, together with my fellow Jewish heritage brokers, what I might contribute to a project of representation and revival that had preceded my arrival. What were my goals, rights, responsibilities, allegiances? What calculus of power pertains when the ethnographer (and tourist) finds it is her own culture that is being documented and put on display by those whom she came to explore? The situation is far from one of unidirectional influence, where "expert" texts shape local understandings. It is closer to what anthropologist Andrew Shryock has called "a shared labor of objectification" in which the agenda of the ethnographer overlaps with that of her subjects: to delineate, create, and disseminate representations of culture, history, and tradition, and to intervene in the cultural landscape.[21] A perspective that is still underdeveloped in studies of diaspora tourism is the role of locals—those whose current home places are visited—in identity projects that implicate the visitors.[22] Non-Jewish Poles are not just consumers of Jewish culture; they are producers as well. Kazimierz has become an influential cultural text on contemporary Jewish Poland, perhaps more democratically written and widely read than any other. "Ethnographic" gazes intersect here in a kind of reciprocity. Observers and observed coexist within the realm of the exotic, the collected, the represented. In this tourist landscape, it is sometimes hard to tell who is guiding whom.

But the quarter is more than a text. The crossing of paths and intersection of gazes here does not only represent an incidental overlap in cultural heritage constructions, with opposing groups crafting images of themselves and others as props for use in separate identity projects. Kazimierz has become a shared project of cultural rediscovery, one that opens a door into the painful process of post-traumatic (re)encounter among members of groups who were former neighbors. The neighborhood is a site of Polish-Jewish engagement: a site in which people of various backgrounds bear witness to, work through, come to terms with, and produce the past. A unique environment, it not only encourages debate but enables implicit, embodied forms of memory to be made more conscious, and to be exchanged and renegotiated both intra- and interculturally. It is thus not only a *lieu* (in Pierre Nora's famous sense) but also a *milieu de mémoire,* where broken strands of memory can be rewoven in new ways and give rise to new kinds of community.[23]

Can Heritage Be Conciliatory?

Reconciliation, argues anthropologist Nancy Scheper-Hughes, has become a watchword of the late twentieth and early twenty-first centuries, and much has been written about officially mandated truth-telling and listening processes put in place by transitional governments to facilitate just peace among members of aggrieved groups.[24] But what do we know about what reconciliation looks like or how it plays out in everyday lives, in everyday spaces of intergroup contact and encounter—including encounters with absence and loss? How do people experience remorse or forgiveness? How is trust built? And "what must happen between people to lead to genuine rehumanization"?[25]

Post-Holocaust reconciliation, particularly in its meaning of reconnection and the creation of new networks that extend across the boundaries generated by group suffering, rarely appears on the agenda of the Jewish establishment.[26] Unlike the cases of differently racialized South Africans or conflicted citizens of North and South American countries, most Jews were separated from their former enemies (due to flight, murder, and related postwar demographic changes). Polish-Jewish reconciliation has not been obligatory, as the two groups no longer inhabit, in any significant numbers, shared geographical space. The Holocaust's primary perpetrator nation, Germany, has been the logical focus of attention regarding real and symbolic reparations. But an opportunity may be missed when human ties between former antagonists—including so-called bystanders (who may themselves be both victims and perpetrators)—are simply severed after violent conflict. The absence of once-significant others allows them to be more effectively mythologized, and opportunities for the kind of nuanced assessments of the past that demand multiple perspectives are diminished. The Poles and (non-Polish) Jews that I met so often expressed desires to revisit, reconnect, and revise their very partial inheritances. It is this process of reengagement, of dialogic working through, of reopening the lid on the past, of making room to think new relationships between past, present, and future—rather than coming to final terms with the past or merging all competing narratives into one—that constitutes my notion of reconciliation.

Addressing the issue of reconciliation in this way requires thinking across multiple, often-discrete conversations: about heritage, tourism, memory, and "transitology." Heritage scholarship, in particular, reveals a recurring preoccupation with themes of conflict, dissonance, negativity, and the undesirability of heritage.[27] Also at issue is a more general neglect of the social life of heritage, in a field of research within which it has been "nearly impossible to discern sentiments toward ownership, custodianship, stewardship, or other forms of possession of cultural heritage on the ground."[28] Central to understanding Kazimierz is grasping the ways that cultural producers and consumers do things with heritage. They use it to imagine and propose both pasts and futures, to connect with those alike and different, to locate themselves in the world and in time. If, as anthropologist Lisa Breglia recommends, we view heritage as practice, then our gaze is shifted toward a range of meaningful negotiations and engagements among heritage producers, brokers, and consumers.[29] It becomes visible that the practice of heritage produces not only "heritage" itself (in material, performative, or even conceptual manifestations) but also particular kinds of social space and relations among those who engage with that heritage. Heritage spaces (and its other products) are tools for stewards and visitors to enact—or act against—particular notions of "us." And if heritage is not simply something that we inherit, but something we do, then we can always do it differently.

Anthropologist Liisa Malkii's work on Hutu refugees of mass ethnic killings illustrates that experiences of identity-based persecution do not directly or necessarily lead to narrow, exclusive, ossified conceptions of identity among victims, but rather that particular socio-spatial circumstances and energetic cultural work are required to produce them. She shows that the rarefied conditions of single-ethnicity refugee camps, for example, are breeding grounds for a sense of embattlement and us-and-them thinking, and that more ethnically integrated spaces of resettlement and the more expansive cultural forms these allow produce more cosmopolitan, fluid identities.[30] Intergroup contact would also seem necessary for social forms and feelings like reciprocity, understanding, empathy, and social networks across difference.

Discussions of memory as it is expressed in the domains of heritage and tourism—particularly the memory of injustice, oppression, and violent cultural destruction—have been constrained by a sense of misfit between ostensible "leisure industries" and the moral outrage and personal and communal pain that accompany tragic histories. Our ability to understand these domains, and to appreciate the potential for productive remembering in everyday heritage sites and by vernacular memorial stewards, is further hampered by discourses of authenticity and normative identity categories shaped in response to particular understandings of the horrors of the past.

Yet along with a global boom in memorial museums, heritage brokering and memory work are taking new forms that redefine our engagements with difficult histories, and push the boundaries of both scholarly and popular understandings of presumed binaries such as fake/authentic, outsider/insider, and commercial/ethical. Like it or not, tourism, museology, and heritage practices today are implicated in some of the most difficult debates about the past, forming cogs in the complex workings of and struggles with such fraught processes as reconciliation after genocide. Indeed, in some cases it is in these realms that the cutting edge of these debates can be discerned.

Amidst the global geopolitical shifts and new media revolutions accompanying the transition from postwar and Cold War Europe to the New Europe, Jewish memory in Poland (and elsewhere on the continent) has been transformed from a terrible void to a key symbol of positive identification for diverse constituencies. But what is this new Jewish memory made of, and how is it being transmitted and reshaped among new generations of Jews and non-Jews? With the opening of Eastern Europe in particular, and the accessibility of its potent Jewish memorial landscapes, what is happening with this wealth of potential heritage? What new configurations are being cobbled out of what was left behind? What impact are increasing encounters between mythologized others like Poles and Jews having on each group's sense of collective self?

In this study, I engage with these questions in four interrelated ways. First, I bring to center stage the role of heritage sites (and those who engage with them) in processes of identity resignification after national trauma. Less and less bound to elite-controlled, univocal expressions of hegemonic memory, built heritage is serving ever-broader transnational publics in stretching, re-conceptualizing, and multiplying ethnic and national identifications. Second, exploring this process of identificatory engagement in public space reveals a facet of national memory construction that has been under-recognized, namely subaltern memory projects that are non-competitive and inclusive, challenging the more visible and more conflictive politics of national memory as expressed in dominant discourses. Third, I show how this conciliatory politics of memory challenges common distinctions between authentic and inauthentic culture that rest on (often unacknowledged) essentialist, exclusiv-ist understandings of culture and identity. Finally, I offer a window onto pro-cesses of post-atrocity reconciliation at the grassroots, as it is lived out in daily experience, in struggles with trust and rehumanization that are experienced by people who inhabit bodies that have been marked and displaced in space and time over multiple generations. The moral and emotional burden left be-hind by the Holocaust is expressed in, experienced through, and grappled with in sociocultural, material, and physical processes and products. While relating to the functions of memory, these domains also partake in present-day aspirations for—and attempts to construct—new moral worlds. If we look and listen carefully, we can discern in unexpected places attempts to ask the difficult, forward-looking question: What should we do now?

Since the publication of Edward Said's *Orientalism,* discussion of na-tional or cultural identity projects have tended to assume that the concep-tion of the other is always a negative foil, affirming and reifying identities in relation to what we frame as their opposite. The qualities attributed to self and other may be imagined (and easier to sustain) without any actual inter-action with or openness to the reality of the other. This perspective is use-ful in understanding both what I call Jewish "mission" approaches to Po-land, and longstanding Polish ethno-nationalist visions that are buttressed by an essential, vilified Jewish other: both positions attempt to eradicate al-terity, negating differences they themselves construct. But this view fails to capture what is taking place, for example, in the case of the growing move-ment of Jewish "quest" travel to Poland, which attempts to find new ways to engage with difference. Here we see another, much less explored kind of iden-tity work, a cross-identification *with* the other that can nevertheless contra-dict the dominant symbolic order.[31] The construction of the self via positive integration of the other is rarely discussed, and, when it is, typically only one side of the equation is addressed—the dominant side. In complex combina-tions of motivations and possibilities, identification, sympathy, and the challenging of norms are generally overlooked when they exist alongside essentialization, commodification, and constraint, and evocations of otherness are thus seen as ultimately at the expense of the other in question.[32] While recognizing practices and structures that "neutralize" the potential of counterhegemonic memory, my goal is to show how both Poles and Jews, in these particular spaces and unique moments of encounter, are led to think more critically about their collective and individual identities, and to rework them in significant ways.[33] Attention to these nuances improves our understanding of the process by which images and stories of people and place influence behavior and policy toward them. We must make conceptual space to grasp emerging, more complex constructions of "otherness" and their uses in heritage manifestations, with particular attention to new discourses about "significant others." Understanding both heritage and otherness calls for a deeper understanding of their nature as processes, for a broader investigation into what kinds of agents, ideas, and spaces animate their concrete manifestations, and for attention to the far-reaching consequences of heritage discourses in shaping understandings of and relations between self and other.

Complementary Subaltern Memory Projects

Interest in Jewish heritage in Poland today is widely assumed to be a superficial fad. Yet the expression of such interest in Kazimierz is in important ways the result of two complementary subaltern memory projects—a local Polish one and a foreign Jewish one, imported by tourism. The Polish project has its roots in earlier activism related to Poland's struggle for democracy, and Jewishness continues to be a key category in post-communist Polish culture wars. In the 1970s and 1980s under late communism, grassroots interest in Jews and activities on their behalf represented a form of progressive politics, of resistance to Polish ethno-nationalism and historical silences in the Church and the government. The latter periodically wielded antisemitism (or occasionally philosemitism) as a political tool, but otherwise it tightly censored Jewish themes.[34] Linked to Jewish de-assimilation and community revival in Poland, this "Jewish memory project" was highly dialogic, with non-Jewish Poles making crucial, personal contributions to restoring Jewish heritage.[35] As sociologist Iwona Irwin-Zarecka notes, "It would often be from these Catholic friends that a Jew brought up in silence learned some basics of Judaism and Jewish history."[36]

Since the early 1990s in post-communist Poland, non-Jewish heritage brokers in Kazimierz have played an important role in cultivating conditions for the flowering and ferment of Polish-Jewish culture.[37] While a Polish urge to remember and reconcile with its Jewish heritage has been a prime catalyst for Kazimierz's development as a heritage site, individual Jewish quests to come to terms with Poland's broader Jewish heritage have also played a part. And while most foreign Jewish tourists travel to Poland to confront the Holocaust, a growing minority seeks more than an experience of evil. A Polish-Jewish memory project developing among foreign Jews has drawn some to confront and reconsider their own community's negation of Poland as a part of Jewish heritage relevant for the formation of the identity of a new generation of Jews, beyond the heritage of destruction. As Amos, a French Jew in his early twenties, told me while sitting in Café Ariel, one of Kazimierz's most popular Jewish-themed venues,

> People come here [to Poland] and say 'It is awful, it is awful.' I say, 'No.' I don't come here to say it is awful. I just come to make peace with people. To *not* say, 'Okay, [see], it *is* anti-Semitic.' To try [instead] to make peace, and to make a place for that in my head . . . It was really nice to try to speak with Polish people . . . I didn't want to go back to Poland to see antisemitism. I want to *stop* this.

While these emerging memory projects follow multiple pathways, Kazimierz is unique as a social catchment, a highly cosmopolitan space with an inherent *genius loci* that brings them into constant, meaningful contact. Over a fifteen-year span, I saw the Polish and Jewish projects not only converge but intertwine, catalyzing and refining each other in the quarter. The result is an evolving Polish-Jewish heritage site, a "conciliatory" space that works against more conflictive notions of Poland's Jewish heritage—dominant in both Jewish and Polish society—that pit Jewishness and Polishness against one another.

Despite their flashy titles, "Schindler's List" and other such tours are often quite the opposite of package tourism. They are opportunities for unpacking baggage long carried but rarely examined—through interpersonal encounter, connection, and the sharing and renegotiating of stories, knowledge, and authority. Self-reflexive, inter-subjective dialogue and reflection on Jewish heritage—what it consists of, who owns it, and what the boundaries of Jewishness are—are the *sine qua non* of much Jewish tourist experience in Kazimierz for those willing to venture outside the tour bus. If this sounds unlikely, consider prominent Polish-Jewish community leader Stanisław Krajewski's statement amidst the hubbub of the neighborhood's twentieth annual

Festival of Jewish Culture in 2008, a nine-day event run and mostly attended by non-Jews. He said, "This place, at this moment . . . is the only place in Poland where being a Jew I feel like a host. This is a Jewish place more authentic than any other in Poland."

* * *

Why do Jews matter to Poland, and why Poland to Jews? Why be concerned about this seemingly optional process of reconciliation, given the more immediate challenges for each party in Europe and the Middle East? For Poland (and more broadly, Europe), Jewish space is a bellwether. The cultural incorporation of this traditional other suggests the very possibility of otherness *tout court*. In ideal terms, if there is space for Jews, there is space for difference. The danger, as has been astutely noted, is that the incorporation of an extremely diminished form of Jewishness simply draws a new line in the sand, allowing Poles and other Europeans to pat themselves on the back while they use a newly embraced "Judeo-Christian" heritage as a bulwark against Islam—a much larger and more animate presence pressing on the New Europe.[38] Yet observation suggests that Poland's Jewish spaces have been spaces of broader pluralism, where other others—like gays, Roma, and some members of the few non-European immigrant groups beginning to trickle into Poland—have found space to breathe, if quietly. To be sure, the lack of a significant Muslim population in Poland makes Jewishness an easier sell as a tool for envisioning pluralism than it does farther West, even as shades of Islam or Arab culture have made tiny inroads into the spaces opened in Poland by Jewishness.

On the Jewish side, Poland matters because if Jews discard Poland, they cut off a thick tangle of the roots keeping their family tree standing. Many Jews I spoke to on (or planning) visits to Poland expressed a feeling of being adrift and unmoored; they wanted to replant themselves in this last remembered site of familiar cultural density. Conversely, to the extent that Jewish rejection of Poland functions as a ritual of purification, a distancing from entanglements with a suspect other, Jews partake in the logic of their enemies. Such essentialization of self and other will inevitably overflow the original setting, and seeing only the bad in Poland blinds Jews to what may be emerging as their greatest national champion on the continent. Finally—and most relevant to this project—Poland today is an extraordinarily rich site that provokes crucial questions about contemporary Jewish identity. While Jews could sit around in New Jersey and discuss who they are as a people two generations after the Holocaust, what they lost, who their others and allies are, and where they fit into a world of continuing inequality and violence, they generally do not. But in Poland—when faced with the traces of their former selves, and the interest others, non-Jews, are taking in these—processes of deep self-scrutiny are frequently triggered. Among new generations of Jews (as well as some older ones), a growing number of individuals are taking sometimes painful steps, in the company of Poles, toward (re)claiming Poland as a rich site of Jewish heritage.

We know the story of loss, even as we continue to discover its depths. We also hear again and again about the ways that Polish and Jewish views of history are incommensurable, a clash of narratives or deep logics about the past. But just as memory can be deployed for ends conflictual or competitive, it is "at least as often a spur to unexpected acts of empathy and solidarity . . . often the very grounds on which people construct and act upon visions of justice."[39] At the few sites where Polish and Jewish heritage projects meet, the confrontation of two very different understandings of a shared past is accompanied by the tentative reweaving of social and cultural bonds. The fraught relationship between Poles and Jews, playing out on the global, mass-mediated field of heritage tourism, offers an excellent frame to consider how historical wounds can be both perpetuated and transcended, how new bridges can be built over old fissures, and the unanticipated companionships sometimes involved in managing the past.

Ethnography of Possibility

We raise new questions for a foreign culture, ones that it did not raise for itself; we seek answers to our own questions in it.
—MIKHAIL BAKHTIN (1986)

This book has many purposes. One is simply to open a conversation about what is left out, and what is distorted, by some current practices of Holocaust memory. But in illuminating a space of possibility in Jewish Poland, I am also fashioning a space for a particular genre in ethnography: an ethnography of possibility. My notion is informed by glimmers in the work of a few intra- and extra-disciplinary predecessors who have dared to talk about love, hope, generosity, or praise in their critical scholarship.[40] It also takes a cue from Tzvetan Todorov's ethics of memory, which asks us not to remember comfortably only our own moments as heroes or victims but to strive to recall the heroics of others and the ways we may have wronged them.[41] Finally, it seeks to recuperate from the disciplinary slur of "salvage" a space for ethnographic projects associated with a sense of cultural loss and recovery.

Ethnography is uniquely positioned to illuminate not only cultural trends but possibilities, pockets of resistant or aspirational culture work that suggest alternative ways of being. As a 1984 review in *Time* magazine put it, Margaret Mead's view of anthropology's ultimate purpose was "to increase a sense of life's possibilities."[42] But this strain of anthropology was and continues to be marginalized in the academy. I would venture that an unanticipated side effect of anthropology's postmodern "crisis of representation"—which produced important strides in self-scrutiny—has been a loss of aspirational space in the discipline. I therefore strive to model an ethnographic approach that documents not only conflict, but also the everyday work of tolerance.[43] Conflict attracts disproportionate attention from scholars. But tolerance, just as its many opposites, is also created in the tiniest details of social life, of speech and action. It is lived, as David William Cohen tells us, in everyday "critical civilities," the "almost invisible little acts of accepting and allowing difference" at a worksite, marketplace, or neighborhood, or among friends at leisure.[44] It seems not only worth asking, but crucial to examine, when, where, and why people behave their best.

Jewish heritage tourism in Poland today is a major form of cultural activism, implicated in struggles much larger and more significant than they might at first appear—struggles for the very souls of the Jewish and Polish nations. On the Jewish side, Poland has been taken up as a symbol and employed as a space by competing projects: Poland as a touchstone for anti-semitism, or Poland as a renewable resource for working through the past and imagining possible futures. On the Polish side, Jews are seen variously as essential, irrelevant, or even threatening to a new Polish national project. Each of these positions provides a partial truth. But as narratives their impact has been vastly unequal. The dominant discourses of Polishness and Jewishness—those that my interlocutors and I, in our parallel projects, have been working against—are much better resourced, and thus more frequently heard and more likely to be made manifest in the world. Thus I have chosen to make ethnographic common cause with those inhabiting the space where the Jewish and Polish projects overlap, with those who claim each other as vital to expansive projects of self-definition.[45] Because they are so little recognized, my written efforts have gone into discerning the good-faith efforts of a small number of Poles to recompense for their national failings vis-à-vis Jews, and the occasional Jewish efforts to swim against their own cultural tide and take a second look at Poland.

On the one hand, this approach draws on oral historian Alessandro Portelli's future-oriented "ethics of amplification," in an attempt "to extend the life and the circulation of narrative, the formation of a new tradition."[46] But it has been difficult—and ultimately futile—to restrict myself to trying to explain the intensity of emotion and sense of meaning in attempts of Jewish travelers (myself included) and local Poles to come to terms with the past. Over time, many of the culture brokers I met—creators of heritage venues, restorers of formerly Jewish sites, founders of Jewish museums—had become accidental activists, and I have increasingly wanted not only to understand them but to emulate them. Their inventiveness in the public sphere has been remaking a Jewish heritage in Poland—the very heritage I had been yearning for: one that was familiar with and connected to the past, but progressive and welcoming of difference. This heritage understood and dignified pain and loss but refused to be defined by these, recognizing that they don't belong exclusively to one group. After years as a perennial tourist-cum-ethnographer, haunting the Jewish cafés, clubs, and bookstores whose work continued to fascinate me, I found I had become part of the scene. It seemed only fitting that I should throw my own hat into the ring.

Thus my project evolved into more than just an attempt at listening and observing generously, only to write my conclusions in academic texts. The examples set by those whose work I was studying led me toward new communicative modes, including a variety of exhibits, installations, popular literature, and translation work.[47] These experimental modes of cultural intervention continue to shape my relations with those people I have been writing about. Anthropologist George Marcus has proposed the notion of "complicity" (rather than the longstanding ideal of "rapport") to describe the changing relationship between anthropologists and their subjects, and the attendant conventions of research, in the fluid mise-en-scène of postmodern fieldwork.[48] This conception captures something of how my own project was inspired and sustained by my subjects, who shared my curiosities and anxieties about the part-foreign, part-familiar cultural fragments that we represented for each other, and how we became involved in each other's projects of social understanding and cultural resistance.

There is a need to push further beyond the still-common conception of ethnographic research as an encounter between "disinterested observers" and "committed insiders" and to highlight instead the complex and interconnected goals and desires of both ethnographers and their subjects. Undoing this language allows us to see how multiple sites and genres of cultural representation and translation practice are increasingly interconnected and mutually informing. It also recognizes and encourages ethnographic practices that are humanistic, creative, collaborative, and responsive to popular needs. We might take seriously Herbert Hirsch's admonition that "if modern social science is unable to construct or communicate memory . . . that induces empathy, we must turn to other alternatives that may be more successful."[49] My Kazimierz interlocutors set an example of how to harness history to imagine expanded identities and create new kinds of community and spaces where Jews and Poles could reclaim lost places together, as former and perhaps future cultural neighbors. If at times I hoped my presence would "[hold] the protagonists to their own idealism," my own goals also shifted as we engaged each other.[50] It no longer felt sufficient to try to apprehend meanings; I wanted to harness ethnography to actively help create and disseminate better meanings.

"Redemptive" representations of violent events and their aftermaths not only distort history and experience; they can lead to further suffering for those who do not recognize themselves in what they may feel are dishonest, sanitized stories. A clear-eyed accounting of the past is thus essential. But given the many genres and domains of representation that engage with difficult histories, should we not risk adding ameliorative narratives and healing spaces? Cultivating a sense of possibility does not mean ignoring the pitfalls that coexist with such an approach. In Kazimierz, superficial, stereotypical, and to some people offensive engagements with Jewishness share space with higher-minded attempts. When I enter Noah's Ark restaurant, right next door to my beloved Jarden Jewish Bookshop, the framed fragments of orphaned Torah scrolls that hang decoratively on the wall make me cringe—not only do religious Jews bury these hallowed, handwritten scrolls when their functional lives end, but their absent owners and the question of their provenance cry out from behind the glass. Yet I recall how many important Polish-Jewish encounters I have witnessed there, how the owner has supported my research needs over the years by lending me restaurant space for interviews and projects as well as the labor of waiters when I needed a helping hand assembling an ethnographic exhibit, and how he tolerated (and even encouraged) my nosy intrusions on his work and customers. The realm of possibility, I often have to remind myself, also means having patience and openness toward unfamiliar perspectives and foreign approaches; the restaurateur may well imagine that framing a page of Torah is a way to honor it. Each observer has their own sensitive spots, their own bottom line—and Kazimierz continues to change as these sentiments are communicated. But possibility also calls for a kind of critical optimism. As historian Michael Steinlauf observed, "A Poland in which an audience could cheer a popular entertainer for donning a *kippah* and performing a 'Jewish' song about a shtetl" may be "well suited to confronting the more problematic aspects of the 'Jewish question' as well."[51]

It bears stating plainly that there are abundant reasons for Jewish pain, anger, and suspicion toward Poles and Poland, due to experiences of murderous violence, betrayal, theft, appropriation, expulsion, or exclusion suffered by Jews at Polish hands—before, during, and after World War II.[52] Poland is felt by many Jews to be uniquely desecrated as the site of an almost incomprehensible amount of Jewish murder. The Polish public is still in the early stages of reckoning its "bill of conscience" regarding its historical record vis-à-vis the Jews, filling in blank spots and outright erasures in their historical narrative and struggling with strains of Polish nationalism in which Jewish claims on Polish history or culture—whether positive or negative—are viewed as occult, corrupt, or polluting. Anti-Jewish discourse is still a not uncommon public occurrence, whether in publications sold at street-corner kiosks, on right-wing radio programs, or in graffiti in more (and sometimes less) run-down parts of Polish towns.[53] More troubling still is the nationalist character of a great deal of Polish public (and occasionally even diplomatic) reaction to new historical scholarship on Polish-Jewish relations, or indeed of some Polish state-sponsored scholarship itself.[54]

On the other hand, while survey research indicates widespread prejudice against Jews in everyday discourse, a 2005 volume on the topic notes that "the mainstream media in present-day Poland give little space to voices of hatred and far more to their opponents."[55] Further, there is little evidence that it is dangerous to be a Jew in Poland today.[56] Antisemitic violence is extremely rare; survey and focus group research suggests that direct personal experience of antisemitism has been very limited; and recent occurrences of harassment have been loudly and decisively denounced at the highest levels.[57] Jewish events and institutions do not entail the extraordinary security measures like armed guards and metal detectors that are the norm in Western Europe, and *yarmulke*-wearing Polish Jewish leader Konstanty Gebert emphasizes that he has been threatened far more often, aggressively, and with much less helpful intervention from bystanders in France.[58] Nor are there reports of institutionalized discrimination against Jews in public life. Indeed, Poland has been called Israel's best friend in Europe.[59] Since diplomatic ties were re-established the two countries have had an impressive record of cultural, economic, political, and military cooperation, with goodwill gestures often exchanged in both directions. More notably, Poland—where criticism of Israel is not a public rallying point—provides little fodder for observers of "the new antisemitism" that has caused much anxiety in relation to countries further west. David Peleg, the Israeli ambassador to Poland through 2008, made a point of stating publicly that "Poland today is not an antisemitic country."[60] On a daily basis, as Poles go to work, enjoy their families, and live their lives, probably very few think—either positively or negatively—about Jews.

The multi-million dollar, avant-garde Museum of the History of Polish Jews being built in Warsaw is substantially government-funded. Teaching about the Holocaust is a compulsory part of the national school curriculum under a 2003 regulation of the Minister of National Education and Sport, and post-secondary Jewish as well as Holocaust Studies is thriving in the form of scholarly institutions, teaching, research and publishing.[61] Since 2005, a National Day of Remembrance for the Victims of Holocaust and Prevention of Crimes Against Humanity has been marked on April 19, the date of the beginning of the Warsaw Ghetto uprising. The list of non-governmental activities on Jewish culture and Holocaust commemoration continues to grow dramatically. Given these facts, why do so many Jews outside of Poland see the country as not just as a site of historical tragedy, but of continuing fear and maltreatment for Jews? And more important, what are the consequences—for Jews and for Poles—of the perpetuation of this image? I explore these questions, among others laid out above, in the chapters that follow.

Organization of the Book

Chapter 1 offers ethnographic context of two kinds: a look outward at the setting of my main fieldwork, and a glimpse inside at the emotional landscape that I inhabited as I undertook this work. It can be read as a love letter to a place, a time, and what was for me a unique—if rarefied—community of cultural seekers. Chapters 2 and 3 address Jewish travel to Poland. Such travel is a very particular type of tourism—it is not meant for leisure, and is not undertaken lightly. As Alex Danzig, a consultant to Yad Vashem (Israel's official Holocaust remembrance institution) and the Israeli Ministry of Education on group travel to Poland, described to me, "The trip to Poland, it's not just a trip to Poland. It's your [perspective on] life. How to [do it] depends what you think about life at all, about history, about your future."[62] Chapter 2 describes the mass, fleeting "missions" that touch down briefly in Poland, their familiar, hermetic Holocaust story written prior to their arrival, scaffolded against new views or voices. Mission tourism forms the backdrop against which my countervailing story of Jewish travel in Poland—the "quest"—unfolds. Chapter 3 illustrates the slower, more multivalent quests undertaken by individuals trying to "unwrite" unsatisfying stories. Many of these people are traveling explicitly against key presumptions of mission tourism, in an effort at defamiliarization, or dispensing with the frames of understanding they have inherited. The inability of mission tourism to accommodate difference is mirrored in the seductions of and struggles with difference enacted in quest travel, triggered by actual encounters with local people. I use the term "tourist" for mission participants and "traveler" for those whose journeys I call quests. This is not to suggest that the first form of journey is superficial and the latter deep, as missions can undoubtedly be transformative. Rather, the terms highlight the distance that mission participants maintain from on-the-ground Polish realities during their trips. If chapter 2 illustrates tourism within the bounds of the dominant narrative of Jewish nationalism, chapter 3 accompanies forays into counter-narrative, following these expanding discursive and experiential cracks and exploring their ecology.

Amidst these criss-crossing itineraries, chapters 4 and 5 address Jewish cultural production in Kazimierz. In chapter 4, I introduce a category of local, under-acknowledged Jewish memory workers: non-Jewish Poles in Kazimierz who have taken as their task the stewardship and perpetuation of Poland's Jewish heritage. Because of their work in lending a helping hand to Jewishness, I call them (as some have called themselves) *Shabbos goyim*.[63] Their efforts, and particularly the ways these intersect with the more indigenously Jewish memory projects, serve to highlight the integral roles non-Jews have had in supporting (and shaping) Jewish culture and heritage.[64] Chapter 5 illustrates how Polish-Jewish dialogues around Jewish cultural production take place in domains beyond the discursive. While Jews themselves are few in today's Poland, representations of them abound; they compose a wordless working-through of history's haunting presence. Especially prevalent in tourist zones like Kazimierz, local Poles and Jewish visitors judge these representations very differently, bringing different worlds of meaning to bear on them. If one single object is a lightning rod in the new landscape of Jewishness on display, it is the wooden Jewish figurine. It is caught in a web of overlapping visual histories: Marc Chagall's flying rabbis, Broadway and Hollywood's *Fiddler on the Roof*, and Roman Vishniac's street scenes of Hasidim (adherents

of various mystical Orthodox sects) on the one hand, and antisemitic caricatures from Nazi propaganda on the other. The figurines embody key problematics of representation, appropriation, commemoration, and commerce.
Tracing their material and social lives, I show how their meanings are negotiated by differently situated social actors, and the ways that both conflict and
collaboration congeal in the final, tangible objects.

Chapter 6 delves further into the complexity of Jewish identification in
contemporary Poland. Population estimates have risen in a decade from specu-
lative counts of 4,000 Jews in the early 1990s to perhaps 20,000 or more today.
Poland's Jewish organizations are facing the difficult task of deciding which
of those many Polish "new Jews" (recent claimers of Jewish group membership, most of whom are not Jewish according to religious law) to accept into
the fold.[65] My interest in these blurrings and margins does not focus on lack.
That is, I take these non-normative Jewish identities not simply as the detritus of tragic history of persecution, hiding, forced adoption, or assimilation—
although these conditions contributed to producing them. Rather, I look at
current practices of identification with Jewishness as a way of coming to
terms with history, through a future-oriented ethics and politics that recalls
what Naomi Seidman has termed "vicarious" Jewish identity. This is particularly true for those "in-between" individuals who embrace a hybrid Polish-
Jewish identity that resists homogenizing nationalisms on both sides. I show
that Kazimierz has provided a space for them to explore and articulate their
senses of self, just as their experiences with cultural heritage tourism there
have helped produce and develop aspects of these selves. Finally, the book's
conclusion brings us up to date on the changes—some quite significant—that
have altered Kazimierz's (and Poland's) Jewish heritage landscape since this
book's central ethnographic moment from the mid-1990s to the mid-2000s.
It points forward to the emergent possibilities enabled by new developments,
while also recognizing lingering limits to change.

This book is not an ethnography of Jewish travel per se. Rather, it is a
story of travels through Jewishness, and how conceptions of Jewishness themselves circulate, are shaped, and are used by Jews and non-Jews for political
and personal ends. To the extent that these projects overlap and interact, it is a
story about Polish-Jewish relations. It is also a story about power: about what
is normative, what is institutionalized, and what is sanctioned. It is about the
ways emotion is implicated in structures of power. And most important, perhaps, it is about places where such power is more and less able to be resisted.

CHAPTER ONE

MAKING SENSE OF PLACE: HISTORY, MYTHOLOGY, AUTHENTICITY

I arrived in Kazimierz for the first time in April of 1990. It was a fortuitous moment; ferried by a hospitable middle-aged Polish painter who had become my and my brother's impromptu tour guide to the city, we drove into the bleak neighborhood under a white banner stretched across the road, advertising the second annual Festival of Jewish Culture. As I tried to grasp this unlikely event, our new Polish friend's white Polonez hatchback rolled to a stop, parking alongside a few other cars in a strip up the center of the spacious, aptly named Szeroka ("wide") Street. We walked the few steps down to the old synagogue, where we saw a small crowd of people—the only sign of life in the otherwise dreary square—filing into the old synagogue museum for a concert. Our host was tickled by his good fortune in stumbling on such an apposite event for his Jewish guests. I was still orienting myself to the idea of Jewish entertainment in what for me was a post-apocalyptic Jewish site, when the evening's performer, cantor Jeffrey Nadel from Washington, D.C., stepped onto the *bimah* and began to sing in a powerful tenor.

I was perplexed by his presence. He represented a kind of contemporary, mainstream American Jewish normality that—foreign to me though it also was—seemed shockingly out of place in this seemingly most marginal of Jewish spaces. He was the Jewish present; what was he doing here in the Jewish past? Looking back, it seems clear that I might have posed the same question of us. But I wasn't yet able to discern the trend of which we formed a part. We were all early evidence of the transnational flows of Jewish people and culture traversing Poland, and Krakow's Kazimierz in particular, which began to burgeon through the 1990s. At times linking to local counterpart projects of Jewish salvage and revival undertaken by Poles (Jewish and non-Jewish), such flows eddied in the quarter. Whereas the Jewish neighborhoods in most Polish cities were destroyed during the war, Kazimierz's core is an architecturally intact, historic Jewish town; the neighborhood today comprises almost a quarter of Krakow's city's historic center. Jewish seekers were drawn by the rich and heavy history, tangible as much through the Jewish human absence as the striking Jewish material presence. But Szeroka Street was also a magnet because it was endlessly surprising, yielding unlikely interlocutors and a regular stream of grassroots Jewish-oriented events, making it an epicenter of ferment, dispute, and development around Jewish and Polish heritage and identities and a touchstone for projects of cultural salvage and development.[1]

In 1993, the iconic Cracovian Jew Henryk Halkowski, amidst a sudden (if small) flurry of interest in Kazimierz on the part of architects and planners, mused about his dream of a Kazimierz that would provide a counterpoint to the dominance and teleological views of the Holocaust in popular conceptions of Poland's Jewish history—the way the memory of Nazi destruction has made everything that came before seem inevitably doomed and rendered everything after it invisible. He wished that the quarter would be developed in a way that balanced attention to the old, absent, and irreplaceable with the new and functional. He saw Kazimierz as a place where such historical and cultural synergy was uniquely possible, where Jews with Polish roots could feel proud of their heritage, a reminder of the everyday Polish-Jewish life that had once been a reality, yet "without [such life] remaining only in the past."[2]

This was a hard sell for foreign Jews. I vividly recall the Argentine-Jewish student who voiced a widespread but usually unspoken sentiment regarding Kazimierz's growing liveliness. "I want to see the synagogue in ruins," he said. "I have to see the ruins because *that's* what I can find here. *Ruins* of a culture, of a cultural group. . . . I just don't like to have so much *life* here."

From my earliest interest in the social life of Poland's Jewish past in the present day, all roads seemed to lead back to Kazimierz. Aside from its local and national magnetism among Polish Jews, the quarter quickly became a kind of "poster child" for (particularly North American) Jewish communal anxieties about the unforeseen, surprising, confusing relationships of local East European populations to "things Jewish" emerging with the end of communism, when it became clear that "antisemitism without Jews" no longer told the whole story. A site dense with tangible evidence of a once-vibrant Polish Jewry and scarred by its more recent, horrific abjection, Kazimierz was an ideal petri dish to observe the materials used for and choices inherent in the (re)making of Jewish space and Jewish selves. Given this symbolic trove of Ashkenazi Jewish experience in more and less tangible forms, what aspects seemed useable, for which purposes, to whom?

These questions drew me to continually return to Kazimierz. I returned summer after summer through the 1990s, talking and listening and taking notes and photographs, and then spent eighteen months there doing my "official" (grant-funded) fieldwork between November 1998 and August 2000. I had already been adopted by the Jarden Jewish Bookshop at the northern end of Szeroka Street; the store formed my base of operations for research and socializing (difficult to separate in ethnographic work), and its owners became my "key informants" and my de facto family. The quarter's rich social and material offerings provided me ample opportunity to develop and consider my research questions. It also forced me, constantly, to reflect on my own, conflicted relation to this past. I touch on my personal story at the end of this chapter, as I was as much a character in Kazimierz's Jewish heritage reckonings as those who became my main interlocutors.

Making, Unmaking, and Remaking Place

Jewish settlement in Poland can be traced back approximately 1,000 years. Jews came to Poland mostly from Western Europe, fleeing from persecution and drawn by Poland's relative tolerance under rulers Bolesław Pobożny ("the Pious," 1239–1279) and Kazimierz Wielki ("the Great," reigned 1333–1370), who offered the Jews significant rights and protections in exchange for their services as tradesmen, merchants, estate managers, and fiscal agents for noblemen. Jews first lived in Kazimierz about 700 years ago. Having been driven out of their earlier settlement in the center of Krakow by anti-Jewish riots beginning in the mid-1300s, the Jews were forced by King Jan Olbracht (reigned 1492–1501) to move in 1495 into a walled section of Kazimierz, itself a separate city surrounded by branches of the Vistula River. Kazimierz has several monumental Christian churches including the gothic Corpus Christi and St. Catherine's, built in the fourteenth and fifteenth centuries, and the eighteenth-century Baroque Skałka sanctuary, a national pilgrimage and honorific burial site in honor of the martyred St. Stanisław (marks of whose blood are said to be visible on a fragment of wood and a stone step from the original eleventh-century church). The quarter has always had a Christian population that lived alongside the Jews, although in parallel, rather than intermingling, fashion.[3] The population of the Jewish section of Kazimierz, known as the *Oppidum Judaeorum* or "Jewish City," grew as Czech, German, Spanish, and Italian Jews flocked to the locale, which became one of Europe's largest districts of continuous Jewish settlement as well as Polish Jewry's spiritual and cultural center. In 1568 due to overcrowding by Jewish immigrants from the West, local Jews requested and were granted a ban on further Christian settlement within the district's walls.[4]

By the sixteenth century, about 80 percent of world Jewry, or 200,000 people, lived in Polish lands. It was a golden era for Jewish Kazimierz, which became a center of talmudic learning; many revered works of Jewish scholarship, still setting standards today for ritual behavior for religious Jews around the world, were produced there.[5] Along with two cemeteries and several commercial and residential buildings, seven major synagogues—built from the 1400s through the late 1800s—still stand today, although only the Remu synagogue has regularly functioned since World War II.[6] Kazimierz's city walls were removed in the 1820s under Austrian rule when the district was administratively incorporated into Krakow, and fifty years later Jews were given the right to vote.[7] During the 1800s the restrictions on Jewish residence were gradually revoked and Jews began to spread throughout the city, but Kazimierz remained the center of Jewish cultural and religious life until World War II.[8] It was a poor area, though, and if people could leave it, they did. Poland, similarly, remained the center of world Jewry—second only to the United States in Jewish population—until the war. While historiographical disputes exist regarding the place of the Jews as "within" or "apart from" the European lands they inhabited (Poland in particular), Jewish history in Polish lands is inseparable from that of the larger Polish nation.

When the Nazis invaded Poland in September 1939, there were approximately 64,000 Jews living in Krakow proper, about 25 percent of the city's populace.[9] The first ghetto was established in the municipality in March 1941, when the Jews were removed from Kazimierz and concentrated in Krakow's Podgórze district across the river along with other Jews forced from the countryside. The ghetto subsequently underwent three consecutive liquidations in which its inhabitants were either sent to the adjacent Płaszów camp or directly to Auschwitz. Those who protested were killed on the spot.

Approximately 3,000,000 Polish Jews were murdered in the Holocaust. Of the 300,000 who survived the war (many in the Soviet Union), few returned to Poland to stay. Many of those who came back felt fearful and unwelcome (either personally or politically) and moved on. About 6,500 had returned to Krakow by the spring of 1945. A pogrom in Kazimierz in August of that year left 1 Jew dead and 5 wounded, and 42 Jews were killed in the nearby Kielce pogrom of July 4, 1946. These events compelled many Jews to leave. Between 1945 and 1948, 120,000 Polish Jews emigrated, and most of the rest followed in the mid-1950s or after a government-sponsored antisemitic campaign in 1968, which was taken by many observers as the decisive end of Poland's Jewish community.[10]

While Kazimierz, unlike other Jewish quarters across Europe, was physically spared, both its humanity and its movable material culture were gone. Already in 1943, when the quarter's Jews were moved to the ghetto in Podgórze, Poles from that poorer neighborhood moved in; after the war, the state distributed still-empty apartments to the needy, probably including individuals displaced from the eastern territories Poland lost in 1945. Despite a few state efforts to reenergize the quarter in the late 1950s and 1960s that supported artists and their projects, the "heritage" of the area was largely ignored. This is perhaps unsurprising given the communist government efforts to keep "the Jewish issue" out of public discourse.[11] For most Poles, the Jewish identity of the quarter had been lost; Cracovians knew it only as a slum.

Kazimierz's remarkable built environment—a complex of Jewish communal structures dating back to the fifteenth century—helped put Krakow on UNESCO's World Heritage list in 1978, and individual cultural seekers began to rediscover Kazimierz in the mid-1980s. But the neighborhood's historical riches made at that time little, if any, impression on the larger city or beyond. In addition to having the worst living conditions in the city, the local population was looked upon as "second class," home to drunks, prostitutes, vendors of illegal home-brew, and feral cats and dogs. Steven Spielberg's choice in 1993 of Kazimierz as the central location for shooting *Schindler's List* put the dilapidated quarter once again on the map for Jewish heritage explorers and jump-started its process of gentrification. But the tri-national Kazimierz Action Plan that produced an elaborate blueprint for the sustainable revitalization of the quarter in 1994 did not manage to move past the idea phase, and alternative comprehensive betterment schemes have remained elusive. Instead, "the vagaries of market forces prevail[ed]," bringing their own problems, central among them the alienation and disenfranchisement of locals from an increasingly fashionable café culture with its attendant late-night noise, tourists, and skyrocketing rents.[12]

Although the "problem" of Kazimierz from an urban planning perspective has been greater than just its Jewish half—as noted, it contains key monuments of Christian heritage and despite the recent inroads of gentrification, a largely socially disadvantaged local population—the Jewish heritage of the quarter has been a particularly thorny subject. Despite the Action Plan's attempts to ensure that neighborhood development proceeded with the interests of local inhabitants in mind, Kazimierz Trafas, professor of cartography at Krakow's Jagiellonian University and chairman of the taskforce behind the plan, explained to me that local people had resisted cooperating with the plan, fearing that Jews would take away their property if they managed to renovate it. Though in more recent years those whom Trafas called "Polish yuppies" began to invest in the neighborhood, in the early 1990s only artists, writers, and a few Jewish cultural seekers were drawn to try their luck as new, makeshift denizens in what would become a grittily hip local address. He singled out the proprietors of commercial venues on Szeroka Street as examples of those few people who had had the vision and commitment to develop Kazimierz in a substantive manner. They were there, he said, "before it was fashionable."

While representatives of the tiny local Jewish community were open to collaborating, Trafas said that American Jews had not expressed interest in investing in the quarter. Indeed, he told me he had trouble getting any foreign Jews interested in the question of what should be done with Kazimierz. Trafas seemed concerned to determine whether Jews felt that local Poles had the "right" to develop the Jewish heritage here. He sought input about what Jews thought about and cared about in Kazimierz. He came away with the sense that foreign Jews simply didn't identify with the place.

For the bulk of foreign Jews Poland has remained resolutely about the Holocaust, and the notion of vibrancy surrounding things Jewish—in the past and especially in the present—is a kind of "undesirable" heritage. Most foreign Jews come to Kazimierz because it is on the way to Auschwitz. Through the mid-1990s I knew many Jewish visitors who arrived in Krakow only to go directly by bus or taxi to the Holocaust's central symbol, returning the way they came. Only a few, perhaps those with specific ancestral ties, would bother with Kazimierz, seeking traces of flaking Hebrew lettering among the ruins, or stopping in entrance ways with visible impressions of *mezuzahs* (small receptacles containing a biblical text traditionally affixed to doorframes) that had been wrenched away in the wake of the Nazis' brutal removal of the Jews. It was easy to be struck primarily by the sense of Jewish absence, "particularly visible, since in spite of the destructive force of the war, the cultural landscape and urban fabric had survived."[13] Decades of economic stagnation made it appear as if time had stopped in the near aftermath of destruction, leaving a monument to the apocalypse.

A major factor inhibiting Kazimierz's organized development has been the issue of individual property ownership. Most local property belonged to Jews murdered during the Holocaust. Many of their descendants—living in the United States or Israel (with whom Poland had no diplomatic relations between 1967 and 1989)—made no claims to their ancestral belongings during the years when Poland was behind the Iron Curtain, for reasons both legal and emotional. Such petitions began to be made in growing numbers in the 1990s, but the situation was chaotic. There were cases of fraud, where individuals pretended to be the legal inheritors of Cracovian Jews who died during the Holocaust,[14] as well as legitimate claims made just after the buildings in question had undergone costly renovations by private and local government investors, significantly discouraging further speculation. And if in reality it was only a minority rather than a preponderance of properties for which no title could be established,[15] a sense of insecurity based on popular mythology and a lack of clarity—combined with the late Polish Jewish business magnate Zygmunt Nissenbaum's purchase of many such buildings on the promise of future renovation that he never undertook—has left even fashionable present-day Kazimierz pockmarked with overgrown, barricaded, empty-windowed ruins abutting its new shiny cafés and clubs.[16]

In 1939, Jews made up 10 percent of Poland's population and 25 percent of Krakow's, the culmination of almost a thousand years of ambivalent coexistence with Catholic Poles. Kazimierz was home to 45,000 Jews. Today, among the quarter's 18,000 inhabitants—according to one local's sardonic (though by no means implausible) estimate of the Jewish population—"there are three." Looking at Kazimierz now, little of this history nor its complex present is immediately visible.

In Spielberg's Wake

For the three months in 1994 during which Steven Spielberg (along with Ben Kingsley, Ralph Fiennes, Liam Neeson, and others) set up shop in Kazimierz to film *Schindler's List,* the quarter was transformed, drawn visually back in time as it was being propelled commercially forward. Spielberg chose Kazimierz over Podgórze, the neighborhood across the river where Krakow's wartime ghetto had been located, because it was free of the office buildings and TV tower that disrupted the historical look of Podgórze's skyline, and for the first time in half a century Jewish storefronts graced Kazimierz building facades and German soldiers strolled the streets. Local friends recounted with amusement watching older Poles staring in shock at the Nazi flag flying high over Wawel Castle, or encountering Nazi officers in full regalia chatting amiably over lunch on the curb with black-clad Hasidim.

Schindler's List was a boon for Kazimierz as a tourist site. It also triggered micro-level entrepreneurship whose echoes remain. Great distinction was bestowed, for example, on erstwhile Café Ariel—the only place on the square at the time where one could sit and have a coffee—by its use as the unofficial retreat for Spielberg and his entourage. Enhanced by the subsequent strategic display of a Spielberg family photograph and autographs of the film's cast members, Café Ariel became the preferred Jewish haunt in the quarter for locals and tourists alike for some time to come. "Schindler's List" tours, tracing both the sites where Spielberg filmed and their historical counterparts, were the brainchild of Zdzisław Leś of the Jarden Jewish Bookshop (the only other Jewish-themed commercial venue present at that time) and began shortly after the film's release, due to public demand. All summer tourists had been coming to his shop "ten times a day" and asking, "Where is this place from *Schindler's List*? Can you show me that site from the movie?" Interest was robust enough to fill multiple tours each day, so Zdzisław hired Franciszek Palowski, the Polish journalist who had had exclusive access to Spielberg during his three months in Poland, to prepare a *Schindler's List* tourist guidebook. The walking and mini-van tours followed.

While dismissals of Kazimierz as a Jewish Disneyland are glib shorthand that erases the cultural-political riches that have helped animate the quarter, there are ways—or perhaps moments—when the label's connotation of "digestible distortion" resonates. For one thing, the re-spatialization of Krakow's Jewishness to the convenient container of Kazimierz erases the more complex, shifting Jewish geographies of the city; not only did Jews begin their settlement just off the city's main square, but by the 1900s those who could had begun to spread across the wider urban landscape. There are unrestored prayer houses and other unmarked Jewish heritage sites in the Old City that—due to signs directing tourists to Kazimierz, Krakow's "Jewish Town"—remain invisible. But if this concentration, even "ghettoization" of Jewishness may obscure historical urban demographics, it is also a boon for the creation of vibrant "Jewish space" in the present day, where the focus and distillation of Jewishness has created a uniquely plural space where a multiplicity of people and interests converge and deliberate. As sociologist Sławomir Kapralski has argued, material, spatial frames are important for new meanings of the past—for example, the progressive Polish intellectual embrace of multiculturalism and the centrality of Jews to Polish history and national identity—to be disseminated at the vernacular level.[17]

The most visible forms of Jewish heritage brokering in the quarter have not always been easy on the eye. Fashionable Jewish-themed cafés and shops that line Kazimierz's main square beckon customers with signs in Polish, broken English, and sometimes faux Hebrew and Yiddish, offering such delicacies as "poultry broth of Jews from Kazimierz," in the shadow of white plaster lions of Judah and a six-foot-high electric menorah. And while *Schindler's List* itself has been roundly critiqued for generating illusions about history, the local detritus of its making also added layers of mediation to the physical traces of historical reality. The imposing mock concentration camp built for the film in an abandoned quarry near the camp's original site (including a road paved with mock-cement Jewish tombstones) stood on the outskirts of Krakow for two years after the filming. Tourist interest led the quarry's owners to transform it into a ticketed destination.

Of course, such attractions may well generate interest in history as much as obscuring or distorting it, but it was still a discomfiting suggestion about the relative value of historical traces and their re-presentation as entertainment to receive a brochure from a U.S. volunteer organization describing the area around Krakow as "a beautifully quaint region which is only a half-hour drive from Auschwitz, the site of the Academy Award winning movie *Shindler's* [sic] *List*."[18] But I felt real concern only on those few occasions when I heard tourists (foreign or local) make comments indicating that they thought the neighborhood's new commercial venues were continuous with prewar establishments, and that Jewish proprietors, families, and neighbors still filled the surrounding apartments and institutions.[19]

Kazimierz is nonetheless impressive. The density of its prewar built environment may be the basis of its claim to world heritage status. But its authenticity for many people comes not from its *yikhes* (Yiddish for pedigree) alone, but from its present-day gifts as an urban social phenomenon, a unique admixture of Jewish, Polish, European, artistic, communal, cultural, and political qualities that the emergence of heritage brokering has acted to catalyze. As a point of comparison, Warsaw, razed to the ground on Hitler's orders, boasts an old city square meticulously reconstructed from prewar renderings by eighteenth-century Italian landscape painter Bernardo Bellotto (Canaletto); the result is an idealized version of what had stood there before. If there is a Disneyland in Poland, perhaps it is in Warsaw. Kazimierz feels like the genuine article, a face-to-face, human-scale place.

Despite its name, tour buses cannot pass through to Szeroka ("wide") Street, the quarter's main square. They park on Dajwór Street, behind the old synagogue and across from the new Galicja Jewish museum. The visitors who leave the bus funnel through the quarter-block of narrow Przejściu ("passageway") Street, into the cobbled plaza. Szeroka is bounded at the southern end by the Old Synagogue—the oldest intact synagogue structure in Poland and now the Jewish wing of Krakow's municipal museum. The museum's entry plaza often hosts children playing ball or lovers chatting on the stone steps. On the northern end the Landau Palace—a tall eighteenth-century façade—houses the Jarden Jewish Bookshop, Noah's Ark café, the restaurant Once Upon A Time in Kazimierz, and a revolving door of variously themed restaurants (Anatewka was the most memorable in recent years) on the ground level.[20] Slightly off-center in the middle of this northern end of the square is a grassy patch, enclosed by a wrought-iron fence with a menorah motif and shaded by a single massive willow tree, evidence of its former life as a Jewish cemetery from the 1400s through the early 1900s. Today it is a favored place for local dogs to relieve themselves. At the southern side of this small green space are the square's only two public benches, flanking a small monument stating that of Krakow's 65,000 prewar Jews, only 2,000 survived.

In the summer of 2008, the eastern side of the square was taken up (from north to south) by the Klezmer Hois restaurant in the old *mikveh* (ritual bath) building, Ptaszyl (a cozy pub with no Jewish theme), the ultra-modern Hotel Rubenstein (named for the Jewish cosmetics magnate Helena Rubenstein, born near that address), the Popper synagogue (set back behind a gated courtyard), Café Alef, Café Ariel, and the Hotel Ester. After the small gap of the alley, a bank stands on the reconstructed building of another former synagogue ("On the Hill"), destroyed during the war. The western side (south to north) contains Ulica Krokodyli ("Street of Crocodiles," a pub named for Polish Jewish author Bruno Schulz's literary work), a new upscale restaurant Szara ("Grey"), and finally the Remu synagogue surrounded by its walled-in medieval cemetery. From the early 2000s through the middle of the decade a sign was bolted on its outside wall with the religious admonition, in Polish, English, Yiddish, and Hebrew, "*Cohanim* [descendants of the Jewish priestly class] beware!!! Only the opposite sidewalk can be used for walking on this street!!! The sidewalk on this side and a part of the roadway have been paved over graves."

With a complex mix of issues implicating a variety of Polish and foreign interests (both state and private, financial and religious), conservation of the quarter has been chaotic, involving conflicts over aesthetic choices, local versus tourist concerns, the identification of former property owners and evolving restitution law, and illegal renovation activities. Commercial trends have simultaneously evolved, comprising cafés and restaurants for different tastes, gift shops, hotels, museums and theaters—all of which host a range of cultural events—as well as local service providers and shops for workaday merchandise. As new initiatives emerge, further debates unfold, and the neighborhood's physical configuration continues to change.[21]

The landscape of ephemera in Kazimierz was similarly rich. Flat surfaces in restaurant or museum entryways invited piles of brochures: A Polish-language flyer from the early 1990s, disseminated by members of Warsaw's young, emerging Jewish community, read: *Do you have Jewish roots? Is this a problem? Or a secret? Or perhaps your passion, pride, or hope?*—and offered an anonymous telephone support line. Another, put out in English in 1999 by the Jewish heritage documentation association Diaspora's Memory, was addressed *To young friends from Israel,* urging them not to look at "us"—at Poles—only in the context of the Shoah. In the mid-2000s stickers began to appear advertising the website of the anti-racism group *Nigdy Więcej* ("Never Again"). Crudely photocopied leaflets advertising free Shabbat dinners sponsored by the American-based Ronald Lauder Foundation, daily round-trip tours to Auschwitz, kosher falafel in Hotel Eden, or a Jewish survivor's trilogy of personal Holocaust films plastered kiosks, wooden fences, and the occasional bulletin board. Over the years these gave way to glossy posters promoting Judaica exhibits at Cracovian entrepreneur Dominick Dybbek's Izaak Synagogue Project or British photographer Chris Schwartz's Galicja Museum. The paper accrued in a thickening crust, its torn edges exposing geological strata riddled with clusters of quickly rusting staples. The foot-long white adhesive strips proclaiming *odwołane* ("cancelled") over July's Jewish cultural festival posters, applied by some anonymous, presumably antisemitic trickster, had become an annual irritation. A stand in the Jarden Jewish Bookshop each year carried an updated flyer proclaiming that Adela Schwarzer is still looking for her siblings, whom she saw for the last time in spring 1942 in the Rzeszow ghetto. Their six young faces gaze out above a plea for information that might lead to a reunion. The 2008 version stated that "she was looking for them until the end," and in 2010 a freestanding banner greeted all who entered the building, as her Swedish children continue the search.

Kazimierz's visible Jewishness stretches some blocks further west—with imposing former synagogues (Tempel, Izaak, Kupa, Wysoka ["high"]) and streets named Joseph, Isaac, Jacob, Ester, Rabbi Maisels—and north with Miodowa/Honey Street and one named for Polish Jewish patriot and freedom fighter Berek Joselewicz.[22] Other hotels, shops, and a couple of nonprofit institutions also openly represent Jewish culture or play on the theme. Some of these appear later in this text. But the heart of the action—and thus my attention—was in and around Szeroka Street. Here, miniature motorized tourist surreys bounced past, their recorded *spiels* about Jewish Kazimierz wafting out from under their red canvas canopies in one of seven languages. They might pull up next to a group of visiting Hasidim on pilgrimage, video-taping each other in front of Remu synagogue, in feigned or actual obliviousness to the presence of this other audience of passersby taking snapshots of them.

The Cracovian brand of small-city urban culture favors leisurely strolling, sitting, coffee drinking, and chatting. This means that once one has entered the square, the possibility that one will linger and be lured into conversation with someone is exponentially increased. As urban planner James Rojas notes, "People activate a setting merely by their presence. Their bodies, faces and movements create an energy that is almost a metaphysical aesthetic."[23] Especially given the heightened emotional state and slightly anxious anticipation in which many Jews travel to Poland, and the tendency to be on high alert for foe or friend, inquiries leading to spontaneous, often fraught exchanges with other travelers, local Jews, or Polish heritage brokers are common.

These are not just any conversations. The four blocks between the quarter's main square at Szeroka Street, and the smaller one—New Square, or "Jewish Square," as locals call it—were scattered with people searching for Jewishness. For the non-Jewish Poles, these forays may be curious, intellectual, or personal, a place to imagine a Poland that contains other kinds of people. Among these Poles are some with Jewish ancestry; for them Kazimierz may be the first Jewish space they have ever entered, a place where they may try on a Jewish identity for size. For Jewish tourists from abroad, the motivation is often memorial. For local Jews the goal is frequently social, a place to meet their Jewish friends. My own aims waxed and shifted, informed by those fellow travelers I met.

Doing Ethnography (or What's a Nice Jewish Girl Like You Doing in a Place Like This?)

Fieldwork was almost too easy in Kazimierz. My apartment's third-floor window overlooking Józef Street was ideal for tourist watching. I would hear them first, the distant babble of Hebrew or English (or sometimes German, French, or Spanish) peaking as they passed below. The guides rarely varied their path: from a stop in front of Izaak synagogue on the southeastern corner of the block, they ambled to the next corner at the rear façade of the Kupa synagogue on the street's northern end. I confess I did stalk the occasional Jewish traveler. I quickly learned how to pick them out on the street, suspecting from their direction that they would likely end up in the Jarden Jewish Bookshop before long; I might hurry over and place myself behind the counter in time to greet them in my occasional role as a shop clerk. Both Jewish tourists and local Poles were often bursting at the seams with untold stories, as if they had been waiting a long time for someone to listen. And while plenty of visitors told their stories to co-owners Lucyna and Zdzisław, or other Jarden employees, being a Jew (and speaking native English) made me a desirable category of listener. As I inevitably revealed my own background, sometimes a cluster of visitors would form around me, trying to figure me out, save me from the presumably horrible fate of being stuck in Poland, or suggest introducing me to a nice young man from their tour group.

As anthropologist Ruth Behar notes, observers are not only visible but vulnerable to their subjects. I often fell in love with mine, those who were trying to put back together what history had broken. My Polish world turned around the forty-five-square-meter Jarden Jewish Bookshop. I wandered in one day in 1994, and in a sense I never left. They simply took an interest in my interest and took me in. I began to record visitors' stories on the couch in their foyer. At some point Zdzisław observed that I'd go bankrupt if I kept buying coffee for my interviewees at the café next door, showed me the shelf where they kept the kettle, and told me to serve from the shop. This also meant that he and Lucyna became, in ethnographic terms, my "key informants." They affectionately called me "our intellectual" (*nasza intelektualistka*). They fished around for others they deemed particularly worthwhile interlocutors. "We have another *victim* for your project," Zdzisław would say with a wink.

Depending on the day, one can get an entirely different impression of Kazimierz, and consequently of Jewish Poland: bleak and empty or buzzing with Jewish life, often temporarily imported in the form of a foreign tour. On my daily strolls I began to expect serendipity. Walking along Szeroka's west side, I might bump into a local Jewish studies student or scholar, a Jewish visitor (or forty of them) from North or South America, Israel, or France, the proprietor of one of the quarter's Jewish establishments, a journalist, the current rabbi—and not infrequently all these characters in a cluster, already engaged in heated discussion. Many people were kind enough to let me follow them on their quests, often traveling to far-flung towns and cities; others asked me to help them in some way (I translated, navigated, advertised, advised, and made sure the *rebbetzin*—whom I barely knew—was fully submerged in the nearby stream that served as her *mikveh*).

There was a good dose of craziness, fakery, and nasty gossip among Jews and non-Jews in Kazimierz, artists and charlatans and scholars and jesters. A lot of documents (old and new), poverty, upward mobility, self-proclaimed experts, scraps of half-learned languages and a lot of pain. There was competition for community recognition and resources that came, on occasion, to blows. I believe this must be true anywhere identities, resources, and social transformation intersect. Sometimes it was too much. There were too many people confronting painful pasts, too many on their way to or coming back from Auschwitz. Some days I just couldn't hear any more grief, anger, remorse, or celebrations of bygone Jewishness. Even interviews with upbeat, curious young people were perpetually accompanied by the often mournful klezmer sound track that animated Kazimierz's cafés. Transcribing these conversations later on, I realized how weary I had grown of that music.

Social Landscape

So whose stories interested me, and why? It seems worth stating what this study is not; doing so will allow me to offer a glimpse of the broader social and institutional landscape in which my research took place. This is not a book about Polish Jews, Jewish Poles, or however one might label the local Jewish population. I did not find a way to relate meaningfully to the few local "old-timer" Jews, the last vestiges of the prewar Polish Jewish world, whose public engagements with Jewishness formed an integral part of Kazimierz's Jewish heritage economy. Difficult to categorize, at the extremes of the spectrum they have been described as the rather hagiographic "Orthodox Jews of Krakow" as well as the more homey (if less polite) "schnorrers" (Yiddish for

spongers).[24] They sat in the Remu synagogue courtyard, sold tickets to enter, requested donations, told their life stories (in Yiddish if requested), and
generally asserted what power they had over the flow of visitors, including
separating men and women, seeing that *yarmulkes* were worn by the former,
and making sure only Jews (more or less) entered during times of organized
prayer. Their continuous East European, if not always Cracovian, residence
since prewar times made them sought after as traces of authentic *Yiddishkeyt*
(Ashkenazic, or East European, Jewishness) for foreign visitors.

There were fewer than 200 of these old-timers in the city in the late
1990s, many of them house-bound; the youngest at the time were in their
mid-sixties, but the average age was much higher. Even those few who attended synagogue (an act rewarded by community subventions for those who
helped meet the obligatory count of ten men—a *minyan*—that Jewish law
requires for public prayer) were not all *halakhically* (legally) Jewish or religiously literate. Many of the men were married to Catholic women, some attended both synagogue and church, and their children (those who remained
in Poland rather than emigrating to Israel or elsewhere) were often kept un-
aware of their parents' Jewish origin or current practice. With a few exceptions these elders had little connection with (or tolerance for) the new generation of self-proclaimed Jews whose identities were not shaped by the suffering
of war and communism, nor for the new, foreign-imported religious representatives sent to Poland to revitalize the community. Both were spoken of
as impostors. When I asked about Rabbi Sasha Pecaric, who lived in Kazimierz and had led services in the Remu synagogue for more than five years, employed by the Ronald Lauder Foundation, one elderly synagogue regular responded, "Rabbi? What rabbi? We haven't had a rabbi here in fifty years." To
them, this young, yeshiva-educated upstart simply did not belong. His enthusiastic, American-bred ideas about Judaism—while breathing keen new life
into their moribund outpost—threatened their hard-won *modus vivendi.*

Nor does my work directly or comprehensively address the identity struggles
of Poland's "new Jews." These Poles, who have discovered and embraced Jewish identities (or new, more visible forms of these) in recent years, have been
the subject of much scrutiny by both older locals and foreign Jews. At issue are their unorthodox (or orthodox) models of Jewishness, their opinions
on the possibility and necessity of Jewish community in Poland, and above
all their very improbability. Most outside observers assumed, by the 1980s,
that the above-mentioned old-timers were "the last of the Mohicans." Indeed,
these mostly elderly Jews saw themselves in these terms. But the new, self-

invented Jews—those whom Polish Jewish community leader Konstanty Gebert, counting himself among them, called "Jews not only from scratch, but from *itch*"—have taken center stage. Others have written about them, and they increasingly write about themselves.[25]

There are other sites of Jewishness in Krakow, both in and outside Kazimierz, that are not featured in my text. The offices of the Jewish community (*Gmina Wyznaniowa Żydowska*), for example, include a soup kitchen providing daily hot meals for needy Jews (and non-Jews who may also show up); in addition, they host Passover seders, dispense aid from the international Jewish Joint Distribution Committee, oversee home visits to elderly housebound Jews, and deal with the immense and complex problem of Jewish property restitution in the Krakow region. For those relatively few foreign Jews who seek out the official Jewish community to answer their questions about Jewish life or family genealogy in Poland, the offices serve as a public relations interface. The minute numbers of this community and the enormity of the issues that they must adjudicate have given rise to a kind of impenetrability to substantive research. I know of no scholarship that illuminates its inner workings.

There was also "the Club" or TSKŻ (*Towarzystwo Społeczno-Kulturalne Żydów,* Jewish Social-Cultural Association). One branch of a nationwide Jewish organization founded in 1950, it remains the largest Jewish organization in Poland today, with 2,700 members.[26] But because it was the only such organization tolerated (and supported) by the communist government, due to its compliance with the party line, it has borne a stigma, particularly for younger people, since 1989. Its character is Yiddishist and anti-religious, and at the time of my fieldwork the Club mostly provided a home away from home for a few old men, a private space to be Jewish, apart from their non-Jewish workaday or home lives. It was set back at the end of a corridor behind an unmarked façade off Szewska Street in the center of Krakow's Old City. Although some American-led Jewish revival efforts in the early 1990s used the club space (there were few if any alternatives at that time), by the time I arrived in Krakow it was largely irrelevant for the young Jews I met.

One could have done an entire study of the copious efforts and intrigues of the Jewish Youth Club, sponsored by the Ronald Lauder Foundation, where "youth" was construed broadly, referring, it seemed, to anyone born after the war—although members of the *Dzieci Holocaustu* (Children of the Holocaust) group also attended its events. It was housed in, yet administratively unrelated to, the Izaak synagogue. An excellent site to observe the deliberate foreign-sponsored efforts at Jewish religious revival in post-communist Poland along American and more-or-less Orthodox lines, it functioned as both a rival to and a collaborator with both older and newer expressions of Jewishness in Krakow. From the mid-1990s through the early 2000s, it was rife with controversy over leadership, resources, and access to space.

The Research Center on Jewish History and Culture in Poland, a unit of the Jagiellonian University situated across town on Batory Street until 2007, when it moved into a lovely courtyard compound on Kazimierz's Józef Street, was another important node in the web of Jewish heritage brokering during the period of my research. Many young people whose Jewish interest began in Kazimierz cafés and bookshops ended up at the Research Center, where they learned Hebrew and Yiddish and could complete an advanced degree in Jewish studies. If to some observers it seemed that such students had graduated from Szeroka Street kitsch to the lofty world of ideas, this view was invalidated by the fact that they were compelled to return at regular intervals to the Jarden Jewish Bookshop, long the only reliable source for the Jewish texts necessary for the university courses. It was at the Research Center that I was first introduced to the historical and cultural complexity of Jewish Poland, as well as its local manifestations, in an American-funded summer program in 1992.

Also present is the Center for Jewish Culture (*Centrum Kultury Żydowskiej*) just off New Square on Rabbi Meisels Street in the former Bnei Emuna prayer house. Beautifully restored and opened to the public in 1993 (funded in large part by the U.S. government), until the late 1990s it was among the most modern buildings in Krakow.[27] Climate-controlled, with an Italian espresso bar, the Center for Jewish Culture was also striking for its clean, publicly accessible (and, unusually, free-of-charge) restrooms, a luxury in the otherwise grimy quarter. Under the direction of Joachim Russek, who cultivated an elite (if dwindling) audience of aging Jewish Polish intelligentsia that gave it symbolic weight, for years the Center was a pioneer in co-sponsoring summer programs on Polish Jewish history and culture (which had been previously housed on Batory Street at the university's Research Center on Jewish History and Culture in Poland) with American universities. But it was beset by organizational troubles. In part because the renovation alone emptied the Center for Jewish Culture's coffers, but also because of identity problems (Whose is it? What is it for? Is it Jewish?), the Center's building long outshone its programming. Financially compelled to rent out space for a range of cultural activities, it often disappointed visiting Jews arriving on emotionally charged pilgrimages. Given the Center's name, such visitors anticipated a

kind of Jewish community center. Instead they found on offer a puzzling assortment of often non-Jewish programs and a staff largely ignorant of sched-
ules and locations of Jewish communal events in the quarter (Shabbat dinner, holiday celebrations, and the like). The addition of an antique shop in the
basement also disturbed some Jewish visitors, who were uncomfortable seeing the occasional Jewish ritual object—its provenance unclear—for sale, further confusing the perceived allegiance of the institution.

Aside from the new Jewish Community Center (JCC)—an entity I discuss in the Conclusion, but which did not yet exist during the years of my
fieldwork—the most significant Polish institution contributing to Kazimierz's
Jewish cultural revival has been the Festival of Jewish Culture. Initiated in
1988 by young local cultural visionaries Janusz Makuch and Krzysztof Gierat
in the Kino Mikro cinema across town, the festival has been held every summer since 1990 in the quarter, growing to major proportions through the 2000s.
It developed, along with the Center for Jewish Culture, out of the late-1980s
democracy movement's engagement with Jewish themes as crucial compo-
nents in reformulating a Polish identity grounded in an ethnically plural history. For years its offices were situated in the courtyard of Kino Graffiti,[28] a
cinema on Saint Gertrude Street adjacent to the Planty park encircling the
Old City. Except for the annual production of its colorful posters that appeared on Kazimierz's many kiosks and fences, the festival's presence was felt
mostly in the summer, when a week to ten days of frenetic activity would en-
velop, enliven, and indeed come to define the quarter, from early morning
walking tours to parties during the wee hours in local cafés, often with spontaneous jam sessions featuring international performers.[29] In the late 1990s
the festival's programming began to diversify and expand through the sea-
sons. Particularly since 2007, when it opened the permanent Cheder coffee-
house on the high-traffic corner of Józef and Izaak Streets, it has formed a
core component of the quarter's visible "Jewish" landscape year round.

The festival has achieved a kind of organic popular acceptance by multiple parties (Jews, Poles, locals, foreigners) in a way the Center for Jewish
Culture has not. In part this may be attributed to festival director Janusz
Makuch's embrace rather than rejection of Kazimierz's grassroots commercial "Jewish" venues, as well as the ties he has cultivated with the local and
international Jewish community. Risk-taking, not inclined to notions of cultural purity, and unafraid of partnerships of all kinds, the festival has—perhaps
ironically—become a highly trusted icon for local and foreign (particularly
American) Jewish organizations, the latter of which provide it with signifi-

cant funding.[30] I discuss the festival in the context of its director's motivations in chapter 4.

I did not take the Remu synagogue, the only fully functioning prayer house in the city, as a focus of interest. It was largely the domain of the "old timers" who used it as much as a place to meet each other and chat, have a *kiddush* snack and drink [social gathering after the blessing of wine on Shabbat], review finances, negotiate with tourists, journalists, or filmmakers, root through bags of donated clothes, or take care of whatever other matter might arise. A fascinating study could be done of intra-religious relations and synagogue cultures as foreign Jewish visitors periodically arrived and sidelined the locals, who, while looked upon as authentic historical remnants, were often perceived as having an antiquated (read Ashkenazic, or East European) and less-than-robust knowledge of liturgy.

I also did not deal substantively with Kazimierz's neighboring Podgórze district just across the river, the actual site of Krakow's wartime Jewish ghetto. The district contains the site of Oskar Schindler's factory (since 2010 housing a cutting edge, multi-media "experience" museum); the historic Pharmacy under the Eagle museum and the small Ghetto Heroes square in front of it (since 2005 a memorial consisting of empty metal chairs); the fragments of ghetto wall along Lwowska Street; and the Płaszów concentration camp site. They all form an important part of Krakow's Jewish heritage tourism constellation. Yet while these Holocaust memorial sites have become increasingly prominent with the economic and cultural infrastructural development of Podgórze in the last few years, during the period of my main fieldwork they were not considered obligatory stops except by those intrepid visitors willing to hunt—with or without the company of a local cab driver—for scattered, unmarked, or inadequately marked sites. Podgórze also lacks the kind of café culture or central gathering place amenable to fieldwork with tourists.

Warsaw is arguably the logical site for a study of Jewish community in contemporary Poland for the simple fact that a relatively robust one had developed there by the late 1990s. The community is largely self-sufficient, self-contained, and somewhat secluded from the surrounding city in an enclosed, guarded compound where all manner of religious, administrative, social, cultural, and educational services take place. It is much less porous and less connected to larger urban processes than Kazimierz. By the mid-2000s, additional Jewish communal options arose in Warsaw: the progressive Beit Warszawa (funded by Seweryn Aszkenazy, a Polish Jewish businessman living in California) and the New York–based Hasidic Chabad House.

Finally, there is Auschwitz. A shorthand for the Holocaust as well as a real place, it casts a shadow over all Poland for Jewish visitors, inevitably informing their trips whether they visit the camp or not. As a site it also partakes of many of the issues that interest me: Jewish and Polish identity construction, historical representation, even commercialization (disputes over a shopping mall and a disco were the most highly publicized of the more general issues). Sensitive scholarly analyses of the site have been undertaken.[31]

I did not exclude any of these places, locales, or venues. Indeed, I could not have, even if I had tried. Given the relatively meager Jewish offerings in Krakow (and Poland) during the period of my research, these various sites and institutions were somewhat interdependent—the Lauder Foundation rabbi led services at the Remu synagogue, the "old timers" got Shabbat challah from the Ariel café, the Research Center students relied on the Jarden Jewish Bookshop for study texts, Jarden is the official representative of the Auschwitz museum bookstore in Krakow, and all these venues are enlisted to host events during the annual Festival of Jewish Culture. These venues are also tied together through a leadership genealogy: Joachim Russek, director of the Center for Jewish Culture on Rabbi Meisels Street, used to administer the Research Center on Batory Street; Janusz Makuch, founder and director of the Festival of Jewish Culture, was the first director of the Center for Jewish Culture on Meisels Street; and Robert Gądek, longtime program manager under Mr. Russek, took over management of the Festival of Jewish Culture under Mr. Makuch in 2008.[32] These shifts were more and less amiable.

One could access a great many of the resources typically provided by official Jewish community venues from the commercial Jewish-themed venues of Kazimierz, in unofficial settings, by unsanctioned individuals.[33] Jewish weddings, genealogical research, kosher meals or "Jewish-style" food, *mikveh* ablutions, Jewish literary, artistic, and musical programs, Hebrew and Yiddish language classes, and Jewish dance lessons were the more visible offerings, but these venues also satisfied less tangible needs: a place for mourning, for meeting other Jews, for sharing one's story.

Dramatis Personae

Before entering more fully into the analytic universe I construct in the subsequent chapters, I would like to offer a series of brief introductions to some of those Kazimierz denizens who shaped my experience.[34] They were part of the quarter's texture, some showing up not only in cafés and on street corners, but also in journal articles, guidebooks, and memoirs about visiting Jewish

Poland. They, along with a variety of prominent Jewish and Polish cultural figures—including historian Jan Gross, former speaker of the Israeli Knesset Shevah Weiss, Israeli ambassador to Poland David Peleg, author Theo Richmond, even (I was told) poet Czesław Miłosz and pop star Kayah, to name but a few—have been browsers at the Jarden Jewish Bookshop and tea drinkers at Café Ariel.[35]

Bernard Offen is a Krakow-born Holocaust survivor, an American who spends winters in California and leads "witnessing" tours in summer from Kazimierz through the Podgórze ghetto and Płaszów camp across the river. A striking seventy-something-year-old with blue eyes and white hair combed into a short ponytail, by the mid-1990s he had made a name for himself as an itinerant voice of conscience. Feeling himself a lone guardian of memory in an amnesiac landscape, Bernard made the daily rounds, urging tourists to walk with him and to watch the films he made about his experiences, which he screened and sold in whichever of the local venues he could convince to accept them. Bernard's endeavors have continually evolved. By 2004 there was a "Bernard Offen Dialogue Club of Krakow," training young Poles to serve as guides in his stead. Bernard also agitated for the Krakow city government to better mark the site of the Płaszów concentration camp.

Allen Haberberg is the owner and proprietor of Hotel Eden on Ciemna Street. His goal was to run what he called a "really Jewish" establishment in Kazimierz. He stumbled onto the neighborhood in the late 1980s on a Jewish-roots mission to his ancestral villages. Jocular and superstitious, Allen told me the story of how he came to open a Jewish hotel with its own *mikveh* and (more or less) kosher kitchen; it was a tale of fate and business acumen combined. He called his hotel's Jewishness the "gimmick that worked," although he added that the sauna, massage, pub, and therapeutic salt grotto also "didn't hurt." The plan for Hotel Eden was nurtured in the Jarden foyer; Jarden's co-owner Lucyna Leś was its first manager, guiding Allen through the nightmarish bureaucracy involved in purchasing and transforming a set of ruined prewar buildings into the only kosher hotel in Poland, to the satisfaction of a wide range of vocal foreign Jewish clientele. In the process Allen married and had children with a Polish Catholic woman. He was also drawn into a Jewish religious awakening, and within a few years he became a cornerstone of the Remu synagogue *minyan*.

Radek is today in his early thirties, a former competitive swimmer and mathematics student who is a trainer at a gym in eastern Poland after trying life in Israel in the early 2000s. He is tall and slim, and in cold weather he wears a white knit hat with the word "Israel" appliquéd across the forehead in black block letters. In the mid-1990s, he found out from his grandmother that he is Jewish. Like a growing number of young Poles who have been burdened with such revelations since the fall of communism, Radek's life has been significantly complicated by this information about his heritage. Radek is also gay. In Poland, Jewish and gay circles often overlap. At Jewish events, gays are a noteworthy presence. In gay clubs or gatherings, Jews who otherwise don't identify publicly may feel comfortable wearing a *yarmulke* or being otherwise open about their ancestry. For Radek, Kazimierz provided a place to be somewhat more himself. Living in Krakow during my fieldwork, since moving away he has more recently begun to return there for the Festival of Jewish Culture in summer and on the occasional weekend to spend Shabbat among Jews.

Menachem is a Belorussian who came west in the mid-1990s to find openness and opportunity. When he wasn't at his job with the international Joint Distribution Committee caring for indigent members of the Jewish community in Krakow and its environs, he played guitar and sang beautiful Yiddish songs—at the Lauder club, for Kazimierz's Jewish cafés, and at bohemian late-night parties in Krakow apartments. A regular at *shul* (synagogue) and Passover seders at the *gmina* (official Jewish community), where he was prized for his knowledge of the liturgy, he was nonetheless trailed by a cloud of controversy, including doubts about his claims to Jewish ancestry and gossip about his lifestyle choices. A born performer, Menachem cultivated a look of stylish Jewish nostalgia, tweaking the standard Orthodox uniform of a white button-down shirt, black trousers, and fedora hat (covering a large black velvet *yarmulke*) with shiny, modishly large-buckled shoes and chic dark sunglasses.

Agnieszka was in her late twenties when I met her, a vivacious Polish woman with a round face and long red hair. I recall her preparing for a trip to Ukraine, hurrying back and forth in the two-room apartment tucked away behind the Center for Jewish Culture, where she had generously agreed to let me stay while she was away. In addition to her roommate, Agnieszka had recently taken in a woman from her church and the woman's small, ailing son, both recently abandoned by the boy's father. There were symbols of Jewishness everywhere my gaze settled: a miniature Israeli flag fluttered in a potted plant, a postcard of tan, fatigues-clad soldiers pressing their faces in prayer against the rough stone of Jerusalem's Wailing Wall perched on a window sill, a water-wrinkled poster of Masada covered the cracked wall next to the toilet bowl. A plaque with the Hebrew *alef-beys* (alphabet) was secured above the sink. Above Agnieszka's small cassette player sat a shelf of cassettes distributed by messianic groups advertising "a joyous celebration of the coming of the messiah to the Jewish people." On the kitchen table was a stack of passports; Agnieszka was in charge of getting visas for friends who were to travel with her. They were going to Ukraine to find and help Jews.

Now in her forties, Agnieszka has spent the last fifteen years of her life seeking out elderly, isolated Jews in Poland and the former Soviet Union and helping them with donations of food, money, visas to Israel, and the organization of soup kitchens and Jewish cultural and religious programs. She told me her work is supported completely by donations from individuals who "believe in what I am doing"; the network includes both fundamentalist Christian farmers in Texas and Hasidic rabbis in Jerusalem's ultra-Orthodox neighborhood of Mea Shearim. Agnieszka's own interest in Jews is intimately tied to her discovery of God in her early twenties. Brought up a "good Communist atheist," she is part of a tiny but growing minority of new Protestants in this otherwise Catholic country. Many of them have a special interest in Jews, whose "in-gathering" will, they believe, herald the messianic age. Some, like Agnieszka, claim Jewish roots themselves. They practice Jewish rituals, participate in Jewish community events and organizations, study Hebrew (and sometimes Yiddish), and go to church (and sometimes to synagogue). On the day of my visit, Agnieszka paused to eat some lunch with me and her other guests. As she sat down, she asked me in English if it would be all right if she told the woman that I am Jewish. "It would be a special joy for her," she said.

Invariably, if you stood in one place in Kazimierz long enough, you would meet Henryk Halkowski. Trained in architecture but an avid autodidact on Jewish themes, Henryk authored numerous books on Jewish thought, history, and mythology that were sold in Kazimierz venues, and grew from being an informal tour guide (for those lucky enough to hear of him) to a somewhat more official one for Klezmer Hois restaurant, which promoted him on their website as "The Only Jewish Guide in Cracow." Secretary of the TSKŻ and a ubiquitous presence in Kazimierz, Henryk, despite his unconventionalities and limited attention span toward the many things that disinterested him, was a cherished presence who could be counted on for his cutting humor, erudite philosophizing, and the most arcane local knowledge. He passed away on January 1, 2009, at age fifty-eight and was buried in the Jewish cemetery on Miodowa Street.

Salvaging Salvage Ethnography

The point of the probe is in the heart of the observer.

—GREGORY BATESON

One could say I first entered my field site at a cocktail party in Cambridge, Massachusetts, in 1992. It was an annual event hosted by a local anthropologist couple, where a very elegant, very assimilated Viennese-born Jewish woman balked at my announcement that I would spend a post-college year in Poland. "Poland!" she exclaimed. "What a horrible country! Why would you *ever* want to go there?" Another woman—a Jew from Belgium, hidden as a child—was more understanding. She touched my forearm with her hand, looked in my eyes, and said, "Find what you are looking for, and then get out."

The last portrait in this section is of myself, partaking of the self-reflexivity that is an acknowledged, even fashionable mode in certain quarters of cultural anthropology. Pioneers of writing in this genre drew attention to the importance, indeed the constitutive nature of, intersubjectivity to the ethnographic endeavor, a crucial contribution to the now general acceptance of ethnographies as specifically situated "partial truths." Even so, most ethnographers are still reticent about the personal cultural projects that may motivate their choice of, and approach to, their subjects. Without wanting to propose that anthropologists themselves should form the main subjects of ethnographic analysis, it seems important to draw attention to the ways that both researchers and their interlocutors are interested, politically and culturally entangled agents, inspired by projects and goals exceeding the intellectual, and constantly subject to each others' influence and incorporation. In this respect, ethnography about Jews has a particularly interesting status in the larger discipline of anthropology. Undertaken almost exclusively by Jews, it has been in no small part a project of identity construction and management, as well as voicing cultural loss, longing, and reclamation.[36] I see my work as part of this tradition, both sharing its concerns and taking them as its subject. So I include something of my own Jewish self here because this book is in important ways about the formation and boundaries of such selves, and particularly the way history and memory provide resources for, as well as impinge on, the kinds of selves available to Jews in this postmodern post-Holocaust moment.

Given my overlapping position as an observer and participant in searches for Jewishness in what historian Michael Meng has called Poland's "shattered spaces," mine is both an ethnography about salvage and a "salvage ethnography" of sorts. I am mindful of the critique embedded in this concept of the implicit claims in works of nineteenth-century (and later) ethnographers to the authenticity, wholeness, and boundedness of cultures rooted in a timeless past, and these researchers' flawed aims of "preserving last remnants" of what was presumed to be former cultural splendor, before they disappeared for good.[37] But my foray into ethnography is nevertheless entwined in my yearning to reassemble something useable out of my sense of broken Jewishness. I wanted to tether what seemed like my own and others' orphaned cultural experiences, to weave these together and have them "redeemed, or recovered as valid and significant, in an age of apparent homogenization and suspicion of authenticity."[38] But why Poland? Jewishness post-Holocaust has been rebuilt elsewhere in communities that see no need to revisit such failed histories except as a negative foil; so why not just go forward along with the rest? It was my estrangement from and disappointment with established narratives of post-Holocaust Jewishness that led me to this project—in part because for me the pre-Holocaust, as well as traumatic shards of the event itself, lingered in insistent ways.

By virtue of my ancestry, my upbringing, the attributions of others, and, in the context of these, some measure of personal choice, I am part of a people who, in living memory, were targeted by a systematic plan to exterminate them. The plan succeeded in eliminating two-thirds of the Jewish population in Europe, and the world's Jewish population was reduced by a third. While it can be difficult to determine or articulate the lingering effects of this genocide on me as I sit writing this in the comfort of my apartment as part of a privileged career, it is a collective tragedy that impinges beyond the generation that experienced it directly.

I went to Poland expecting to find nothing. Like the ninety-odd percent of American Jews who trace their roots to Eastern Europe, the "old country" for me existed only as the vague and caricatured setting of family memory; it was not a place to visit, because our Poland no longer existed. But expecting to find nothing is not the same as having no expectations. The Poland I anticipated was a gray and vaguely malevolent one, a product of Cold War propaganda made more sinister—and more significant—by references to it by my parents' prewar European-born Jewish acquaintances as "blood-soaked ground" and "the largest Jewish cemetery." I grew up in a leafy New England town where my parents had taken refuge from history. My mother is a real refugee from Nazi-occupied Vienna; my father, I like to joke, is a cultural refugee from the great Jewish homeland of Brooklyn. Due to choices they, and later

I, made, I was twenty before I experienced being in a large room filled with young Jews. There was a dazzling sense of physical self-recognition. Yet they seemed *different*, comfortably, Jewishly American in ways I had never felt, wasn't taught to be.

Neither did I have a clear sense of the old world. It had been only shortly prior that I discovered photographer Roman Vishniac's famous images of Jews in prewar Eastern Europe in *A Vanished World*, and then the photograph, taken in the same era, of my great-grandfather; he looked just like them, long-bearded and wearing a black hat. I stumbled across my grandfather's *tefillin* (phylacteries) in a wooden box carved with the name of a small Polish resort town. Some time after, rifling through basement boxes, I found my grandmother's Polish schoolbooks and wedding invitation. It was only years later, after my own language studies, that I realized that the "other" language my grandmother spoke with her lady friends over tea wasn't the usual German she spoke with my mother. Why didn't I know this language, this culture? Why were the women at the cocktail party so negative? Where had this Polishness gone? The "field" that began that evening continued in a series of arrivals and departures—my own and others'—spanning three continents and the next two decades. Of course, there was the obligatory period of formal (that is, university- and foundation-sanctioned and supported) fieldwork. But it has been a longer, slower accumulation of experiences that allowed me to begin to answer some of these questions.

Poland—and ethnography—drew me for what they revealed about the force of history in shaping the most intimate worlds of meaning in which groups of people live, make choices, and relate to others; the often quiet ways that the past lives on in minds and bodies; and how echoes of earlier evil have an enduring power to both inflict damage and inspire positive action in sometimes unanticipated ways. I do not take as a given that Jewish life in Eastern Europe today is defined by ruins. Almost as soon as my own quest began, I realized mine was just one among a range of overlapping, vibrant Jewish cultural projects that operated across geographic space in ways that variously delineated and conflated past, present, and future, us and them. The experience of traversing them unsettled familiar narratives, memories, and identities.

Poland was one of the few places I have been where my particular gaps, lacks, and preoccupations made sense in a way they never did growing up in my suburban American town, where Europe was ancient history even for the Jews. Going to Poland put me in the company of other young Jews—Polish ones and foreign visitors—who were, like me, rediscovering and reclaiming a heritage and "deassimilating." But it wasn't just Jews who seemed familiar and necessary to my project. Rather, I found myself alongside a cosmopolitan assortment of intellectual, multilingual, multi-ethnic, and multi-national Jewish cultural seekers, and felt surprisingly at home among them. In Kazimierz, I spent my days traipsing from Alef to Singer to Noah's Ark, drinking a tea in each café, collecting stories, checking out the crowd, hearing the news. Much of my work was done—even during the light of day—in candlelit cafés with heavy wood credenzas and lace-clothed tables, grandfather clocks and samovars, dark oil paintings in thick, heavily-gilded rococo frames. It was as if I had stumbled upon my parents' secret back room, with all the material culture they had stored or thrown away, all they had replaced with Danish modern blond wood and futuristic white veneer. In my childhood, my grandmother's pedal-driven Singer sewing machine—an enticing link to our family's old-world past and immigration story—was relegated to a closet; in Kazimierz versions of it stand as centerpieces on café tables and in store windows, looking unabashedly back in time.

I stayed. That was the main difference between me and other Jewish tourists to Poland. While it may not be clear to the non-Jewish reader what the big deal is about staying for a time in Poland, it was not clear to me at first, either. Because I wasn't enculturated into mainstream communal American Jewishness, I didn't realize the invisible boundaries I was crossing, the taboos I was breaking, the political statements I was making by straying from the prescribed route. Staying is what revealed contours of Jewishness that had been ossified by historical trauma and the cultural and political currents, forms and structures this trauma had generated. And staying is also what enabled me to pass—at first unwillingly—beyond the visible surfaces of a Polish landscape that most Jews view, at turns, as death or Disney.

The connections to Poland that I developed over the course of my many visits—Polish friends, the Polish language, and living in Poland—clarified unspoken boundaries of Jewishness. I could feel Jewish visitors I met trying to make sense of me. I looked like a nice Jewish girl. But I was in the wrong place. I knew the wrong facts. Worst of all, I had renegade emotions. "Oh gosh," said one Jewish visitor mid-conversation, seeming suddenly awkward after hearing me express some empathetic sentiment about the wartime experience of Poles. "I didn't realize you were *Polish*."

Narratives of Jewish "return" to post-communist Poland, written by Jews who have never been there before, invoke remnants, shadows, silences and voids. Published on websites, in community newsletters, and in college news-papers, they detail angry, tearful trips "back," filled with trepidation and ironic asides about grey skies, bleeding Jesus statues, Poles picnicking on sites of wartime destruction. Search the web with keywords like "Jewish," "Poland," and "trip" and you will find them. I wrote some myself.

I recall sitting on a train in the early 1990s, hurtling eastward from Berlin to Warsaw, staring out across the countryside as it changed slowly from highest-tech to dilapidation. Trains carry unintended freight in this part of the world. Every clackety-clack of the wheels turning against the tracks tugged me more insistently backward in time. Watching the deep green of thick pine forest broken by an occasional field—how many Jews hid in that grove? Did the nearby farmer give them food or turn them in? Poland as a real, present-day place where flowers grew and young people went to dance clubs was difficult to assimilate. But anger and suspicion are hard to sustain in the absence of negative feedback. "Write about it while the wound is still fresh," a friend—a fellow anthropologist and a Jew—told me after my early trips to Poland. But a scab had already formed. The inevitable dulling of pain was itself unsettling; it had been such a constant companion. Subsequent trips to Poland were like trying to force a blade ever deeper into my stubbornly healing flesh, in a vain attempt to preserve the original hurt. And then that, too, passed. Signing up for aerobics classes in Krakow forced my mythic Poland to make room for an everyday Poland.

The modernizing urban landscape was particularly hard to swallow. The shiny new constructions that began to fill the toothless gaps between build-ings in Kazimierz made it feel like a door on memory was closing. The more the visible past receded, the less comfortable I felt. But hearing my own un-ease voiced outright by others—like the earlier Argentine student demanding ruins—gave me pause. If the physical landscape seemed to be shedding some of its mnemonic potency, the social landscape retained a special power. Po-land's relative homogeneity as a society means that Jews (real or imagined) are still *the* significant Other. The past—a past that includes the culture-altering loss of the murdered Jewish population—is a half-healed wound for Poles, and one that the renewed presence of Jews traversing the landscape abrades. While the response to this irritant can be ugly or awkward at times, the Poles I met were overwhelmingly kind and generous and interested. Some were un-deniably inspiring, like Jan Sasak, the small-town Catholic stonemason who had built a Holocaust memorial with his own hands, changing forever my understanding of memory's vectors.[39] Either way, I found something simply welcoming and cathartic in the popular acknowledgment that the past is not over. Whether in the form of accusations or apologies, fascination or simply a desire to reconnect with something tragically, violently, but incompletely lost, Poles approached me in myriad ways to say, simply, *I remember.* I wanted to remember with them.

CHAPTER TWO

THE MISSION: MASS JEWISH HOLOCAUST PILGRIMAGE

Anyone who anticipates and focuses only on the known and familiar finally sees nothing.

—DEENA METZGER

A few days after arriving in Warsaw on that first East European trip in 1990, which had been inspired by the revolutions of the previous months, my brother and I found ourselves circling the city's central synagogue. The building's somber, grey exterior matched the sky and still-leafless trees, and we wondered who, if anyone, would be inside. We also wondered what we were doing there. We hadn't explicitly considered any Jewish-themed itinerary for our journey, beyond the map our father had hastily photocopied at the last minute and in which he had underlined the few ancestral place names he could recall, today all well east of the Polish-Ukrainian border: Otynia, Hadenkowce, Kołomyja, Czernowitz ("*kleyne* [little] Paris").

If we didn't know what we wanted to see nor what we expected, it was in any case not what we encountered. The doors of the synagogue flew open and out poured a stream of Jewish American teenagers. One of the first identifiable sounds was a girl yelling, "Jews Rule! (Ooh baby!)," as she and her girlfriends marched astride, clutching each other and waving their brightly manicured hands in the air. It was difficult not to stare. We approached two middle-aged women who appeared to be with the group, standing guard outside; they had been eyeing us warily. I asked about the nature of the trip. They told us that it was the March of the Living, or more precisely its Pittsburgh and Washington contingents, out of the 3,000 teens who came "from *everywhere*." In response to my question about the trip's purpose, I received a terse recitation of statistics about the vibrant prewar Jewish population in Poland and its ravaged postwar remnants. Still trying to comprehend what this enormous parade of American teenagers was up to, I asked what they had been doing in the synagogue. Each of my questions seemed to position me, in the chaperones' eyes, further outside the particular Jewish "us" being celebrated by the group. "Praying," one of them said curtly.

My journal entry that evening was cynical. This was the Jewishness my parents had avoided. It was loud, it was conspicuous, and it seemed to value an accident of birth as an end in itself. It was also inherently suspicious of outsiders, with a large chip on its shoulder. That year would have been my third in college, which I had postponed in a classic middle-class quest of self-exploration. Although it was not a particularly Jewish self I had sought, it was dawning on me during our trip that Poland was home not only to a heavy history—we spent the first three days on that first trip in the Warsaw Historical Museum confronting the city's astounding wartime destruction and postwar reconstruction, at market square displays on the Solidarity movement, and wondering at the early inroads of capitalism—but in some way a home to us, as well.

As my relationship to Poland developed over the years, I revisited this early encounter often; it stood out among the difficult issues I was beginning to discern. How were images and experiences of Poland being produced and disseminated among Jews, and what models of Jewish memory and identity do these support? The ways that large, organized trips framed Poland and Jewishness and the relation between the two became increasingly uncomfortable, especially as I was moving in the opposite direction from many other travelers—toward the complicated, the disquieting, and the unknown—as I tried to work through inherited baggage and forge my own answers to the nagging questions of the past.

* * *

"Jewish tourists photographed themselves yesterday against the backdrop of antisemitic graffiti."[1] This was the caption under a large photograph that accompanied an article in the Polish daily *Gazeta Wyborcza*. The article, headlined "Swastika on Museum," reported on vandals who had spray-painted a swastika and the Nazi German phrase "Jude Raus" ("Jew Get Out") on the *Apteka Pod Orłem* (Pharmacy under the Eagle), today a museum on the edge of what had been Krakow's wartime Jewish ghetto, commemorating the non-Jewish pharmacist who had used his position to aid Jews. The composition, selection, and prominence of the photograph suggested that in addition to Polish concerns about antisemitic graffiti, there are concerns about Jewish tourists' relationship to such graffiti—specifically, how it functions as a destination for such visitors, and how they fashion from it a key souvenir of their trip to Poland.

Graffiti employing Jewish slurs is not uncommon in Poland—from stars of David depicted dangling from gallows to the slogan "Jews to the gas" ("Żydzi do gazu"). Such scrawled messages can remain for months, even years—often near train tracks or highway underpasses, but occasionally as a backdrop to Polish families taking tea on a café veranda, or emblazoned on an official government building. The reasons why such graffiti appears in an almost Jewless country and why it often lingers there are complex.[2] They are, of course, related to a widespread acceptance of (or blindness to) antisemitic discourse in the general culture, but also to soccer hooliganism and the damage that massive postwar population transfers and a half-century of communism have done to such civic sentiments as the public good and neighborhood pride. In response, an increasing number of Polish youth organizations have formed in the last decade to remove such graffiti and to raise public consciousness about it.[3]

The juxtaposition of text and image in this news item links the problem of antisemitism in present-day Poland to the question of how popular knowledge about such antisemitism is created and circulated among foreign Jews. These two domains come together in the phenomenon of tourism. There is troubling antisemitism in Poland, and much work remains to be done to create a public culture that condemns this prejudice unequivocally. Yet the antisemitism experienced by many Jewish tourists is not the antisemitism they think it is. Rather, they experience a seemingly eternal, de-historicized antisemitism that is in no small part a product of their own imagination, or a reaction to their own behavior. Diana Pinto has noted the way Jewish Holocaust memory relies on an image of Europe fossilized in the near aftermath of World War II.[4] In particular kinds of Holocaust memorial travel, we can see one of the mechanisms by which this ossified perception endures. The approach of much Jewish tourism to Poland perpetuates the country's "unseeability," and works against the sense of ethnographically informed possibility that I set out in this book's introduction. Anthropologist Jack Kugelmass captures the problem best:

There is something unique about Jewish tourism to Poland. Jewish tourists see nothing quaint about the local culture either Jewish or non-Jewish; their interest is in the dead rather than the living. They go back as antiquarians rather than ethnographers; consequently, they bring back with them no experiences that deepen their knowledge of the local culture. The experiences they remember are likely to be those that enhance an already existing negative opinion. Indeed, they are the experiences they expect to have in Poland, and because they confirm deeply held convictions, they are almost a desired part of the trip.[5]

"Mission" as a Mindset

A key mode of Jewish travel to Poland today is the "mission," a term used in Jewish communal circles for a range of organized Jewish group travel experiences, almost always advertised as an opportunity to enhance one's Jewishness. Building on older forms of more literal nation building through kibbutz volunteering in Palestine/Israel, Jewish missions grew with the development of tourist infrastructure and Israeli university foreign-student programs through the 1960s and 1970s, and until the late 1980s a robust industry of mission tourism consisted largely of American youth trips to Israel.[6]

Mission tourism has grown to comprise a key part of "a broad [Jewish] institutional and organizational terrain" that Jewish studies scholars Caryn Aviv and David Shneer have called the "diaspora business." The purpose of this industry, they assert, is "to shore up the perceived diminishing religious, ethnic, and cultural identities of individual established Jewish communities around the world."[7] Mission tours are advertised as something much deeper than a normal trip. They offer a chance to make a difference, have a spiritual awakening, or undergo a life-changing experience. They attempt to transform communal ideology into embodied reality. They create group memory.

Certainly other ethnic groups strengthen group identity through organized travel; Chinese, Irish, Armenian, Greek, and Lebanese communities have all sponsored homeland tours for diaspora youth, and African American groups make pilgrimages to Africa. But Jewish mission travel is notable because of the serious communal investment it garners. This is in part due to a historical intersection: in the 1990s, American (and to some extent Israeli) Jewish anxieties about waning Jewish/Zionist identity and intermarriage were rising.[8] At the same time, communism had suddenly come to an end in Eastern Europe, and with it the rallying point of Soviet Jewry. And the last eyewitnesses to the Holocaust were dying. Their passing has simultaneously provoked and, to many, appears to have imperiled the "imperative to remember [that] has motivated and mobilized Jews around the world to de-vote millions of dollars and countless hours of creative energy toward docu-menting and rendering visible" the Holocaust's ghosts.[9] Jewish missions to what was then a newly accessible Poland have become a powerful tool in the pursuit of this imperative.

While most Jewish communal resources still go toward the majority of Jewish missions that travel to Israel, Poland is now the second-most-visited destination. Much of this tourism is institutionalized. Every Israeli eleventh-grade class makes a trip to Poland; about 40–50 percent of all Israeli youth participate, approximately 30,000 student travelers per year.[10] The March of the Living (MOTL)—the single most popular youth tour to Poland—each year takes from 6,000 to 10,000 international Jewish youth there, mostly from the United States and Canada, reaching Auschwitz for Holocaust Re-membrance Day (*Yom HaShoah*). From there, like many smaller American-origin missions, MOTL tours continue on to Israel, just in time to celebrate Israeli Memorial Day (*Yom HaZikaron*) and Israeli Independence Day (*Yom Ha'atzmaut*). Exact statistics on Jewish travel to Poland are impossible to ob-tain, but a 2002 *New York Times* report estimated the number of American and Israeli Jewish visitors to Poland in excess of 100,000 annually.[11]

Jewish mission tourism to Poland is also unique in that unlike the vast majority of ethnic identity tours, which bring participants to various home-land sites to cultivate a sense of positive connection with a place, these trips are constructed largely around rejection. Poland is presented not as a Jewish place, but as an anti-Jewish place, perhaps even more than Germany.[12] Be-cause Poland was the site of all the Nazi extermination camps during World War II, many Jews consider the country's very ground to be desecrated, and even missions organized around the theme of "heritage" often take the Holo-caust as Poland's central Jewish inheritance.[13]

It has been said that Jewish educational travel is "less about sustaining al-ready existing connections and memories between individuals and commu-nities than it is about inventing new relationships between American Jews and other Jewish places,"[14] and mission travel to Poland is a case in point. Jews take part in a range of Polish itineraries in the present day. Young Israelis line up at the Polish embassy to take advantage of inherited citizenship so that they can acquire Polish passports enabling them to live and work in the Eu-ropean Union. Hasidic pilgrims journey to Galician villages to pray at graves of famous rabbis. Jewish families from many countries make genealogical "roots" trips to ancestral villages and regional archives. Yet mission travel is a dominant force in the Jewish travel arena, and because it targets youth it has particular power to influence not only the relationship of new generations of Jews to Poland, but also their stance toward otherness more broadly.

Despite the visibility and investment of large Jewish mission tours to Poland, I define mission tourism not in terms of group size or sponsorship, but rather as the single-minded pursuit of a particular experience. The mission is a mode of travel that attempts to ensure a pre-determined outcome. Employing aspects of pilgrimage—with its exalted moral purpose and expectation of personal transformation—missions provide a strong framework through which the participants' experiences are meant to be interpreted. Experiences during the journey that do not fit this frame are less likely to register, or, if they do, they may well be discounted as irrelevant. Such selective attention is, of course, a characteristic of all travel, and indeed of all experience. But the mission is a particularly highly scripted form of travel. It reflects and seeks to reinforce the dominance in Jewish communal life of certain memorial priorities and narratives of Jewish identity.

What kinds of Jewish selves and sentiments do these trips encourage? What kinds of relationships with others do they promote? And what are the consequences of the trips, both immediate and in the long term, intentionally or inadvertently? As sociologist Shaul Kelner argues of Birthright Israel tours—free, community-sponsored ten-day heritage trips to Israel for eighteen- to twenty-six-year-old Jews—such trips are political instrumentalizations of culture.[15] Yet despite the significant efforts that go into their ideological conceptualization and operation, they are not hermetic systems. Nor are trip participants utterly impressionable; they actively negotiate with tour structures and agendas, sometimes resisting them, and sometimes using them to their own ends.[16] Anthropologist Jackie Feldman, in his observations of Israeli youth tours to Poland, rightly differentiates "the steam engine of the State apparatus" from "the sincere, deep, and creative search for personal identity" that may animate individual tour participants, drawing our attention to "how state agendas and personal meaning interplay."[17]

But the structure of mission tours—in both of these authors' observations, as well as in my own—ultimately delimits the range of meanings participants are likely to glean from their travel experiences. While counter-narratives to the one built into the tour may begin to form, tour formats and frameworks—particularly given the journeys' intimacy, intensity, and the impressionable age of the teen participants—do a great deal to influence experience and channel emotion.[18] Especially notable is how the physical and temporal realities of missions, as they traverse the Polish landscape, structure the way young Jews and Poles experience each other.

*   *   *

Travel is a potential site of critical, progressive memory work due to its capacity for broadening horizons, forging transnational connections, and expanding "imagined communities."

Jewish observers of Polish nationalism often express legitimate concerns about ethno-national definitions of Polishness, conceptions of belonging that inherently exclude Jews. Jews paid an enormous price for the historical inability of the Polish majority to view them as part of a shared collective self, particularly when the Nazis exploited the fault lines separating the two groups. Jews traveling to Poland on "quests"—as we see in the next chapter—often raise parallel concerns about constructions of Jewishness. Quest travel facilitates participants' consideration of the limits of essentialist understandings of (Jewish) ethnicity, the boundaries of (Jewish) culture, and what kinds of allegiances with others Jews may anticipate. But mission tourism is engaged in a different kind of memorial endeavor. Rather than questioning the ethno-national thinking that has historically made Jews (and other minorities) a key problem in Europe, missions simply invert it, offering a paradigm of Jewishness with its own ethnic exclusions: in this case, of Poland as a legitimate home for Jews, of Poles as belonging to the Jewish universe of obligation, of lessons of the Holocaust that do not involve Zionism. Despite the fact that these Jews are going *to* Poland, their trips aren't really *about* Poland or interested in Poles; rather, they are focused narrowly on Jewish national memory and identity enacted on and against their Polish equivalents.

The MOTL's own research proclaims that the trips are successful in meeting their goals.[19] These goals are mostly related to strengthening Jewish identity, faith, practice, and community, maintaining vigilance against antisemitism and Holocaust denial, and increasing Jewish youths' connections to and support for Israel. Participants have also claimed a higher commitment to combating genocide and racism, and to human rights and tolerance for other groups. But in considering these (secondary) universalist issues, the nearest other toward whom Jewish youth might exercise their new tolerance would seem to be the Poles whose towns and cities they traverse during their tours. And yet ethnographic research suggests this is not often the case.

Leaving aside the limitations of the MOTL's survey research methodology, my observations suggest that the missions' speed, decontextualization, and emotional tenor leads participants to patterned forms of (mis)perception of Poles and Poland; encourages "us vs. them" thinking; obscures historical, moral, and social complexity; and distracts from the potential for cultural and social change. The trips work against humanistic forms of identification, encouraging instead a sense of Jewish embattlement. They also inhibit young Jews from an awareness of the increasing number of Poles who are working, on the grassroots and diplomatic levels, to challenge antisemitism and narrow forms of Polish ethno-nationalism.

Experiencing the Holocaust Firsthand: The Pedagogy of Affect

A number of scholars, including Jackie Feldman, Jack Kugelmass, Rona Sheramy, and Oren Stier, have discussed the motivations and ideologies of Jewish Holocaust tourism to Poland, characterizing such tourism in terms of religious pilgrimage and ritual.[20] While I begin by highlighting key aspects of their arguments below, I am primarily interested in how ethno-national subjectivity is shaped by the politicization of emotion—how group membership is defined in important ways by the cultivation of powerful, shared feelings. An understanding of how collective sentiment is formed demands attention to sites, mechanisms, and experiences surrounding the transmission of traumatic memory to new generations, as well as the relationship between affect and subjectivity—themes that have often been relegated to the domain of psychology.[21]

There are differences between the two main institutions of mission travel: the largely diasporic MOTL and the Israeli school trips to Poland that eleventh-graders make. A basic distinguishing feature—given the participants' differing citizenship—is an inherently different conception of what it means to be part of the "Jewish nation," an identification each tour works to strengthen. Israeli youth go back to defend the Jewish state they live in, while diaspora youth return to other national homes. But for the purposes of understanding Jewish-Polish relations and processes of reconciliation, the differences are relatively insignificant when compared to the similarities.[22] This is especially so because MOTL has "come to dominate the culture of [Holocaust] memory tourism," and "its structure and itinerary are paradigmatic of . . . the large majority of such tours."[23] Both North American and Israeli missions enact a Zionist narrative in which Poland functions as a visceral object lesson in Jewish alienation, victimization, and destruction, a decontextualized "end" to European Jewish history.[24] And both rely centrally on the activation of sentiment as the key means for achieving their goals.

Gary Weissman argues that there is an increasing popular yearning for personal, experiential forms of witnessing the Holocaust.[25] Fulfilling this desire is facilitated by encounters with "authentic sites," and mission travel employs an experiential pedagogy that capitalizes on the sense that one can approach the Holocaust by approaching Poland. As Sheramy describes MOTL,

> Within a compressed period of time, participants 'relive' the Jewish past, moving from sites of death in eastern Europe—the culmination of which is a silent procession from Auschwitz I to Birkenau—to sites of life and vitality in Israel. Before and during the March, lessons and activities emphasize the price of Jewish powerlessness and victimization and the need for Jewish strength and autonomy. . . . Participants move emotionally, physically, and ritualistically from intense sorrow in the Diaspora to cathartic festivities in the Jewish national home.[26]

The goal of this pedagogy is "to inspire 'memory' of the Holocaust and the founding of Israel in a generation that lack[s] personal recollections of these critical events." Orchestrating emotion is deemed more important than remembering dates, places, or times.[27] The study guides, itineraries, and a range of collective rituals that physically embody mission ideology forge an entire "sensory envelope" that surrounds participants with the desired meanings and relegates any others to an extraneous background. The pace of the trip, as I experienced myself as a guide, is exhausting; the itineraries offer little respite from a blur of tragic sites. The most intimate aspects of tours are engineered to heighten the sense of physical hardship and alienation in Poland, including the quality and timing of food and music. The goal is to produce a present-day experience of trauma that functions as an implicit corollary to the Holocaust.

Participants are instructed when to wear the blue and white sweatshirts or jackets with Star of David logos or the word "Israel" framed with barbed wire; this uniform marks conformity within the group, difference from those outside it, and collective visibility in the Polish landscape. Producing a "powerful sense of affiliation," it also enacts the supposed denigrated, alienated relationship of the diaspora Jew to his physical environment, heightening the sense that one is reexperiencing Nazi Europe.[28] A kind, enthusiastic Israeli teacher and tour leader described to me her own innovations for achieving this end, which included having students squeeze themselves into a tiny cupboard in an old Warsaw apartment to feel what it was like for a Jew in hiding. Scholars Aviv and Shneer argue that such mission travel "reaffirms communal solidarity through memory, sadness, and fear."[29]

Most relevant to a consideration of Polish-Jewish relations and reconciliation is the way that mission travel presents Poland to Jews as fundamentally other. The MOTL advertises itself as "a study in contrasts," and—using tactics shared with the Israeli school trips as described above—delivers this contrast in temporal and spatial as well as physical and emotional ways. The sense of hostility and austerity created in Poland is followed by an equally engineered experience of safety and pleasure in Israel. A MOTL souvenir book describes how participants go from "glacial Poland to the luminous warmth of Israel," and conduct guidelines remind participants that "in Poland modern music may be less appropriate than in Israel," where they will be welcomed by crowds dancing and singing.[30]

Even Polish-born Alex Danzig, a long-time expert consultant to the Israeli Ministry of Education on youth tours to Poland, has been a trenchant critic of the way mission travel is organized. He told me that while the motivation for students to go on such trips is *szlachetna* (Polish for noble), structural flaws inhibit the tours' potential from being realized. These include the enshrined practice of taking Holocaust survivors along on the trips as "witnesses." Danzig feels these individuals, who are treated as sacred in the Jewish community and therefore unquestionable, obscure participants' view of the larger, complex historical and social contexts essential for a balanced understanding of both the past and the present. "Security, tour agents, and survivors are obstacles," he said.

Danzig, along with the scholars cited above, make clear how the structure, and to a large extent the ideology, of Jewish missions to Poland anticipate antisemitism. During my fieldwork in Poland I had a number of experiences with groups that shed light on the ways that such patterned expectations of Poland often result in patterned experiences there. My Polish vantage point offered a window on the ways mission tourism frames antisemitism, conjures it, and in some cases may even provoke it.

Anticipating Antisemitism ("Itching for a Fight")

While mission tourists generally present their feelings of hostility toward Poles as resulting from their experiences with them, close observation suggests that aggression may in fact precede any actual encounters. I was employed as a guide for the Poland portion of the MOTL in 2000—an opportunity that presented itself fortuitously during my fieldwork—traveling with a caravan of three tour buses containing 150 Jewish teens from the American Midwest. But my experience of the MOTL as an organization began in Israel. I was recruited at the last minute on a visit to Tel Aviv during my fieldwork; they suddenly needed another guide for the Poland portion. I had no previous experience as a guide or youth leader. But I would be in Poland, I was Jewish, and that seemed to suffice.

Edward Bruner, an anthropologist of tourism, wrote about the "delicious ambiguity" in his dual role as ethnographer and tour guide, as well as the challenges of such an in-between position.[31] The draw for me was twofold as well, although it felt anything but delicious. Rather, it foregrounded a painful tension that wends its way through this project. I was suddenly inside the belly of an impressive entity I had previously experienced, along with other awed local bystanders, only from the outside, when the MOTL had marched into Krakow. But like my Polish friends who were just discovering their Jewishness, I shared some yearning to belong. Here, it seemed, was my chance—I would wear the jacket, carry the backpack, feel the collective effervescence. But I was almost immediately reminded of the downside of in-group warmth: the creation of otherness. Sitting in the MOTL office waiting for instructions, I was taken aback as the Israeli MOTL coordinator yelled into the telephone that *no* Polish guides (who accompany the tour buses for translation and navigation purposes) should be allowed to use the bus PA system under any circumstances. "Don't let the Polish guides say a single word!" she said. "They don't tell the truth!"[32]

The coordinator gave me a small packet of information before wishing me luck and sending me on my way. On the plane back to Poland, I read the MOTL's two lists of security precautions for students to observe during the Polish and Israeli portions of the trip. The list for Israel, where the threat of bombs in public places is part of everyday reality, comprised four items. The first and second of these addressed the need to keep cool and hydrated in the hot climate; the other two points required being aware of strange, unattended items and asking permission from the group leader before going off on one's own. The instructions for Poland—a comparatively uneventful country—consisted of eighteen points of detailed admonition, including "draw all window curtains so that the room cannot be surveilled from the outside," "do not wander into stores or other areas," "do not reveal information pertaining to the delegation's plans or timetable," and "avoid joining strange people, especially at their invitation."[33] No rationales were given.

Sheramy notes how these trips "cast Poland as the embodiment of non-Jewish hostility towards Jews and of the ongoing threat to Jewish safety."[34] The extent to which mission groups arrive in Poland primed for conflict was evident when I met my group at the Krakow airport a week later. The rabbi accompanying the group walked out, his full beard making him easy to spot. He was in animated conversation with an Israeli security guard. I introduced myself. "*Already* we had a problem," he said. "On the plane, someone was drunk and pulled one of the kids' *tsitsis* [ritual garment with fringes] while he was *davening* (praying). They arrested him the minute he got off the plane." While the arrest indicates the seriousness with which the Polish authorities take antisemitic behavior, the rabbi's emphatic use of "already" suggested that he had been anticipating trouble, if perhaps not so soon, and his immediate outpouring to me as well as his choice of Yiddish inflection and vocabulary implied that he took me as an insider who would share his sentiments. Indeed, such bonding around expected adversity buttresses the sense of group belonging and reinforces the experience of embattlement the trip is meant to provide.

While I was looking forward to providing a kind of bridge between the group's Jewish concerns and the Poland I had come to know, given the polarizing framework in which they were traveling, the kids weren't sure what to make of me: if I was "one of us" (a Jew), what was I doing living in Poland? For the first couple of days they were stand-offish. For my part, I was trying to acclimate to the rarefied atmosphere inside the insular tour bus. I soon gave up trying to deliver information, as the kids were tired, distracted, and seemed to listen only when the rabbi boomed out mostly logistical directives at each stop we made ("Get organized, we're going to have a ceremony here!"). Otherwise I was trying to screen out the sexual chatter of the teen boys in the seats behind me. One student finally broke the ice. "I don't mean to sound offensive," she said as we milled outside the bus, "but how can you *live* here? I mean, I've only been here two days and it sucks!" I asked her how it sucked. "The people are *rude*," she said, "on the plane, on the street . . ."

The MOTL, at a cost of over $1,000 per person and drawing heavily from Jewish communal cores, is biased toward sheltered teenagers who have been privileged to grow up in "safe spaces," surrounded by peers with similar backgrounds. Confronting them with unfamiliar sights and behaviors in the heightened atmosphere of the mission predisposes them to finding the alien incendiary. Further, it would be understandable that their approach to what is outside the bus (Poland) is influenced by what is inside of it: flirting, fitting in and bonding with the group, creating personal capital in a developing social microcosm. These teens are not, of course, motivated to go on these trips by hatred. For most of them the opportunity is simply to take an international trip with friends and to have an exciting life experience. More elevated intentions—to preserve the memory of past suffering—undoubtedly animate some of them. Yet the very nature of the trips makes it difficult for its participants to tap into their higher selves. Rather, multiple factors encourage their confinement to a bubble filled with adolescent distractions and easy answers to enormously difficult questions.

Mission literature and casually circulated anecdotes prepare tourists for the kind of experience they should expect to have, and thus young people in particular often arrive, as Jackie Feldman put it, "itching for a fight."[35] As a student from a mission group told me, "We were almost . . . like waiting for someone to take a swing at us so that we could just fight back and get out our aggression. . . . We were just so pent up with hatred . . . it was like oozing everywhere, and we just wanted somebody to do something so we could just have an opportunity to lay into these [Polish] people."

Aggression may be a common coping mechanism among adolescents, but the idea that Poles are deserving of such aggression does not originate with them. While I heard many angry statements, one that was told to me second-hand illustrates with particular acuity the depth and tenor of sentiment I have heard uttered by adults. A MOTL official told me, off the record, that an adult chaperone of a special tour contingent sent to repatriate a Torah scroll to a Polish congregation had said, "I'm here to shove this Torah up the asshole of Poland." If such aggressive frameworks are modeled by adults who lead these tours, what can we expect from the adolescents who travel with them?

Framing Antisemitism ("Everyone Took Pictures")

As Edward Bruner notes, "The tour is a story in the making. The vision of the posttour telling, which will be delivered in a living room full of family and friends once the traveler returns home, is present in the tourist's mind during the tour, and it structures the actual tour as lived [as tourists are] directing their actions toward encounters that will form the basis of future stories."[36] In cyclical fashion, these encounters-that-will-become-stories are, Walker Percy suggests, selected and remembered to the extent that they conform to the "preformed complex" of ideas that travelers have brought with them—a complex in no small part shaped by the stories of previous travelers.[37] Travel photographs add a visual scaffold to this process by which travelers-to-be learn what to expect of the tour. Such images underline items on the tacit to-do list of experiences that subsequent tourists will anticipate and seek out. A successful trip means seeing what others saw. For Jewish visitors, a trip to Poland without an experience of antisemitism would be incomplete. As Ronit, a student I spoke with in Israel the summer after her class trip to Poland in 2000, told me, "Everyone was looking for [antisemitic] graffiti on the walls. And when one person found it, everyone took pictures."

Jack Kugelmass talks of Jewish travel to Poland as a way of "symbolically reversing reality: [tourists] are transposing themselves from what they are currently perceived as—in the American case highly privileged, and in the Israeli case oppressive—and presenting themselves as the diametric opposite of privilege, as what they in fact were."[38] Going to Poland is a safe experience of danger, but it provides evidence that the danger still exists, out there.

Photographing oneself smiling before evidence of vandalism—as captured in the *Gazeta Wyborcza* news article—may also represent an attempt at a historical inversion of power, a pose suggesting that one has dominated antisemitism by reducing it to a tourist snapshot. Yet the domination is not complete, as the Jewish visitor is precisely that, a daring and intrepid visitor, to a Poland imagined as a perpetually genocidal time-space. Such photography echoes the Plains Native American practice of "counting coup"—a demonstration of bravery in which a warrior in battle rushes in to touch his enemy with a stick and returns unharmed, proving his courage. Evidence of proximity to danger heroizes its owner. Photographing oneself next to antisemitic graffiti thus achieves a double move: in having "survived" Polish antisemitism one may feel both that one has *partaken* in the fate of the original victims (in whose footsteps one is walking) but also overcome the threat, and in this way avenged the victimized ancestors. While Jackie Feldman describes how Poland trips are viewed by many young participants as "an adventure into a dangerous unknown," Oren Stier notes these young tourists are encouraged to think of themselves as transformed by their trips into "the next generation of survivors and witnesses."[39]

In his essay "The Holocaust's Life as a Ghost," prominent Polish Jewish sociologist Zygmunt Bauman pointedly describes a "sense-giving reassurance" that Jews may draw from real or imagined signs of hostility toward them, and the "eagerness" with which they may interpret any behavior as an expression of hostility. "In a world haunted by the ghost of the Holocaust . . . assumed would-be persecutors are guilty in advance, guilty of being seen as inclined or able to engage in another genocide."[40] My observations in Poland suggest there is something to Bauman's theory. Feelings of fear on the part of mission tourists are often taken as evidence of malevolence on the part of Polish locals. As one student recounted: "We're standing on the street corner and every bus and every car that went by, people just *stared* at us, and glared at us, and people were walking around on the corners and like, fiddling in their pockets as they went by, and like, we were all *terrified*."

Mission travel creates a template that alternatively screens out the everyday and transforms otherwise banal moments into extraordinary experiences that serve the goals of the trip. To those who assume they will encounter violence, normal behaviors from a Polish perspective—like staring at large groups of obvious outsiders in a small town or hanging around on street corners with one's hands in one's pockets—are perceived as evidence of antisemitic hostility, or even threatening preludes to violence. There are, of course, negative Polish responses to such tour groups, as I elaborate below. But the tours' frameworks overdetermine the possible interpretations of Polish behavior. As tour organizer Michael Berl of Heritage Seminars in Jerusalem told me, "Every time there's a minor altercation [in Poland]—a drunk, someone spitting—the kids look at it as 'They hate us.'"

Such inability to imagine a local perspective that is different from one's own is a fundamental weakness of mission travel. The resulting erasure of subject positions includes those of local Jews—particularly frustrating to members of Poland's Jewish community, who are constantly called upon to justify their decisions to live in what is perceived to be hostile territory. Antisemitic graffiti—iconic evidence to Jewish tourists of an active threat to Jewish well-being—is seen rather differently by local Polish Jews. In response to the newspaper article about the graffiti, Tadeusz Jakubowicz, head of Krakow's Jewish community, published a brief statement: "For me this is not an expression of antisemitism, but rather run-of-the-mill stupidity. Those who painted the wall have undoubtedly never met a single Jew. . . . But it's hard to explain to young people from Israel that there isn't any Jew-hatred among Poles, when the museum is painted with anti-Jewish slogans and a swastika."[41]

One can certainly disagree with Jakubowicz's premise; antisemitism does not, to be sure, depend on having met a Jew. One may even see in his posi-

tion a timid gesture of public relations on behalf of his tiny minority community that relies on the goodwill of the majority—the idea that there isn't *any*
Jew hatred in Poland is clearly untenable. But particularly because Jakubowicz's comments invoke the gaze of Israeli youth (a gaze captured in the photograph), his statement also contains the embedded suggestion of an issue of
shared concern among Polish Jews and non-Jews. It goes something like this:
*The Jewish world is watching us. They assume you (non-Jewish Poles) are anti-
semites, and we (Polish Jews) live in conditions of persecution. We both know
this is not true. But we've got to do better in the public realm if we want them to
believe it.* Jakubowicz's somewhat weary tone points, in effect, to the ongoing
erasure of a complex local Jewish reality by the dominant Jewish discourses
coming from the West.[42]

The effects of this discourse blinker visiting Jews from important nu-
ance. The fearful student anecdote above about the glaring Poles continued,
"We climb[ed] up on the bus and look[ed] out the window, and on the wall
[was] written in spray paint 'Nazis won.'" Yet these words do not mean in Polish what they do in English. A common graffiti tag seen in Poland says, "Żydzi
won," Polish for "Jews, get out." But increasingly one sees another Polish tag—
the one the students saw—which says, "Nazis won"—meaning "Nazis, get
out." A tag written by anti-fascists in rejection of antisemitism, it was read instead *as* antisemitism. While an understandable misreading by English speak-
ers, this example highlights the problems that arise when meaning is made in
terms of imported context. In this case there is an additional lesson: hyper-
vigilance against presumed enemies can inhibit one's ability to discern potential allies.[43]

Conjuring Antisemitism ("Imagining What They Thought about Us")

Embellished versions of ahistorical claims circulate among tour participants,
implying, for example, that Polish antisemitism was the reason Hitler built
the extermination camps in Poland (rather than because the largest concentration of Jews was in Poland). Further, contemporary antisemitism, whether
real or imagined, is framed as a direct continuation of wartime participation
in the Holocaust among segments of Polish society, promulgating what one
MOTL participant called "a view of Poland as unchanged since the 1940s."[44]
Such a static view is suggested by the comments of a mission group leader, a
professor of philosophy and child of Holocaust survivors, who told me, "Every place we went there was antisemitic reaction to us. . . . After all those

years, and after fifty years of communism, and now with democracy and with the openness of everything . . . *none of this has passed.*"

Poles are blamed for living today in proximity to Nazi-era atrocity sites, cast as front-row witnesses to Jewish extermination—even if such nearby apartment blocks were postwar constructions. A "fact" I have heard repeated by mission tourists—insinuating the imminent potential for another Holocaust—is that the "fully intact" Majdanek death camp "can be made fully operational in 24 to 48 hours." Since Germany is rarely mentioned in the context of these trips, presumably it is the local Poles who are envisioned as the camp's potential new operators. A related problem is what anthropologist Sharon Macdonald calls "material suggestivity," in which any perceived flaws in the physical state of (Holocaust) sites are perceived as a direct expression of the weak or distorted historical consciousness and moral apathy of such sites' de facto local and national stewards.[45] An associated "behavioral suggestivity" can be discerned in the comments of a young North American Jewish woman visiting Poland during a college semester in Israel, who wrote of the Nazi camp in Krakow, "The saddest aspect of Płaszow [*sic*] was not even that thousands of Jews that were killed here, but today people picnic on this memorial ground, a clear indicator of their indifference towards the horrors of WWII."

I had the opportunity to observe how an antisemitic "incident" was produced through perception and narration. It began when I first met members of an American college Holocaust study trip. They had signed up for the Jarden Jewish Bookshop's Schindler's List tour, and, after receiving permission from the paying tourists, I was invited to take the tour as well as part of my research. The tour was led by Janina, a graduate student in Jewish history and a well- educated guide. She talked in detail about the historical situation of Jews in Krakow and related personal anecdotes and information about Holocaust survivors she knows. She was clearly both accurate and sympathetic regarding Jewish suffering; when discussing Jews and Poles imprisoned in Nazi camps, for example, she stressed the fact that conditions for Jews were much worse than for others.

After interim stops, including the Heroes of the Ghetto square and Schindler's factory, we drove to Płaszów, the former concentration/labor camp on the edge of the city. The mini-bus ferried us to the top of the old quarry that contained the former camp, where we got out. The grassy hills rolled off in all directions. A few mountain bikers in colorful sports clothing wheeled past, and families strolled along the dirt road. We walked up to the small Jewish Holocaust monument and Janina translated the inscription. One of the students lit a memorial candle as the rest of the group ambled in the direction of the bus. I stood looking toward the massive, socialist-era monument to the victims of fascism: a grey stone block at the very edge of the site, looming many meters high, with a row of bowed figures, a void in the rock slashed across their chests.

I saw a group of people silhouetted as they emerged over the crest of the hill, black cutouts in sharp relief against the setting sun. They appeared to be young men, but at a few hundred yards it was hard to tell. I held up one hand to shield my eyes from the sun's rays and gazed at them for a few moments. Suddenly it seemed they were looking back at me—one of them was standing as I did, with hand up at his forehead. I realized that it didn't make much sense for him to shield his eyes from the sun because the sun was behind him. I suddenly felt uncomfortable. Was I being mocked? I thought I might hear laughter. But I wasn't sure. I took out my camera and took a picture of the Jewish monument, with the larger monument and the young men in the background, although some of them had already disappeared around the edge of the stone. We all got back into the car and drove on.

At dinner that evening I interviewed the group's professor and four of his students who had not been with us that day, and they volunteered stories of Polish antisemitism, including the following: "We heard that some of the kids were on a trip out seeing one of the monuments on their Schindler's List tour and there were a bunch of skinheads there yelling things at them." I was curious when this might have happened—had there been another Schindler's List tour besides the one I took? I was unsure what to make of the comment, and in any case the conversation moved on. After dinner the five of us wandered to Krakow's main square. As we sat on benches in the middle of the square, five more students from the group—those who had been on the Schindler's List tour with me—happened to be strolling nearby and joined us, standing in the chilly night air in the mostly empty square. Despite the quiet surrounds, the conversation immediately lapsed back into a dramatic, emotional recounting of the myriad ways in which the group had felt unwelcome in Poland. The student who had lit the candle at the Płaszów monument recounted the incident with the silhouetted boys. His version was strikingly different from my experience.

I was lighting a candle at the monument, and these guys, they looked like skinheads, were yelling at me, they kept yelling probably the only thing they knew in English, 'Motherfucker, Motherfucker, Motherfucker!' And I was like shaking, imagining what they thought about us. I had so much rage. And I didn't see, but I bet that monument was painted up and down with swastikas. I haven't ever felt that much rage. And when I got in the car, Elisa [another student] just squeezed my knee. I mean, I don't know what they were thinking, but I can imagine . . .

The key words here are "probably," "bet," and "imagine." They enable the teller to include in his story unseen evidence of Polish antisemitism ("yelling" and "swastikas") and a lack of English skills as if these had been confirmed. I had been standing no more than fifteen feet away from this student when he lit his candle, and no farther away from the silhouetted boys than he was. Could I have missed the violent yelling the student heard? And what led him to determine the silhouettes were skinheads? When I later asked our tour guide, Janina, if she had heard or seen anything, she said she had not. This experience reveals the range of sensitivities and interpretive frameworks that differently situated individuals bring to the same events—the way we all imagine the social worlds we move through. On mission tours to Poland, in particularly decontextualized and overdetermined scenarios, imagination is collectively solidified into experience. Back home again in North America or Israel (or elsewhere), any cracks in this souvenir story will fade still further beneath the patina of myth that an expanding circle of tellers brings back from their journeys.

Provoking Antisemitism?

Poles are keenly aware of how such Jewish groups see them: "As murderers."[46] But there appears to be comparatively little consideration among mission tourists of how they are perceived by Poles. While missions are undertaken in response to historical violence, the notion that mission tourism could itself be perceived as a form of aggression from a Polish perspective may come as a surprise to tourists. Yet such tourism has an impact on the landscape it traverses, both in real time and cumulatively. The thousands of Jews who fill the streets of Polish small towns may be attempting to symbolically reclaim lost space and "creat[e] memories of empowered Jews in Europe" for themselves.[47] But for Poles such tours may appear hostile incursions into their own home spaces and symbolic places. The MOTL, in particular, "marks the takeover of Auschwitz (the camp) and Oświęcim (the town). . . . Traffic between Auschwitz and Birkenau is blocked for the event, and stalled residents wait at intersections, watching the procession in silence, while marchers observe the observers, sometimes taking photographs of them."[48]

Great indulgence has been shown Israeli and international Jewish groups during Holocaust pilgrimage season, where contingents of Polish police help their Israeli counterparts manage the passage of visiting groups through the towns they traverse. Yet on the most basic level, it is hardly surprising that tourists—particularly large groups that are discouraged from participating in the local economy—are not universally welcomed by residents. Loads of teenagers emerging from long hours in cramped buses do not make favorite guests under the best of circumstances. But add to this the hostility toward Poland that is structured into these trips, and one can imagine entirely different kinds of incidents than those generally reported by the tourists themselves.

There is, at minimum, resentment on the part of Poles whose daily lives are disrupted by Jewish missions as tour security imposes roadblocks and frisks local Poles on their daily errands. Journalist Ruth Gruber noted that what MOTL participants take for antisemitism may in fact be a response to the disruption that the marchers cause in the towns through which they passes. She quoted Jerzy Bebak, a Polish journalist and an active member of the Polish-Israeli Friendship Society living in Oświęcim (Auschwitz): "The village of Brzezinka (Birkenau) is virtually cut off by security and preparations for the march. Local people can't get to work or go about their normal business. Naturally they don't like that."[49]

But even for the majority of Poles, who do not come into direct contact with Jewish youth tours, media images leave a lasting impression. The spectacle that mission organizers attempt to create through their numbers, costumes, and choreography—of "victorious representatives of Israel in enemy territory"—fits into a broader framework of successive invasions central to Polish historical memory.[50] Paulina, a veteran guide for Jewish groups in Poland (and Polish groups in Israel) and also a non-Jewish Pole who learned fluent Hebrew, told me:

Israel [is] the only nation coming [to Poland] with flags. . . . And it seems to be very nationalistic. . . . But I think it's not a good idea. . . . Nobody is coming and walking along the street with flags. Not even Polish people. . . . You know which people [were] walking with a flag? Russians. So this is the bad background. Everywhere Russians with huge flags. This was typical for the Communist period. . . . These parades. Parades, and these flags. Flags, flags, flags, flags. Immediately, when you see a group of people with flags, you are going back to previous times. And then back to the war. Who was doing that? Germans. Huge flags with swastikas. All over the town. They were marching with flags. So this is very bad relation. It's difficult maybe to explain, but this is what people think immediately. . . . War and communism and now this.[51]

Given mission travelers' comments about being "almost eager for [a] confrontation," it should not be surprising that they have occasionally provoked one. Popular Polish frustrations with the missions bubbled over into the media in a 2007 article in the Polish weekly *Przekrój* ("Cross-section"). Titled "Young Israelis Run Amok in Poland," it reported accusations against Israeli students and their security detachments for traumatizing locals, trashing hotel rooms, and harassing Polish flight attendants. The article prompted responses from both Polish and Israeli diplomats.[52] In June 2009 it was reported that the Israeli Education Ministry had announced a new code of conduct and educational preparation for students traveling to Poland, "follow[ing] several years of reports of poor student behavior, including drinking, gambling and violence."[53]

Jews are obviously not at fault for antisemitic slurs, graffiti, or any acts of hostility against them. But there is a kind of circularity built into mission tourism. As Bruner describes, tourists have the power to change the culture of the places they visit. "In what might be called 'tourist constructivism,'" he says, "present-day tourists find in the local society the cultural enhancements that their tourist ancestors had fashioned."[54] Poles are offended by Jewish hostility and condescension. They retaliate in petty ways. As Jackie Feldman describes the resulting cycle,

> These insults, in turn, must be countered with increased security, which, in turn, further increases the group's visibility. These [petty] manifestations of Polish antisemitism, though not planned by the organizers, serve to confirm the image of the world constructed by the voyage: "You see?" said one [tour] organizer, "nothing has changed. Would they do the Shoah again if they could? You bet they would!"[55]

Collateral Damage

What does Jewish tourism look like from a Polish vantage point? How do experiences and interactions in tourist-local contact zones influence historical memory and national and cultural identification? While much institutionalized Jewish tourism to Poland is explicitly and overwhelmingly about "preserving memory" for the Jews who travel, such tours also create memories *of* Jews among local people—both Polish Jews and non-Jews—in the places they visit. During my fieldwork, major Jewish youth tours hurtled periodically through Kazimierz in ways that contributed to the quarter's character, if not much to its community or economy.[56] Each spring, strapping armed members of Israel's Shin Bet security services take up posts along Szeroka Street. Their ubiquitous close-cropped hairstyles, wrap-around sunglasses, and steely expressions give Kazimierz a new dimension. To my young friends among Krakow's newly Jewish—those who had grown up without knowledge of their ancestry—these guards portended the arrival of the "real" Jews, of whom my friends stood in awe. These masses of loud, proud, often tanned Jews with their Western clothes and accessories represented an unattainable level of self-assuredness and authenticity. At the same time, to local Poles (Jewish Poles included), the Jewish missions had also become something of an annoyance.

Kazimierz pulsated. One moment it was quiet; the next, throngs of Jewish youth would pour into the main square, dispatched from tour buses parked as close as the narrow cobbled streets would allow. Guides offered fifteen seconds of information in front of the Remu synagogue, and then the groups would turn to the nearby doorframe at Szeroka number 38 where there is a visible impression from a long-ago *mezuzah*. One by one the kids would dutifully photograph this sign of Jewish absence. And then they, too, disappeared.

There are deep feelings of anxiety among Poles that guilt is being displaced from the Nazi German perpetrators of the Holocaust onto Poles. While important new historical work is helping to break down Poles' own self-mythology as only heroes or victims during the Nazi occupation,[57] an unintended side effect may be the further erasure of Polish victimhood and suffering in popular Jewish discourse about Poland. Beyond ignorance of Nazi crimes against ethnic Poles, there is a visible slippage in which Poles are at times retroactively cast as Nazis themselves. In a combination of legitimate corrective and nationalistic defensiveness (the latter of which can at times slide into historically familiar anti-Jewish conspiracy theorizing), a campaign by the Polish government has attempted to combat this historical conflation. In March 2006, the Polish culture ministry petitioned UNESCO to officially change the name of what had been called the Auschwitz Concentration Camp to the Former Nazi German Auschwitz-Birkenau Concentration Camp.[58] The motivation for the change is often attributed to concerns about the frequency of foreign media reports that describe former Nazi-run concentration camps, including Auschwitz-Birkenau, Treblinka, and Majdanek, as "Polish" death camps.[59] The vigilance in this campaign, to be sure, is also in reaction to the perceived blows to Poland's international image due to recent revelations about Polish complicity in the Holocaust.

But earlier actions that attempted to improve Poland's image targeted mission travel specifically as a source of perceived misinformation. A 1999 government-sponsored booklet—one of a few of this genre—was aimed specifically at "marchers." *Poland: A Few Words about Its History, Culture and the Present* places key issues within a historical and contemporary context that missions tend to dismiss. The introduction addresses the reader personally:

> If you are convinced you have come here to remember, let others stand next to you, let them express their *solidarity* and remember together with you. . . . Be sure that there are many friends here waiting for you, ready to be understanding and willing to be understood. . . . People living here would like to feel they are hosts and a visitor usually likes to know a bit about his/her host. When you *look around,* see that the hosts are honored with your visit and willing to become your friends.[60]

Many Polish youths are keenly interested in meeting Jewish tour groups, but this aspiration is rarely reciprocated; such meetings are seen as marginal to the mandate of most Jewish groups. A meeting is set up only when a particular group leader pushes for it. Indeed, even when scheduled—and when a Polish class may have prepared for months designing a program involving learning Hebrew or Yiddish songs and polishing their English skills for conversation—the Jewish group may drop out (even by text message, in one reported case) or not show up due to a last-minute scheduling conflict, creating frustration and disappointment on the Polish side.[61]

The rejection of Poland that is built into mission travel is directed not only at non-Jewish Poles. Polish Jews, too—especially young, contented ones— have presented a problem for mission narratives, as they disrupt the image of Poland as a Jewish cemetery and as a fundamentally anti-Jewish place. Contemporary Jewry was long written out of MOTL materials. The "adjectives 'Judenrein' and 'Judenfrei'—the sinister terms coined by the Nazis to denote an absence of Jews, were often applied [by Jews] to Poland."[62] A 270-page study guide for the MOTL, printed in 1995, does not discuss general Polish history or culture at all, and devotes only thirteen pages to Polish *Jewry* before World War II.[63] When I was hired to lead an American MOTL group in 2000, the educational materials I received still contained nothing about general Polish history. The MOTL's 2011 "Curriculum Chaperone Guide" compiled by UIA Federations Canada, out of 100 pages, offers no information on Poland's history or contemporary society.[64] While Poland's present-day Jewish community has begun to be acknowledged—most commonly with visits to a synagogue or the Krakow Jewish Community Center if the trip includes a sabbath stay—it has been with studied ambivalence.[65] In response, Polish Jewish community members have called MOTL "a plague," "the opposite of ambassadors of goodwill."[66] As community leader Konstanty Gebert described the discourse of such trips, "A thousand years of Polish Jewry's wonderful history is reduced to five years of murder."[67]

Beyond the exclusion of contemporary Polish Jewry from the mission storyline, Polish Jews themselves were also physically excluded from the MOTL through 1998. This was most acutely felt in the MOTL's main event, the somber, defiant mass walk from Auschwitz I to Birkenau (the complexes' main killing center, also called Auschwitz II) that takes place on *Yom HaShoah*, Holocaust memorial day. On this afternoon, all the geographical sub-groups of teens, who have been touring other Polish Holocaust sites in staggered convoys of tour busses, come together for a demonstration that numbers in the several thousands. In 1999, my Polish Jewish friends struggled to feel a part of the proceedings; despite now being officially welcomed, they had not been given the blue MOTL jackets worn by the U.S., Canadian, Israeli, Latin American, Australian, and other groups, and were relegated to a spot in the far rear of the procession. At the ceremony at Birkenau during the 2000 MOTL, I stood with a twenty-three-year-old "new Jew" named Radek in the bitter cold as the keynote speech was made in Hebrew, English, German, French, and four other languages. Not a single word was spoken in Polish. Radek said he felt sorry ("jest mi przykro") for the elderly Polish Jewish survivors in our group, as they could not understand the speeches. "They've been forgotten [o nich się zapomniało]. They must feel very lonely," he said.

Change and Constraint

Mission trips have been criticized by Jewish academics, politicians, and public intellectuals—particularly in Israel—for their manipulation of the Holocaust to ideological ends, the radicalization of participants, and the priority by organizers of profit motives over moral reflection.[68] The Israeli class trips, it is noteworthy, take place just prior to participants' enrollment in military service. While the Polish and Israeli governments have always worked closely regarding the logistics of these trips—with Israeli youth groups flown in on non-commercial flights and shepherded directly to tour buses with special Israeli security measures at both ends—there has also been public out-cry in Poland.[69] As broader diplomatic relations between Poland and Israel have evolved, the tenor of hostility toward contemporary Poland and Poles on the trips has somewhat attenuated. The original MOTL program textbook, *To Know and To Remember,* included this text: "Everywhere we will be sur-rounded by the local Polish people, and our feelings toward them will be am-bivalent. We will hate them for their involvement in the atrocities, but we will pity them for their miserable life in the present." The passage was removed in the mid-1990s.[70]

Even in the context of highly structured, ideological tours, the potential for progressive memory work is sometimes realized. Indeed, the very con-straints that have been placed on young people during travel in an attempt to engineer their experience can backfire, causing some participants to mistrust the trip's motives or rebel against its strictures.[71] During my brief employ as a guide for the MOTL, I witnessed this kind of revolt. A handful of students met at night in one of their hotel rooms to consolidate their concerns and the next morning voiced these to the two rabbis who were the group's leaders. The students asked that the strict rules preventing them from leaving the hotel during unscheduled time be changed. They wanted the opportunity to con-nect with Polish daily life, to go shopping, to go to a club, to meet some Poles. Their entreaties were politely declined, in part due to concerns about what would be *shabbosdik,* or appropriate on the sabbath—basically Saturday—the one substantially free day of the tour. "You're not letting me have my *own ex-perience,*" one girl protested. Another student on a smaller tour described to me his discomfort with the way the group leader imposed his harshly nega-tive view on everything they saw. A number of news articles in recent years have given voice to a range of similar frustrations.[72]

Local efforts to change the character of mission tours—with most of the organizational energy coming from the Polish side—have slowly begun to bear fruit, as individuals inside and outside the trips have worked together to begin dialogues. Indeed, a bilateral "Program of Cooperation on Youth Ex-change" between the Polish Ministry of Education and the Israel Youth Ex-change Council was established in 2006 to build upon these grassroots ef-forts.[73] It mandated that visits be reciprocal (Polish students should also visit Israel), that they promote tolerance and mutual understanding, that "preju-dices and stereotypes in the perception of common history" be reduced, and, perhaps most relevant, that all Israeli tours meet with Polish youth groups. Yet the policy has proved difficult to enforce, and despite some sporadic funding made available to Israeli educators and guides who wanted to visit Polish schools, an insider estimate suggests that perhaps only 10 percent of the Israeli school groups have met with their Polish peers.[74]

Non-governmental Polish groups like the Warsaw-based Forum for Dialogue among Nations and the city's new Museum of the History of Polish Jews have also begun to organize intercultural meetings in both Poland and Israel, with increasing success since the mid-2000s. By 2009 they had run twenty meetings of 300 students each. Individual Polish or Israeli teachers who have managed to make contacts with their counterpart schools have also organized meetings independently, preferring smaller, more extended exchanges—often with older students—over large, harried trips. Certain Polish municipalities have developed triangular relationships with both Israeli and German towns. New Israeli citizens of Polish descent have also played a mediating role, using personal networks to design local Polish itineraries. The mayor of Wrocław sponsored a group of young Jewish and Arab Israelis to meet with Polish youth in the summer of 2008.[75] But money is short, language and security (on the Israeli side) are barriers, student enthusiasts grow up and get real jobs, and the lack of well-trained dialogue facilitators means that meetings can also backfire. When interethnic encounters don't go well, the damage can leave the two groups even more polarized.

If Polish diplomatic pressures may have laid the groundwork for incremental shifts in the agenda for Israeli youth missions, individual voices on the North American Jewish side have also called for change. Phil Lieff-Greif, a leader in the Los Angeles MOTL branch, drafted the 700-word vision document "Los Angeles March of the Living—A Different Paradigm," that counters the notion that the tour emphasizes Jewish victimization as the norm of diaspora living. The text characterizes the Los Angeles program as one that "differs dramatically" from what many perceive the MOTL to be "in basic philosophical assumptions, educational objectives and . . . day-to-day activities." Indeed, Lieff-Greif notes that most of the teens on their trip come "with deeply rooted negative feelings about non-Jewish Poles," but that their itinerary works to "challenge their stereotypes" through opportunities to meet and engage with "some remarkable Polish people." He describes how "a full day is spent in the [Polish] town of Otwock where our teens meet the local Catholic teens, engage in basic dialogue and socializing activity and then work together on restoring the local Jewish cemetery. They have an opportunity to confront their own stereotypes" and to move the conversation "away from 'What "they" did to "us"' to 'What we must do'; away from a perspective of 'victim', towards one of personal responsibility and personal growth" and to "try on new ways of relating to the world." This motivation to swim against the tide is impressive and facilitates useful social and cultural defamiliarization. Yet such an approach is constantly threatened by other ideological or logistical priorities of most such trips.

An interview with Eli Rubenstein, the founding director of the Canadian national branch of the MOTL and a consultant for its international umbrella, shed particular light on this problem.[76] Rubenstein is a model of self-reflection and openness. He grew up in an ultra-Orthodox Jewish community in which he heard a great deal of anti-Polish sentiment. But he came to realize the importance of Polish-Jewish dialogue for MOTL participants through his own experiences. Poles whom he respected expressed pain at the MOTL's various distortions, particularly his use of the phrase "Polish concentration camps," but also the fact that the only Poles with whom his student charges had contact on the MOTL were the bus drivers, hotel staff, and navigators who served them. Rubenstein's Polish acquaintances were also bothered by the absence of Polish at the MOTL's ceremonies in their country. He said that previously he had "no idea about the depth of Polish suffering" during the war, nor how offensive the notion of "Polish camps" could be to Poles who had themselves been imprisoned in these Nazi German camps (built on what had previously been, and is today again, Polish terrain). Hearing these sentiments expressed by Poles was a transformative experience for Rubenstein. Today he says "it's a sin to spend a week in a country and not connect with the [local] students." He has developed an armory of stories, parables, and life lessons drawn from the Torah (*divrei torah* in Hebrew) that he uses to inculcate messages of tolerance and humanism into MOTL participants.

Yet due to the diffuse structure of the MOTL as an organization, Rubenstein says there are limits to the impact his personal convictions can have. Each Jewish community's "Federation" (a core confederation of social services) organizes MOTL participants, leaders, and programs separately. Aside from a single paid staff person, the organizers and chaperones are volunteers, some of whom make large donations. Most of these individuals see dialogue with Polish youth as simply irrelevant to the goals of the MOTL, which is already tightly scheduled. Jacek Olejnik, an employee in cultural affairs for the Polish embassy in Israel (and formerly for the Israeli embassy in Poland) who has spent years working to organize Jewish-Polish youth meetings on the Polish side, described the sentiment of some Israeli parents—who pay a lot for these trips—to such intercultural programming. They ask, "Why should my kid waste time meeting Polish kids when they could see another death camp?" Moreover, a vocal minority of parents and community members finds such programming antithetical to the missions' goals of Holocaust education and building Jewish identity. Rubenstein recounted having quickly assembled a dialogue group on the spot during a 1996 trip, simply out of frustration. "When it was over, I was almost lynched" by the chaperones, he told me. "*Lynched. By my* people."

While there has been an attempt to modify Israeli security measures in recognition of new diplomatic sensibilities (Polish youth can now, at special request, join their Israeli counterparts on the tour buses), there are still impediments to true interethnic experiences. Israeli youth are, for example, not allowed to stay with Polish host families. In addition, armed Israeli guards and guides who warn Israeli youth not to speak Hebrew in public are not incidental to the experience of the trip; in fact they help constitute it. Mike Urbaniak, a young member of Warsaw's Progressive Jewish Association "Beit Warszawa," said he stopped accepting invitations to meet with visiting mission groups after participating a few times, because they always asked him the same questions: "How can you live here? Are Jews attacked on the street? What are the signs of antisemitism?" He said he wished they would ask where they could find a good nightclub.[77]

* * *

While mission tourists may have been described in unflattering terms—particularly by Polish Jews—they also provide an undeniably potent infusion of energy into Polish Jewish settings. The perpetual problem of assembling the ten adult men necessary to form a *minyan* (prayer quorum) in Kazimierz was made more poignant by the periodic influx of religious missions that delivered more Jews than could possibly fit in the small Remu synagogue. They packed the pews, praying flawlessly and singing with gusto where most local Jews had either forgotten, or were struggling to learn, the liturgy.

During a visit to Poland in 1996, I spent Shabbat with Basia, a seventeen-year-old Polish woman I met at the Ronald Lauder Jewish summer camp near Warsaw. As with many Jews who were raised as Catholics or atheists and were newly experimenting with religion as a form of cultural engagement, her experience of coming out was fraught and tentative, and I quickly dropped the idea of interviewing her; she seemed pained by my questions and I didn't want to heighten her sense of being a curiosity. When she took me to the Warsaw synagogue, I came face to face with a major source of her discomfort. We sat upstairs in the women's gallery overlooking the main floor; if there was difficulty making a *minyan* among the men down below, the women were a far sparser resource. Sitting next to her on the wooden bench, I followed her lead in the prayer book she was learning how to use. From time to time the upper gallery doors opened as a woman or girl would come or go, but at one point a stream of women, very well dressed with colorful hats and scarves, bustled in. A cluster of them made their way directly to the back of the gallery where I was sitting with Basia and a few other young Polish women. They sat down all around us and began asking questions. I wondered how their expensive jewelry must look to Basia, who lived in meager circumstances. When I told them I was American, like themselves, they began to focus their questions on Basia. "Are you Jewish? Do you have a boyfriend? Is *he* Jewish? Why don't you move to Israel or the States?" Basia struggled to come up with answers and was clearly eager to leave, which we did as soon as the service ended. "They're horrible," she said of the tourists, adding that such incursions by groups of American Jews are one of the hazards of going to services. She's not always up to the challenge.

Still, some of the young Polish Jews I knew looked forward to the arrival of these groups, especially the young ones. My Jewish friends in Krakow envied their numbers and vibrancy, and often seemed content to simply bask in their glow. There was something powerful and sexy and beautiful about all that youth, confidence, and just plain noise in the synagogue. But these were often bittersweet encounters. Along with three or four other tentative locals, my friends were used to being the lone stalwarts in the dank women's gallery of Kazimierz's Remu synagogue, chatting or observing the men, the one or two prospective converts tracing the lines in the Hebrew prayer book with unsure fingers. Nineteen-year-old Naomi's wide-eyed awe at those she thought of as "real Jews"—these glittering, confident young Jews who sang with gusto and *davened* [prayed] at top speed, often from memory—dimmed somewhat as an influx of fashion-forward, dark-tressed Israeli or American girls piled in, often sidelining her to the barely visible edge of the suddenly packed gallery. When services ended, these foreigners would smile politely at the locals, say "Shabbat shalom," and then disappear to their hotels for festive Shabbat dinners lasting far into the night. As Tadeusz Jakubowicz, head of Krakow's Jewish community, murmured as we watched the sea of youths in their Star-of-David shirts at their ceremony on the steps in front of the Old Synagogue in Szeroka Street, "How nice it would be if they stayed."

I tried during my stint as a MOTL guide to create cracks in the monolithic narrative into which the participants were being initiated, to pose some of the many questions that had arisen for me in the course of my months in Poland. I don't think much was heard amidst the adolescent din. But an older man who had accompanied the group as a chaperone approached me as I stood watching their ceremony in Kazimierz's main square—a mass of blue-clad teens listening to songs and speeches under Israeli flags. The man was grappling with emotions he didn't expect to have in Poland, and his own ambivalence seemed to make him uncomfortable. "This morning, I saw hatred in people's eyes," he said to me. "Now it's a nice night and I'm enjoying myself. I took pictures of three pieces of graffiti today, but I didn't take a picture of the one *you* pointed out." It was an image of a Star of David next to a cross, with the word "Tolerance" [*Tolerancja*] written in Polish above them. "Because that's not what I wanted to see."

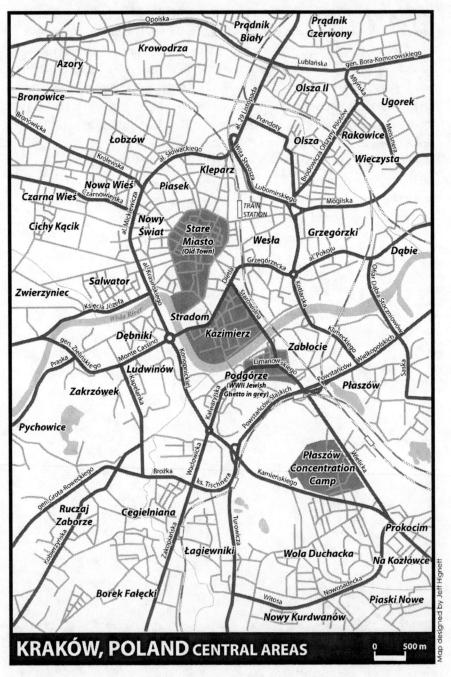

Figure 1. Map of Krakow's city center, showing the old city *(stare miasto)*, Kazimierz, Podgórze, and the Płaszów concentration camp site *(Obóz Koncentracyjny)*.

Map designed by Jeff Hignett

KAZIMIERZ KRAKÓW, POLAND

1. Remu Synagogue & Cemetery
2. Once Upon a Time in Kazmierz Pub
3. Noah's Ark Café (to 2011)
4. Jarden Jewish Bookshop
5. Klezmer Hois Restaurant & Inn
6. Popper Synagogue
7. Café Ariel (the "other" one)
8. Old Synagogue (museum)
9. Centre for Jewish Culture
10. Tempel Synagogue
11. Isaac Synagogue
12. High Synagogue & Austeria Jewish Bookshop
13. Kupa Synagogue
14. New Jewish Cemetery
15. Jewish Community Centre (JCC)
16. Jewish Community ("Gmina") Offices
17. Galicja Jewish Museum
18. Cheder Café
19. Jewish Cultural Festival Office
20. Jagiellonian University Jewish Studies Institute
21. Ethnographic Museum

Figure 2. Kazimierz street map. Jewish Kazimierz is East of Krakowska Street.

Figure 3. View down Szeroka Street, the main square of Kazimierz, in 2010.

Figure 4. Szeroka Street.

Figure 5. Windows were cut into the western wall of the Remu cemetery in the late 2000s, presumably for visitor interest. Photo 2010.

Figure 6. In front of Remu Synagogue on Szeroka Street, mainstream tourists purchase souvenirs while Hasidic pilgrims photograph and video each other.

Figure 7. *Gazeta Wyborcza* article, "Swastika on Museum," 2000.

Figure 8. March of the Living in the town of Auschwitz/Oświęcim, 2000. Participants look at locals looking at them.

Figure 9. Polish and Israeli security on Szeroka Street during Holocaust pilgrimage season, 2000.

Figure 10. Jarden Jewish Bookshop entryway. The poster text reads: *We are all born, live, have our hopes. 1 = 1. Intolerance = 0, All different, All equal.* 2000.

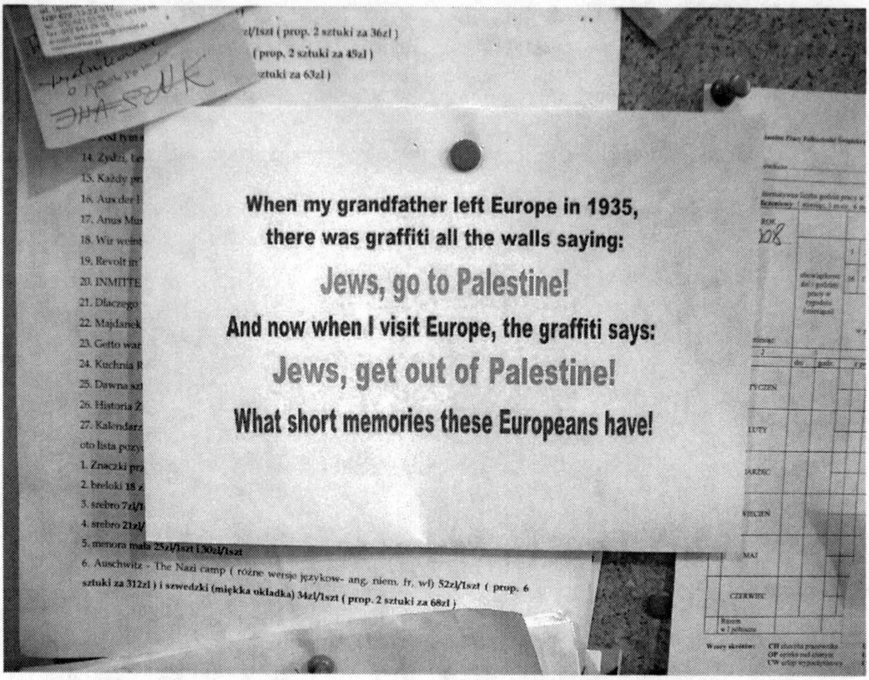

Figure 11. A political poster inside the Jarden Jewish Bookshop office, 2010.

Figure 12. Lucyna Leś helps an Australian Jewish visitor interpret wartime family documents, July 2011.

CHAPTER THREE

THE QUEST: SCRATCHING THE HEART

We Polish Jews . . . We, everliving, who have perished in the ghettos and camps, and we ghosts who, from across seas and oceans, will some day return to the homeland and haunt the ruins in our unscarred bodies and our wretched, presumably spared souls.

—JULIAN TUWIM

poland / we have lain awake in thy soft arms forever

—JEROME ROTHENBERG

At the Jarden Jewish Bookshop and Tourist Agency in Kazimierz, I bumped into Max Rogers, a forty-year-old Hasidic Londoner who travels to Poland frequently on business. Max had been involved in numerous local projects and delights the employees of the bookshop with his periodic gifts of falafel. He brings the mix from London or Jerusalem and cooks it at Noah's Ark café next door.

"Jews who come to Poland? What Jews?" asked Max rhetorically, in response to my description of my research. "The only Jews who come [to Po-land]," Max announced to me and to the non-Jewish Lucyna Leś, the book-shop's co-owner and coordinator of much Jewish traffic through Krakow, "are those who go to pray in some cemetery of famous rabbis, and leave."

"What about you?" countered Lucyna. "You came, you wanted [me to take you] to see Chmielnik"—the hometown of Max's father.

"But my *father* didn't," Max retorted. "Why should people want to see places that they were thrown out of? Where they suffered? The only reason I wanted to see Chmielnik is because I hate the people who are taking over my father's house."

"But you sent me there again! You wanted me to take pictures!" Lucyna prodded.

"Okay," Max admitted, "but *only* of the synagogue, the cemetery—not the house!"

Max mimed his father looking at the photograph of the Chmielnik synagogue that Lucyna had taken and Max had brought home to London. He studied the imaginary picture for a few moments with a furrowed brow, then a slight smile developed and he gestured at a detail with his finger. "I remember, we went in this door," he said. The smile faded and Max was suddenly back with us, reiterating that he wanted to go to Chmielnik only to confront those people living in his father's house and demand to know "how it is possible [for them] to live here."

Several weeks later I encountered Max again in the bookshop, looking a little pale. Lucyna was sitting and smoking. I said to her and husband, Zdzisław, "*On nie wygląda bardzo dobrze dzisiaj*" (He doesn't look so well today). They agreed.

Max asked, "What does it mean, '*wygląda*'?" We explained it means "look," as in "appear," and gave him some examples. "My mother always used to say that: '*Wygląda, wygląda . . .*,'" Max said wistfully. "Beautiful, beautiful . . . I should speak such good Polish! You're so lucky," he told me.

I asked him why he thinks so.

"I don't know!" The question seemed to irritate him. He ran his hand up and down his arm and said dismissively, "It's in the blood."

I again raised the issue with Max about his wanting to visit Chmielnik.

"Okay! Maybe I wanted to see Chmielnik because I heard every day in my house growing up in London 'ChmielnikChmielnikChmielnik . . . ' And so what? Poland for us is finished. If not for the cemeteries, the holy men, there's nothing here."

To quell my questioning once and for all, Max finally settled on a metaphor to explain his feelings for Poland. He asked if I had ever had a boyfriend and then broken up. He said Poland is like that. "Who would want to go back and see an old boyfriend with whom you are not together any longer? Going back to Poland is like going back just to look at such a person, what they are doing now—we don't want to do it," he said.

"So what brings people back?" I asked.

Max shrugged. "You scratch the heart? It speaks."

Many Jewish hearts are being scratched these days, judging from the number of Jews traveling to Poland on exploratory personal journeys, beyond the thousands of Jews who visit the country each year on insular mass missions. Mission tours, under one or another banner of Holocaust remembrance, employ a conventional, distancing, and generalized stance toward Poland, in large part enacting a disavowal of the country as anything but a site of tragedy for Jews, now redeemed by the existence of the State of Israel. But other Jewish travelers are engaged in journeys to Poland designed to transcend this story. Such trips are motivated and informed by travelers' struggles with absence, fragmentation, cultural displacement, and longings for a living connection to the intimate past, a sense of being at home in the world, of positive connection to other-cultural neighbors—perhaps more enduring if less acute wounds of the Holocaust. The trips are often experienced and sometimes planned as radical, connective, even "ethnographic," sometimes opening out into deeper explorations over time, sparked by meaningful Polish encounters. I call this very different mode of travel a quest. Quests are seeker's journeys, undertaken out of a sense of lack, in pursuit of what can only be fulfilled through an expedition into the unknown. They do not follow prescribed paths, and thus are often subversive, even if accidentally. The richness and diversity of quests offers a glimpse of the myriad Jewish connections to Poland that mission travel attempts to erase, and of the complex, intimate ways the Polish past inhabits the Jewish present.

In recent decades scholars have found memory a useful counterpoint to history as a way of apprehending the past. Particularly as a source of voices that rarely find their way into archives, memory is valued as a site of resistance to narratives and discourses associated with and disseminated by institutions of power. But what happens when memory itself becomes institutionalized? When collective expressions of "our past" (through monuments and memorials, oral history archives, education, family storytelling, or rituals such as mission travel) themselves begin to ossify, constrain, and limit both our understandings of the past and our sense of possibility for the present and future? Jewish quests to Poland suggest a mode of struggle with these forms and the gaps in personal knowledge and experience they leave in their wake.

I became interested in the motivations and meanings of Jews visiting Poland on quests because these travelers tended to be the ones I met around Kazimierz. Unlike mission tourists' harried, hermetic huddles, questers travel alone, with a friend, or in small family groups, and they have the time and inclination to talk to strangers. While quests crisscross Poland, heading for ancestral towns or other Jewish centers, many pass through Krakow. Quest travelers often have questions or projects, and Kazimierz's "Jewish" venues provide a place to seek both answers and support. I was drawn by the way these visitors wandered into the Jarden Jewish Bookshop and lingered, looking for opportunities to connect. They brought documents to decipher, place names they wanted to find on maps, ancestral stories to parse. They laid generations of burden out on the shop counter. Some wept.

If not the most representative figure among visiting Jews, Max Rogers became part of Kazimierz's motley group of chronic visitors. He turned up on weekly, monthly, or annual cycles, always as though he had never left. On my own periodic returns, I would often find him sitting in the green shag couch in the bookshop foyer, smoking and chatting with Lucyna, or making ribald jokes or half-cocked business plans with Allen Haberberg, owner of the kosher Hotel Eden two blocks away. Despite his uniqueness—as a Hasidic Jew from an insular community who found some personal freedom in Krakow—Max eloquently illustrates a memory problematic shared by a broader spectrum of Jews of his generation.

On the personal level, Max labors under "postmemory," a condition literary theorist Marianne Hirsch characterizes in part as "grow[ing] up with such overwhelming inherited memories . . . be[ing] dominated by narratives that preceded one's birth . . . having one's own stories and experiences displaced, even evacuated, by those of a previous generation."[1] Mission travel, in a sense, is postmemory writ large. Growing out of the important struggle to have Holocaust survivors voices heard, legitimized, and dignified, it has also limited the ways new generations of Jews can engage with Europe Jewishly. The desire to reconnect or reconcile has had little communal support and much informal sanction.

Jackie Feldman has shown that unauthorized Jewish experiences are consistently policed, eschewed, and submerged during mission travel to Poland.[2] But quest travelers also struggle with the strictures of memory—whether present in public discourse or intimate family experience—that they have at times internalized and inevitably must navigate. In part this is because the Holocaust developed a singular and simplified national meaning, most intensely engendered by Zionism and the exigencies of the young State of Israel (and the growing focus of American Jewry on these). As historian Anita

Shapira notes, the massive terms in which Holocaust memory was always related, "six million Jews; Auschwitz; Maidanek; Treblinka," overshadowed and
silenced the "private holocausts" and personal experiences of survivors.[3] The
"private" memory of individuals was gradually legitimized as Israel's physical
reality and identity became more secure, along with a parallel shift in the
United States from ethnic assimilation to assertiveness. But the overall relationship between public and private memories, individual and group identities, remains a highly charged issue.

It is still the tiny minority of Jewish travelers who make a journey to Poland that is "entirely personal rather than communal," based on family connections or simple tourist interest. Communal ideology discourages it. "Because visits to Shoah territory . . . touch on . . . the sphere of the enduring
past," literary scholar Susanne Klingenstein writes, "such visits are paid by individual Jews as representatives of and on behalf of all Jews. They become collective, historical acts and hence have restitutional power."[4] Jewish travelers
are thus seen by the community as emissaries, embodied statements, speaking in the name of "The Jews." (Indeed, Klingenstein's characterization of return travel may itself be seen as an expression of the dominant communal
ideology, reinforcing the sense that a Jew cannot—should not—"just" take a
simple trip.) Individual memories of Jewish Poland always carry the danger
of exogenous identification, of pulling away from the group toward a broader,
humanistic identity. Thus, despite the recent ascendancy of private memories
of the Holocaust in the public realm, their expression is guided by powerful
templates that make some stories more tellable and hearable. Indeed, these
templates enshrine "ideal" stories and demote, ignore, or silence others.[5]

Max struggled with his own emotions, his own longing for roots, not
only because of inherited family trauma, but also because of specific Jewish
cultural work that stifles those emotions. Max's formulations highlight the
difficulty in narrating multifaceted personal sentiment toward Poland within
the procrustean bed of communally prescribed forms. Jews can, of course, la-
ment the Poland of the pogroms and death camps. The Poland of Jewish communal ruins, represented by mostly despoiled cemeteries and synagogues, is
also provisionally acceptable as a site of mourning (and for Hasidic Jews, of
continuing religious significance in the form of annual pilgrimages to pray at
the graves of dynastic rabbis). But for Max to justify his interest in his ancestral home, he is forced to switch from a connective mode of narration to a distancing, accusatory one, directed at his family homestead's current Catholic
Polish inhabitants. He is also compelled to shift to a collective mode ("we"

don't want to come back) that belies at least an aspect of his own sentiment, revealed in his repeated visits and displays of nostalgia. Finally, to resolve the tension, this Londoner absolves himself of any claim to, and hence responsibility for, his "errant" sense of connection to Poland. He does so by means of an embodied metaphor: Poland—like some kind of genetic handicap—"is in the blood."

Crying Someone Else's Tears: Postmemory and the Jewish Order of Things

What are quest travelers looking for when they come to Poland today? What does Poland offer them? Quests, like missions, are motivated by difficult memory. But quest travelers, as opposed to mission tourists, can be characterized by their openness to—indeed often their seeking out—unfamiliar perspectives and "others'" memories. Quests make efforts to work through the difficulties, to question prescribed memory, to consider its consequences. For many travelers, quests are about reestablishing what anthropologist Jack Kugelmass calls "genealogical memory," or more simply "the desire to know who [one's] grandparents were and how they lived."[6]

As anthropologist Jonathan Boyarin notes of Polish-Jewish émigrés in Paris and their very French children, while "the loss of homeland and family is a recurrent theme in Jewish popular memory . . . the loss of one's children to a different cultural world . . . remains in large measure an unalleviated source of pain."[7] But what about the pain of losing access to a cultural world that shaped one's parents? Of living with elders whose cultural performances are cryptic or misplaced in their current settings? We know Holocaust survivors' memory constructions and cultural struggles are painfully complex. But what about those who come after? Those carriers of postmemory, who "remember" Poland through scraps of language, inherited anger, and the occasional photograph?

Studies of children of Holocaust survivors suggest that their parents' history is experienced by the offspring as simultaneously absent and burdensome, smothering and yearned for, because the history is incomplete. While such children may struggle with their parents' wounds, they also often remain loyal to or even replicate their emotional states, living as if their parents' pasts were their own. They reconstruct and seek to reexperience their parents' and grandparents' lost cultural worlds because it is these imagined landscapes—not the comparatively secure, mundane landscapes they physically inhabit—that feel familiar, defining, authentic.[8] Yet despite studies of survivor-descendants' attempts to reconstruct their families' histories, and an outpouring of memoirs and films addressing such "return" travel, most scholarship has remained in the clinical or discursive realms, and almost none has explored the way such descendants attempt to physically encounter their ancestral places through travel.[9] With the rise of tourism studies and "mobile methodologies,"[10] the opening of Eastern Europe, and the growing primacy put on experiential modes of encountering history, the question arises: what does Holocaust postmemory look like "on the road"?

Jewish immigrants or exiles from Europe are different from other European ethnics. Irish immigrants, French, Italians, or even Poles could—in theory—return. Their descendants can and do visit the homeland to reconnect with linguistic, geographical, and cultural roots. But since the Holocaust, there has been no "old country" to which Jews might return. As a decimated diaspora, the intimate human infrastructures that make up much of the experience and lived memory of a home place—embodied in native ethnic kin, language, institutions, and local knowledge—is gone. While some remnants of physical infrastructure have remained (and, as I discuss, form powerful mnemonic devices for visitors), what made Poland a Jewish place— the little of it that was not destroyed—moved elsewhere, in a divorce that left Jewish and Polish memory largely irreconcilable stories.

If Jewish mission travel works to maintain a particular story by constraining experience and channeling emotion, quest travel encompasses a broader range of sentiments and cultural projects. This other mode of Jewish travel represents a countercurrent to the cultural politics of mission travel. A significant component of quest travel—judging from the travelers I met and published memoirs—is made up of descendants of Holocaust survivors and other Polish-Jewish refugees. Such descendants can, of course, also be found among mission travelers. But these others, having lived particular struggles with parents and community, seem to have felt particularly compelled to break through inherited silence and aversion regarding Poland and to need to see this hypocenter of the Holocaust for themselves. To put it in therapeutic terms—an idiom the questers whom I encountered often used—if missions aim for traumatic repetition, quests pursue resolution. Quest travelers approach Poland seeking understanding, self-transformation, and an enlarged group narrative, by means of identification with and connection to cultural milieus beyond those sanctioned by familial and communal institutions.

Even before she had made her first Poland trip, Szifra (pronounced "Shifra") Feld anticipated it would have a curative outcome. "Poland," she said, "is like a blank, but a blank that contains toxin and horror and loss. I need my own image to put next to this." Szifra was seeking a "second image" of Poland that has speakable substance and human scale, one that is not over-determined by her parents' suffering. Her expectation was that if she experienced Poland herself, "then maybe something will shift. Something will be lighter, or different, or I'll cry the tears for the *right* reasons, and they'll be *mine*. I'll be grieving [for] what my parents never could and finding something that's new for me."

Such "post-Polish" Jews like Szifra best illustrate the dissonance between institutionalized Holocaust memory and their own, particularly pressing memory needs. Anita Shapira notes the centrality of descendants as a linchpin connecting the public and the private memories of the Holocaust, as they are uniquely "products of both memory systems."[11] Post-Polish travelers struggle to navigate their fragmented, often conflicted inheritances. Yet these descendants' desires to recoup truncated family histories also situate them uniquely as memory workers—in a critical yet conciliatory role—in the ongoing life of Jewish and Holocaust memory.[12]

While "quest" travel may be intensely personal, it is also political. If descendants of survivors experience the loss of roots and a tension between constricted narratives and lived experience most acutely, their struggle converges with a broader generational project. Marianne Hirsch makes clear that post-memory is a condition not confined to actual children of survivors, but is a position that can be empathetically inhabited by further-flung "inheritors" of mediated history. And if the central pull toward Poland may be the compelling claims made by the Holocaust's difficult memorial legacies, there may be an even more widespread push: Andreas Huyssen suggests that the anxieties produced by the fracturing of time and space brought on by modernity have led many people to a search for "extended forms of temporality and to secure a space, however permeable, from which to speak and act."[13] Poland, it seems, offers a glimpse, for some Jews, of just such a space—a familiar, intimate place, perhaps a kind of home. This search for place runs across diverse Jewish projects, from those that seek to reembrace Hasidism (a religious tradition with Polish roots) to those drawn to secular Yiddish culture or Poland's history of experiments with Jewish politics. What these projects have in common is the desire to excavate, rekindle, and reincorporate cultural elements discarded by previous generations. New models of Jewish identity are being sought, and Poland is a newly accessible archive to trawl for inspiration. As Marisa Davidson, a doctoral student in Jewish history, told me, she went to Poland "hoping to connect." "Israel wasn't doing it for me," she said. "I wanted to find another way of thinking of myself as a historical Jew."

Jewish quest travelers engage in memory work by embracing cultural elements that feel familiar and fitting, but exceed what is authorized by mainstream Jewish identity discourse. Such self-developmental work may blur ethnic categories and threaten ideologies that other strands of dominant, institutionalized memory work seek to reinforce, with implications for the boundaries of Jewish identity, for definitions of "us" and "them." Quest travelers are pushing the boundaries, trying to envision selves and ancestors in a past and present Polish context. The post-1989 accessibility of mythologized East European sites of Jewish memory thus can function as an opportunity to challenge as well as to reinscribe inherited memory. Travelers I spoke to characterized their trips to Poland as in part a search for an identity that contains more than victimhood, a ground-level struggle that mirrors scholarly charges that Jewish history has too often been written in a "lachrymose" mode.[14] Approaching Poland as a place not only of Jewish loss, but of Jewish imagination, affection, and possibility, can both dignify and vivify the fragments of a cultural world that the traveler feels might have been—or could still in some way be—his or her own.

Because most Jewish travelers have ambivalent emotions, "mission" and "quest" are not clean categories. I thus include among "quests" those journeys on which self-transformation or intra-cultural critique may not begin as primary or fully formulated motivations, and even trips where an instinctive negativity toward Poland is present. For example, Nate Birnbaum, a thirty-four-year-old American who visited Poland with his wife, mother, and kids, admitted to me that he wished he had been wearing a T-shirt in Poland that said, "I'm a Jew. Fuck you."

But my definition of quests refers not only to the emotional but also to the structural. The fact that these trips are relatively unscripted in character, and that they are undertaken in less hermetic fashion, positions them to denaturalize what missions naturalize. The restrictions and staging employed in mission travel inhibits contact with Poles, the key source of the humanizing experiences that generate important epiphanies for quest travelers. Traveling alone or with a family group with no prefabricated institutional program or leadership that would constrain movement or channel emotions opens travelers up to serendipity. Such free exploration of present-day Poland and meaningful contact with contemporary Poles (including Polish Jews) risks not only conflict—as mission travel would have participants believe—but also unplanned empathy, intergroup identification, and a broader range of historical and ethical questions, all potential threats to the mission agenda.

Sławomir Kapralski, a Polish sociologist long involved with the few Jewish heritage study programs that have been run for American college students in Poland, described to me the process of "demythologization" he has observed among his charges during the course of their encounters with Poland. "After the first meal on their own, they think, 'Okay, we ate Polish food and we didn't die.' Then they go out for an evening, and think, 'Okay, we went to a Polish disco and no one attacked us,' and so on. Each experience they 'survive' normalizes Poland for them." Yet this process can easily be derailed if students are not allowed to have such unscripted individual experiences, or the space to interpret them freely.

If nothing is standing in the way, "places possess a marked capacity for triggering acts of self-reflection, inspiring thoughts about who one presently is, or memories of who one used to be, or musings on who one might become."[15] As Nate told me with some wonder, "I thought we'd just come to look at the sites. I couldn't have imagined the amount of introspection. I could imagine my grandmother [here] working as a seamstress." A major part of my time in the field was spent listening to Jewish visitors express the sudden coming into focus of previously inchoate feelings of connection to Poland—an unexpected sense of deep familiarity, like that expressed by Daniel Mendelsohn while researching his book *The Lost*. Mendelsohn was struck by the particular cadences of Yiddish-inflected English among the Jews he met in present-day Ukraine (formerly Poland): "Very few people I know anymore talk that way."[16]

I, too, had such experiences. I remember wandering in one small Polish town under a hot spring sun with my brother in 1990. In a bakery window we saw crumbly yellow cookies, their two ridged halves glued together with seeded red jam. Even the way the small brown paper bag was folded prompted a singular thought: *Grandma*. Indeed, I recall successive shocks in the early 1990s as I encountered *chała* (challah) in a bakery, *maca* (matzo) in a corner grocery, *kiszka* (kishka) at the butcher shop, *placki* (latkes) at a restaurant, and *bajgełe/obwarzanki* (bagels) sold from sidewalk carts. Hearing the words *cymes* (tsimmes), *szmata* (shmatta), and *kibic* (kibbitz)—some of my favorite Yiddish words—emerging from Polish mouths was astounding. Didn't they know those words were mine? More jarring still was being told that the traditional Polish Christmas eve dinner consists of *karp po żydowsku* ("Jewish-style carp")—basically glorified gefilte fish. Such unanticipated encounters with fragments of "Jewish culture" in Poland can be unsettling recognitions that what one has always taken as cultural boundary markers may equally be intercultural bridges.

* * *

Sitting in Noah's Ark café in Kazimierz one day, under an arched wall where a biblical passage telling Noah's story was stenciled in English, Hebrew, and Polish, I overheard a portly, dapper, middle-aged British man ask the waitress, "Excuse me, do you know how many Jews still live here?" She didn't understand his English well enough and looked over at me, at the nearby table I often occupied, with distress. I introduced myself and said perhaps I could help him. It was as if a dam broke. "I just feel overcome," the man said, in a trembling voice:

> My family was from here. This is my first time in Poland, but I just feel this is my place. I walked down the street and came directly here as if I knew exactly where I was to go. I got off the tram and just came straight here, and this atmosphere, this Jacob's Ladder [he points to a painting on the wall], it just all feels like it exactly fills the holes I feel in myself.

The man shook with emotion, repeating over and over how deeply he felt he knew this place, that he'd been here before. When we parted, he clasped my hand and kissed it.

Max Rogers's comparison of Poland to a lost love—despite his defensive insistence on the country's simultaneous meaninglessness and negativity in Jewish terms—captures the sense of yearning and intimate connection to Poland that can accompany more obvious feelings of anger and rejection. Indeed, these other sentiments seem to make anger and rejection all the more understandable. Max's conflict—the ways he attempts to wriggle free of his connection to Poland at the very moment he asserts it—points beyond a straightforwardly nostalgic model of Jewish-Polish heritage, to one that is inherently fraught. But neither is this heritage captured by the flat, negative caricature of Poland in which mission travel often traffics. Instead we are faced with a much denser tangle of conflicting emotions, a tension between repudiation and desire.

Subjunctive Identity

Jewish quests to Poland are explorations in identification. They are a way to step into the flow of family, community, and history from which one feels displaced. As Feldman describes,

Israeli teenagers, when they reach a point in their development when they begin to ask themselves who they are and where they came from, would like to be able to rummage for an answer in the houses and dusty attics of their grandparents. But the houses are often also their tombs. Many don't exist any more. The way back, for many young Israelis, leads through Auschwitz. It is this search for roots, for a tie to Jewish history, that leads many—myself included—to Poland.[17]

Some quests are undoubtedly motivated in part by the desire to "experience the Holocaust" through the iconic landscape, a purpose shared with missions. "It was these exact tracks," says Adam, a twenty-two-year-old Jewish Australian with a Jewish day school background, wide-eyed while recalling his gut reaction during the train ride to Krakow. "They hid behind these very trees." But Adam did not stop with these discomfiting wartime images. "My grandmother is from Poland," he told me, adding quickly that his grandmother hates when he expresses feelings of connection to Poland and had protested his visit. "She doesn't want me to think this way, but besides the atrocities, I know this is where [she] grew up. I see people on the street, going into fruit shops just like my grandmother did. I see their faces and think it's amazing, all these people who look just like my grandmother *would have* looked here."

The subjunctive is a grammatical mood that expresses doubts, wishes, and possibilities. The use of the subjunctive in memory work, then, suggests a relationship with identity in which one considers the possibility that things might have been different—or proposes that they might yet be so. Adam is imagining his grandmother back into Poland, back into a picture he wants to see. By doing so, he is also imagining himself into a relationship with the place, reestablishing Poland as a meaningful link in his own chain of generations. This sense that one has been displaced by the Holocaust is articulated poignantly by Momik, the child of survivors in Israeli novelist David Grossman's *See Under: Love*. Momik struggles to interpret his parents' veiled and cryptic references to their experiences in Poland because he feels "unable to understand my life until I learn about my *unlived life* Over There."[18]

Psychiatrist Aaron Hass illustrates such "subjunctive identity" in a particularly place-based way that reveals the powerful imaginative connection between place and identity that can connect us to places we have never been:

When asked "Fin vanit bist du?" [Where are you from?] by someone from the old country, I would respond "Ich bin a Lubliner" [I am a Lubliner]. Even though before 1978 I had never been to Lublin, Poland, where my parents and grandparents lived before the war, I felt *as though that were* my home. Through a series of circumstances beyond my control, my life was displaced from where *it should have* taken place, from where, I believed, I *would have* led a far more contented existence.[19]

Hass's comparison of "what might have been" with the frustrations of his actual life—a theme echoed in other quest narratives—smacks of classic nostalgia: things were always better "back then." But longings for an imagined past among quest travelers are accompanied by attempts to imagine or establish a living connection to Poland in the present day. Critical nostalgia thus emerges as a meaningful political project, what oral historian Alessandro Portelli calls "memory as alternative," or the art "not only of what happened but also of what did not happen, what could or should have happened."[20] To that I would add "what might yet happen," or the art of possibility. Adam, the traveler from Australia, seemed taken not only by how his grandmother might have looked in her past, but how she might look alongside these familiar-looking Polish old folks today. He even attempted to "try on for size" such a contemporary Polish connection with his grandmother directly. Before his trip he had asked her if, when she watched the 2000 Sydney Olympic games, she had felt any connection to the Polish teams. He had expected that she might. With both dejection and confusion, he recalled that "she said absolutely not, none at all, it has nothing to do with her."

Memory work like Adam's attempts to imagine a positive Jewish connection to Poland, a connection that one suspects his grandmother may also feel despite (or because of) her resolute rejection. Longing often underlies and is entwined with the terrible pain and anger that people displaced by violence also feel toward their former home places. But such recuperative memory work undertaken by quest travelers must contend not only with the fraught sentiments of family members based on their direct experience, but with the way such negativity toward Poland has become more broadly embedded in Jewish memory culture, taking root in generations that have no memories of their own that might complicate increasingly uni-dimensional representations.[21] "Don't kid yourself," Adam's father (the son of the once-Polish grandmother) had told him scornfully in response to his son's enthusiasm about visiting Poland. "Poland is one of the most antisemitic nations in the world." Adam pointed out to me that his father felt that way "even though he has no personal experience with Poland."

The public performance of boundaries between self and other are central to the creation of group identity. Jewish travel to Poland that blurs this

boundary may be taken as "an affront, really, to both Jewish and Polish per-
ceptions of each other and the antipathetic nature of their relations before,
during, and after the war."[22] It risks being considered a "bad Jew" among Jews,
or even throwing one's very Jewishness into question.[23]

Max Rogers and I were zooming in a Polski Fiat through Nowa Huta, the
once-proud communist steel town on the outskirts of Krakow. We passed gray,
greasy-looking villages where tired locals wearing old clothes and carrying
worn plastic shopping bags milled about the main streets. Uneven concrete-
slab walkways, muddy patches of grass, and rusting, twisted metal grates divided soot-streaked, crumbling gray-stucco buildings. Max shook his head
at the sights, "tsk, tsk"-ing periodically. Suddenly he asked me, "Don't you
think it's a curse, that Poland looks like this? Like a hundred years ago?" "A
curse for what?" I asked. Coming from the West, I shared his disconcerted
perspective on the battered landscape and people that languished beyond the
fast-gentrifying city centers, if not his sense of supernatural causation. He
rolled his eyes in disbelief, leaned toward me, and loudly mock-whispered,
"Are you *Jewish*?" Then he spoke matter-of-factly: "For bad behavior during
the war."

Such assertions—of connection and distance, of kinship and otherness, of now and then, of "our" and "their" places in the geochronology of
generations—define much Jewish travel to Poland today. The struggles articulated by quest travelers illuminate the dominant discourses and structures of sentiment that constrain and direct institutionally supported concepts of Jewish identity. They also reveal shifting grammars of identity that
Jews employ to inflect those structures.

"To Carry My Own Story . . ."

As Daniel Mendelsohn explains in *The Lost,* "Auschwitz is the gigantic symbol, the gross generalization, the shorthand, for what happened to Europe's
Jews; but it had been to rescue my relatives from generalities, symbols, abbre-
viations, to restore them to their particularity and distinctiveness, that I had
come on this trip."[24] Listening to post-Polish Jews, I got the sense of a generation that lacks its own stories. They have been overwhelmed by—and have
struggled to domesticate—an inherited narrative of unwieldy proportions.
The dominance of "capital H" Holocaust memory over human-scale narrative in public discourse may be critiqued on its own terms. But descendants
of survivors share a deeper problem; generalized representations of "The Holocaust" have displaced their own personal stories.[25]

Twenty-three-year-old Amos Teitelbaum sat with me in Café Ariel in Kazimierz on a Sunday afternoon in January at a small table by the fire sharing
tea and "Pascha" (Passover) cake. Amos was dressed scraggily, his shoulder-
length brown curly hair pulled just off his forehead with a blue bandana. His
dark eyes were framed by darker, heavy brows. I had met Amos the previous
Friday evening at the Lauder Foundation's weekly Shabbat dinner across the
square. It was easy to spot unfamiliar faces there. Newcomers had an air of
aloofness as they hung back at the door, unsure of what they had stumbled
into. I had called over in my American English, "Hey, where are you from?"
and watched as Amos took a moment to make room for me among his expectations of this place and event. Whatever he imagined finding on his quest to
Poland, I was not part of it. "Why did *you* come to Poland?" I asked Amos,
after explaining my own presence. I learned that Amos lives in Paris. "I'm visiting because my father's parents are from Poland. . . . Finally I want to see,"
he told me, grasping at the air with his hand. He clutched the edge of the open
door next to us and said, "This is the real place. . . ."

Amos's grandfather died in Auschwitz and his father committed suicide
when Amos was a boy. "The only Jewish identity I had during my childhood
is the war story," Amos told me as we sat, klezmer music wafting in the background. Amos's trip to Poland was part of a larger quest to find a clear, positive, life-affirming place in Jewishness, which had been largely an inherited
burden. He sought to differentiate his story from collapse into the generalized
Holocaust narrative. Amos sought a story of his own, one not reducible to the
Holocaust:

> We mix these unconscious stories, you know? It's like there are knots between
> me and [others] that I don't want. For example there's a very close friend I met
> when I was nineteen years old, and his mother is from Poland also, and it is like
> I mixed up our stories. I feel I don't know where I am, I have no mark on this
> earth, you know? Because I am searching, because there is no ancestry. And in
> coming here it was to make me go into my own story and to take care to carry
> my own story and to be with my own story and go with my own story, and not
> to mix it with others' stories.

Amos' self-analysis points to some of the contradictions in the transmission of trauma. Parental silence regarding the past is a central issue in
Holocaust survivor families. The silence, far from being empty, was packed
with messages about prior experiences that these children's own could never
match. Some of the silences were about the Holocaust and unspeakable suf-

fering. But others had to do with what else had existed, besides the Holocaust, and before it. As Szifra, the daughter of Polish Holocaust survivors, put it,

> In my family you don't talk about Poland. You know, "Poland sucks." Besides the fourteen rote sentences that got said, no one ever asked my parents anything about Poland. I'm fifty-one years old, and I haven't had five minutes of conversation with my siblings about Poland. And we talk a lot. I think I had honored my parents' pathological or adaptive need to just go forward. We all got the message that this was the forbidden room. How many generations grew up in that country—grandparents, great-grandparents, great-great-grandparents—and it was like this country didn't exist. This vacuum feels bizarre. I have to fill it in some way.

Szifra had warned me she might cry as we talked on the telephone about Poland. She was planning her first trip there in the spring of 2002. And she did cry periodically, but she didn't let it interrupt her story. She was one of many people referred to me by friends; once people heard about my research, it seemed that each one had or knew someone who had a Poland story, and most were eager to tell them. They represent a different kind of post-Holocaust loss that the opening of Eastern Europe has made visible—and perhaps speakable, or even perceptible. Although Szifra admitted she couldn't quite pin down why she wanted to visit Poland, she said, "I feel like I *have* to go."

> This is a pilgrimage for me; no one [in my family] has gone back to Poland. My parents essentially disowned the Polish part of them; they were Jewish, not Polish. I don't feel Polish at all, despite a name which can be pronounced instantly only by Poles. My father was very wealthy; none of his property was reclaimed. It will be an incredibly emotional time for me; I know that. The Holocaust has undoubtedly been the central organizing principle of my life.

What does it mean when the central organizing principle of your life is an absence or distance? The silences of Holocaust memory are often pregnant with tension and encoded with powerful nonverbal communiqués.[26] These have produced a sense of both loss and yearning among descendants, a need to make sense of what has been central but cipher-like, distressingly decontextualized, in their own lives. The various metaphors for missing coherence that come up in conversations with and writings by survivor-descendants suggest that a key goal of Poland quests is the search for a kind of missing "frame," the borders of a jigsaw puzzle into which one could fit inherited cultural fragments to give them meaning and stability. Szifra's ancestral cultural context had been fractured, leaving her genealogically adrift. Her parents, from Lodz, had tried to disown their previous Polish context, but traces remained. These intimate, tantalizing shards—her name, unclaimed family property—point Szifra to a social elsewhere, another milieu where she, or at least part of her, might yet be recognized and rooted.

A Genealogy of Details

Most American Jews are of East European descent. To the extent that a sense of place was conveyed in parents' or grandparents' old-world narratives, it was often unconnected to actual, present-day geographical places. Even the names of prewar East European hometowns are often untraceable in Jewish families; deemed irrelevant by emigrants, those that were passed down were frequently done so in their Yiddish forms, and thus not rendered on most published maps. In *Landscape and Memory*, British Jewish historian Simon Schama suggests this predicament with reference to his own life:

> And just where, exactly, was this place, this house, this world of stubbly yellow cigarettes, fortifying pulls from grimy vodka bottles, Hasidic songs bellowed through the piney Polishe velder? "Where was it?" I pressed my mother while we sat eating salad in a West End hotel. For the first time in my life I badly needed to know. "Kowno gubernia, outside Kowno, that's all we ever knew." She shrugged her shoulders and went back to the lettuce.[27]

On the most mundane level, post-Polish Jews are faced with a documentary gap, often forced to "imagin[e] a world without the aid of one picture or memento."[28] So much material Jewish culture was destroyed during the Holocaust. Concrete details help slake the desire for tangible evidence, sensually fleshing out family history and combating both the void and the generalization. The swell of North American Jewish genealogical conferences, books, and services that has developed in the wake of the opening of Eastern Europe speaks to a yearning for roots, and to some extent re-correlates Jewish geography with concrete European terrain. But such at-a-distance reconstructions still often abstract Jewish lineages from the surrounding other-cultural environments. Actually visiting a former home place, on the other hand, offers the possibility of a much different quality of "return."

Poland quests are thus based not on what Jack Kugelmass calls mere "antiquarian" interest, but on each traveler's urge to understand and to experience his or her own place with reference to both a physical and a sociocultural landscape, in some partial way inherited but never seen or experienced. Nate Birnbaum said, "My mom had told me stories of September 1, 1939, about walking on the road away from the Germans, and I wanted to be there on that road." And Israeli traveler Ryan Kedar told me, "I really never knew anything about what the Polish climate was like and what it is like to breathe and how does the skin feel when you are in Poland." But individual experience is not always enough. Many quest travelers seek to share this new horizon of genealogical memory with family, to both stabilize it and weave it back into the flow of generations.

One way to perpetuate and propagate this newly made memory is to share in the experience of making it—to remember together. As Nate said, "I wanted to be *with my mom* when she saw her hometown for the first time since the war," as if sharing in his mother's reexperiencing her natal home could not only repair her severed Polish roots, but graft him in by proximity. But quest travelers also pursue more straightforward documentary work in many forms. They undertake interviews, observation, archival research, artifact collection, visual and audio documentation, and journal writing. From these they produce annotated photo albums, videos, websites, blogs, and narratives typed up and distributed to family and friends, publishing articles in synagogue newsletters, Jewish and general newspapers, and academic and literary journals.

Barry, a trustee at an Israeli university, gave me a copy of his 130-page document titled *The Streets of Kazimierz: A Personal Journey Back to Poland and Jewish Kraków—Second-Generation Perspective,* which he wrote after his trip in the summer of 1997. Noting in the introduction that the trip "was one of the most important experiences of my life," he created the document because he felt it was "necessary to pass [the experience] along to my own children when they come of age."[29] Such self-authored travel documents are not inert souvenirs or another layer of fragments to be stored in the family archive. Along with creating them, their authors animate them through circulation, making them the basis of emotionally significant dialogues. They are intended to create new experiences that mend perceived ruptures in the flow of family memory, to not only record what little "direct" family memory can be captured, but to inspire the further elaboration and proliferation of such memory.

I took a walking tour of Krakow's Kazimierz neighborhood with Julie, a forty-three-year-old American Jewish lawyer whose grandfather was born and spent his early life there. "You might wonder why I'm in Krakow in the winter," Julie said, telling me the story of her father's advancing cancer, which pushed her to drop everything and travel to Poland "before it is too late." Her father had always wanted to see Krakow, his father's home. His father, Julie's grandfather, had lived on Kupa Street; other family members lived on Jozef. As we walked, Julie pulled from her bag a seven-page transcript of her grandfather's memories of Kazimierz—which he had dictated in Yiddish and which an aunt had translated into English for Julie. Julie also shared archival photocopies listing her great-grandfather's and other relatives' Kazimierz addresses, occupations, and causes of death. When she got home to New York, Julie e-mailed me, saying that she took the photographs she had made in Kazimierz, "put them in a scrapbook and annotated them with explanations and excerpts from my grandfather's narrative," and sent the scrapbook off to her father "along with a whole lot of books from Krakow."

Szifra's mother, her only living parent, was suffering increasingly from Alzheimer's disease. Szifra seemed anxious to reweave dangling strands of her family's memory of Lodz. She decided to videotape places in the city where her parents lived before World War II and bring them back for her mother to "annotate." "There are so many pieces she's never talked about," Szifra said. "Pre-horror. Cabinets, rooms. So little family history is documented. I need it for my kids."

Remembering Bodies

What Pierre Bourdieu calls *habitus,* or acquired dispositions including "ways of talking, ways of moving, ways of making things," forms another kind of document, "exist[ing] in, through, and because of the practices of actors and their interaction with each other and with the rest of their environment."[30] For this kind of document, the body is the archive. If Jewish and Polish memory were rendered irreconcilable, and their boundaries were ossified in ways that have imaginatively isolated Jews from their one-time neighbors, it has been at the expense of recognizing the cultural interpenetration resulting from centuries of territorial co-habitation and interaction. Hence quest travelers' astonishment at the cultural familiarities they find in Poland. I encountered Neta, for example, a fifty-something Israeli woman sitting and speaking in Hebrew-accented English to Zdzisław in the Jarden Jewish Bookshop entryway's upholstered chairs. "My parents were really very Polish," Neta mused aloud, as if thinking the thought for the first time. "[Coming here] I was shocked how much I understood—not just the language, but the culture. How people move, how they fold things, how they behave with one another."

Post-Holocaust generations have been unable to comprehend—and thus perhaps to mourn—the loss of cultural roots because the intimate contours of what was lost have been obscured. With the ascendancy of Zionism, Ashkenazi Jewish collective memory and identity was unlinked from the places where it was generated. Israel became the official "homeland" to which Jews were to orient, and the demands of post-genocide cultural reconstruction involved triage: new, if culturally unfamiliar, roots were to be sutured on. Israeli scholar Yael Zerubavel captures this transformation—which undoubtedly occurred more starkly in the Israeli context—in an anecdote about discovering that a memorial volume about her grandfather's life obliterated his formative years in Eastern Europe, making his life "[appear] to have begun only when he immigrated as a young man to Palestine."[31] Zerubavel notes the power of commemorative indoctrination in recalling that during all her own formative years, she never noticed anything amiss about the book's truncated narrative. It was only "when she returned to it as an adult and as a mother, involved in the active transmission of family memory," that she noticed the gap.

If many thousands of Netas are walking around in Israel, North America, and elsewhere, carrying unrecognized remnants of Eastern Europe in their postures, gaits, eating habits, and senses of humor, traces of the context in which this Ashkenazi habitus was formed still exist in that part of the world today, in a way that connects Jews to their non-Jewish former neighbors. But it is a fraught connection, shot through with ruptures that separate or at least experientially mark Jews within this "familiar" social landscape. Particularly when societies are damaged by events that induce social suffering or institutionalized oppression, "memory processes [are] sedimented in gait, posture, movement" in a way that "merges subjectivity and the social world."[32] Just as with the "normal" transmission of embodied culture, embodied traumatic memory does not necessarily disappear with the death of those who had primary experiences. The Jewish body has been so pathologized in European history—most recently and starkly during the Holocaust—that it would be surprising if many Jews did not carry some awareness of or response to being cast as corporeally different.[33]

This kind of abject physical postmemory, particularly among descendants of those who directly suffered systematic racialized violence, may also be activated in proximity to a historically charged landscape. If anxieties about visible difference are stoked in the context of mission travel, Jews on quests also navigate them. As Amos explained to me, "What is funny is when I come to Varsovie [Warsaw] it is really . . . when you go out . . . I'm paranoid . . . [it's] something very strange . . . [I am] very paranoid; they'll know I'm Jewish or something." And Nate said, "In San Francisco, I rarely feel Jewish ... but here I have constant thoughts, I'm looking at people's faces, thinking, 'What would they think if they knew I was Jewish?'" I, too, was at times fixated on whether or not Poles could discern my Jewishness at a glance. I wasn't sure which I hoped for. I asked Zdzisław, the non-Jewish bookseller, "Can everyone tell I'm Jewish?" He assured me that I looked "like any other Polish girl."

Problematic as such physical reductionism may be, it should be recognized as a kind of "deep memory," a "more basic core of experienced memory that runs beneath the banal reassurances of common memory."[34] Especially in a situation of traumatic inheritance, activating such deep memory can function "as a continued lived testimony, an ongoing witnessing."[35] Experiencing one's body as different—different in historically and culturally specific ways that may run counter to dominant stories of community belonging—is another kind of memorial practice, one that points to more complex vectors of identification.

Being recognized as Jewish while visiting Poland can feed feelings not only of anxiety, but of vindication or shaming, as Nate's aggressive earlier comment suggests. Racialized experience, though, is not inherently negative. Being pointed out as physically, Jewishly different in Poland can be a source of positive distinction to a traveler as well—especially when that distinction is welcomed by locals. Especially in smaller towns, I was often recognized as a Jew on the street by older non-Jewish Poles. The obvious problems of racial essentialism aside, at times this felt oddly comforting, as if my Jewish history—largely irrelevant and unnoticed in the United States—were legible here.

This heightened attention to bodies functions in multiple ways. As I illustrate in chapter 6, visiting Jews often try to determine if the Poles they meet—particularly those involved with Jewish heritage brokering—are Jewish based on appearance or activity. "Jew-dar," American slang for the instinctual interpersonal sixth sense used to determine whether unfamiliar individuals are Jewish (characterized alternately as a sensible social navigational tool or a self-conscious minority tic) is set on high sensitivity among Jews traveling in Poland.[36] Such physical self-consciousness during travel need not, however, be based on a sense of *difference* from the majority. On the contrary, it can provoke a visitor's realization that he or she, for the first time, looks like everyone else, at home in the phenotypical landscape. Tamara Lesser recalled during her trip

being really, really surprised that I felt that people really looked like me. I thought that was really weird because I am Jewish not Polish, which my dad's told me like a thousand times, you know. Because if anyone [ever said,] "You're Polish," it was like "No, no, no," because my *Bubbie* (Yiddish: grandmother) was *not* Polish, she was *not* Polish, she was *Jewish*. . . . So I was walking around and just really looking at peoples' faces. And like I said I have traveled a lot, I have been all over Latin America and . . . the Middle East [and] I went to Israel and I was in Egypt [and] India. But this was the first time that I had been somewhere that I felt . . . like "*these people look like me.*" It was weird and I felt *wrong* to think that, because my dad, his voice is always there [saying], "You are *not* Polish, you are *Jewish.*"

The idea that Tamara could be (a)kin to Poles had been deliberately and vociferously disavowed, to the extent that she herself was taken aback when she perceived a visible similarity directly while in Poland. Tamara invokes repeated family interactions in which a distinction between Jews and Poles had been built and reinforced; indeed, she describes an apparently frequent *slippage* between them in a contemporary North American context, and the categorical rejection of such blurring by her father. Tamara seems fascinated to have found a kind of new "home" place in the world—a place indeed more familiar to her than even Israel—based on her own observations of bodily resemblance. But she expresses moral ambivalence in even entertaining these observations (and their implications of Polish-Jewish relatedness) due to her father's reproach and assertion of a clear distinction between the groups.

Tamara's musings reveal not only the truism that the boundary around Jewishness (or any ethnic group) has an imaginative component that requires maintenance. Rather, they show a misfit of generational and culture-political (Jewish) sensibilities about the function of boundaries, the experience of physical difference, and the meanings of belonging. The father's distinctions likely speak to his more recent memories of Jewish persecution in Poland, not to mention his closer proximity to a time of starker cultural and religious differences between Jews and Poles. But his (potential) emotions, moral judgments, fears of assimilation, and understandings of history are not those native to his daughter. For Tamara, bodily similarity seems not only surprising, but suggestive—of relatedness, of identification, of meaningful forms of *possibility.*

Whether experienced as positive or negative, such bodily recognition and categorization confers a sense of social and historical situatedness on the traveler abroad. These recognitions—like quests themselves, in the context of which they occur—are not unmotivated or disinterested. Israeli Ryan Kedar, whose grandmother is from Poland, was drawn to Poland by the anticipation of phenotypical fit. "A big part of why I never felt at home in Israel," Ryan said, "was that . . . I sunburn extremely easy and am totally sensitive. I knew that my genetic makeup was just not suited to being in the desert and yes . . . I was born there and was Israeli but in so many ways I was also Polish." One can hear in his comments a desire to deconstruct and inflect his Israeliness with reference to deep, abiding diasporic connections, precisely the kind that Israeli Zionism has sought to obscure.

As both Tamara's and Ryan's comments suggest, discerning similarity between their own bodies and (non-Jewish) Polish bodies is transgressive, pushing against racial logics prevalent in both popular Jewish and Polish discourse. If "the fundamental efficacy of ritual activity lies in its ability to have people embody assumptions about their place in a larger order of things," then Jewish quests to modern-day Poland can be seen in part as an emerging Jewish ritual that attempts to question the larger order of things with reference to their own bodies.[37]

Turning Poland Back into a Country: Quests as Therapy and Activism

Mission travel is an institutional product of Jewish communal demographic and memorial anxieties that encourages Jews to see themselves as a permanently embattled group. But this approach has itself produced new anxieties, to which quest travelers are responding. Quest travelers struggle with family and community rejection of Poland in the face of what seem to be obvious cultural affinities. This tension points to the Jewish version of a broader cultural conflict in post-Enlightenment identity formation, in this case heightened by the Holocaust: a clash between appeals to group loyalty and universalism, or in Jewish terms "*yiddishkeit* versus *menschlichkeit*" (Jewishness versus humaneness/compassion).[38] How to mourn one's own group's suffering without perpetuating alienation from broader humanity? A deeply inculcated sense of difference and victimhood—despite its source in the very real suffering of these travelers' forebears—is at odds with their own everyday surroundings and experiences today. It doesn't sit right with these young Jews to feel a particular way about Poland at the turn of the twenty-first century, just because they are Jewish.

Quest travelers often expressed their trip experiences to me in the idiom of therapy. They took their trips in the active pursuit of "counter-experience" that might shed new light on burdensome inherited perspectives. All Amos knew about Poland before his trip was "the Hasidic stories of Martin Buber, and that the Poles were all antisemitic." Given Amos's tragic family story, he knew he would be traveling with heavy baggage. He said he was left, after his father's suicide, with the task of sorting out what his father could not, in a desperate attempt to "find my own karma." His psychoanalyst said a trip to Poland might save him a year of analysis.

> I think [my father] was traumatized by the Second World War—he never met his [own] father—and also traumatized, fatally, by his mother, who survived but was psychologically ill. I think he was asking himself a lot about his identity. I think my father was not able to speak about this. Otherwise, if he had been able to, he would not have committed suicide.
>
> I think because of this I have this big karma with my father and I think it is the Jewish problem. . . . He didn't have a place to open [up to his problems of identity]. And I have to open [up these problems], because if I don't, it will mean death. . . . I have to carry it in another way. [My father] never came here [to Poland]. He never saw where his father was from, he never made a move, so I have to make a move to live. To keep life in a good way . . . in a better way than it is now. That is my goal.

Travel to Poland for Jews often involves pain and fear projected onto Poles and the Polish landscape. But travelers in the quest's self-questioning mode are highly introspective about their own ambivalence, confusion, and self-described "paranoia" vis-à-vis Poland, as well as regarding their own tendencies to make assumptions about the place that might negatively distort their experiences there. Tamara Lesser told me that during her trip to Poland she constantly heard her father's voice in her head:

> "The Poles were really bad to us, the Poles were really bad to us . . . don't be nice to them, they hated us and they still hate us!" So the whole time we were like, "Are they antisemitic? I don't know. Did you see that guy? Did you see the way he looked at me? Was he antisemitic? I don't think so. Yeah I think so." It was totally, like, this constant game of "They hate us." "No, that guy was nice, they *don't* hate us."

While she could have easily deferred to her father's admonitions, and interpreted her interactions with Poles in a uniformly negative fashion, Tamara wrestled to square his inherited voice (urging continued vigilance and suspicion) with her own empirical observations.

Part of these travelers' motivation is a desire to challenge received or prescribed sentiments, and thus to change their relationship to both the past and the present. Szifra recounted a conversation she had with a Peace Corps volunteer who had lived in Poland for a few years in the early 1990s. The non-

Jewish acquaintance had described places she had lived in Poland, the land-scape, the topography, Polish friends. Szifra had finally burst into tears.

> I wanted to muzzle her. Poland is about the Holocaust, period. That Poland is a real country, with mountains, with nice people, it was just too much. It was like a file that was getting uncompressed when I hadn't pressed "unstuff." But I knew that when I got home, I had to look at a map, I had to do something that makes this country into a country.

Herein lies the connection between individual, self-described therapeutic aspects of Poland quests and their function as cultural critique. Jack Kugel-mass proposes that many American Jews travel to Poland to reconfirm their sense of victimhood, an inherited sensibility that does not square with Jewish success in the United States nor Israeli power in the Middle East. But I found that many quests to Poland are as much or more about Jews questioning their victim status. Amos told me,

> When I was young it was an "Auschwitz" atmosphere. It was really trauma-tized. Still nobody can think about it. It is still like an open blister and we keep saying, "It is horrible." It *was*, okay? But we are not changed; we are not trans-formed by any kind of message. I think it is now fifty years later, and we have a lot of horrible things that happened in the world, but we still say "*this* is hor-rible, *this* is horrible" [meaning the Holocaust]. But what is the responsibility that comes to us? I mean, there is some problem with keeping this [attitude of] "*We* suffered, *we* suffered."

Amos made agonizing sounds, beating his breast and wringing his hands for effect.

> You know? It is true: I really understand—really—because my grandfather died there [at Auschwitz]. My father committed suicide. I think a lot about this. But I think we have to move our head a little bit forward because it is not pos-sible to keep this [suffering].

Amos in no way wants to deny his forebears' suffering; his concern is with halting the damaging effects of and responses to this suffering that entangle subsequent generations. His use of the word "responsibility" and his invoca-tion of the many other "horrible things" that have happened since the Ho-locaust suggest that he feels a need to work against a kind of cultural, even moral malaise that has mired his Jewish intimates in a closed loop of trau-matic memory, impairing their ability to act morally vis-à-vis—or even to live fully in—the larger world. He is thus among the quest travelers I met who were using a reencounter with Poland as an attempt to break a traumatized, mythologized, inward-looking relationship to the tragic Jewish past.

The efforts of quest travelers are deeply connected to the needs of their ongoing lives; they are explicitly present and future-oriented. Instead of idealizing the past, quest travelers seek to confront and interrogate received histories. Many descendants of survivors are traveling to Poland with the explicit goal of reassessing their ideas about that place and its relation to their Jewish selves. Jews on quests resist what writer Walker Percy calls the "approved confrontation of the tour" and the "radical loss of sovereignty" it engenders.[39] These travelers use Poland otherwise: to explore Jewish identity boundaries and to express or construct a Polish component to their ethnic heritage in the face of the general denial and disavowal of such identification by mainstream discourses of Jewish identity. Ryan Kedar explained that, unlike most Jews, he went to Poland with a very positive outlook:

> I just had that expectation that I am going to love [the Poles] and because of that I looked really positive[ly]. If I had gone looking for the negative I would have found that too. I have heard of so many people who have gone to Poland and see a town and think: "Oh my God, where are the Jews? Oh my God, this person is talking behind [my back], whispering something, he must be saying something negative about me because they are anti-Semitic." [But] I didn't go looking for that and that is why I didn't find it. I remember just talking to people as people, and they were just really amazing people. . . . Really, I was looking for home. I was looking for *my* home. So you don't want to come to the place where your family lived . . . with negative feelings toward it.

Ryan even avoided the ritual visit to Auschwitz:

> I wasn't there [in Poland in order] to experience the terrible six years but to actually see the hundreds of years, more than 600, let us say 1,000 years of Jewish life and my family's life in Poland before that and to see what the Poles are—the living Poles, not the dead Jews. That is what I was looking for.

Amos, too, steered clear of Auschwitz. For him the critique of victim-centered Jewishness is related to the way it has evacuated more positive Jewish cultural content.

> I didn't want to go back to Poland to see antisemitism. I want to stop this [practice]. I don't want to go to see Auschwitz. I don't want to see the place. I don't have anything to do there. I could go, but I don't want to. Because I think it

is already alive in me. Or I would make a ritual there, or make a prayer. But I don't know the prayer. So I don't go.

Like the other quest travelers I met, Amos used the encounter with Poland, on his own terms, as a kind of therapy designed to speak to a preexisting sense that something was amiss in his relationship to the world due to the Holocaust and his family's response to it. Such travelers' inherited relationships to Poland as an ancestral place—a basic resource for self-making—were experienced as damaged, even *morally* damaged. An encounter with this country offered a way to expand their sense of cultural resources and to enact a broader politics of reconciliation.

Confronting the Neighbors: Intersubjective Encounters

Quest travelers seek moorings on which to tie Jewish memories cut adrift by trauma or displacement. But if in Poland the landscape endures—and serves as the major resource for the kind of memory work carried out by missions— the neighbors also remain. For quest travelers, Poles themselves are being rediscovered as significant memorial partners. In a review of Larry Mayer's quest narrative, *Who Will Say Kaddish?: A Search for Jewish Identity in Contemporary Poland,* Polish sociologist Alina Cała criticizes the "Judeocentrism" of such trips, noting that non-Jewish Poles barely show up in the narrative, or only as minor actors, because "Poles are not necessary to the inner journey of the authors."[40] But as I illustrate, encounters with Poles— Jewish and non-Jewish—are transformational moments in many quests, and a major catalyst of perceptual shifts.

Nate Birnbaum surprised himself by how deeply he began to ponder his own Jewishness and experiences during his visit to Poland. Encounters he had in Poland prompted epistemological questions about his own and others' understandings of Jewishness, Polishness, and antisemitism. He recounted meeting a Polish Jewish woman who challenged his perspective on current Polish antisemitism:

I was telling her how I don't feel antisemitism in the States. She got very upset and said, "In thirty-five years in Poland we haven't had a Jew killed, and in LA there was just this shooting in the Jewish camp.[41] How can you not feel antisemitism?" The point is that facts distort truth. I have the *experience* of living in the United States, but she has the facts. [Similarly,] she feels *Polish,* and I had trouble understanding that.

Although Nate told me "the idea of antisemitism is pervasive of this trip," it was clear that how he viewed antisemitism and its role in his own life had been made significantly more complex due to his Poland travel experience. He seemed to be digesting a new appreciation for the distinction between— on the one hand—incidents, statistics, and labels (like "antisemitism"), and— on the other—day-to-day lived experience of place, identity, belonging. His own country's narrative of exceptionalism, in tandem with a traumatic Jewish communal perspective on (particularly Eastern) Europe, made the notion of a Jew living happily in Poland hard to imagine without going there and meeting such a person. "Talking to that woman gave me a perspective unavailable in the United States," Nate said.

Jewish quests, like missions, often contain embedded desires for confrontation—to see how Poles will respond to the implicit accusation embodied in one's presence as a Jew, to see "what they have to say for themselves." But where missions tend to stoke these passions while providing limited opportunity for interpersonal contact with Poles, quests allow encounters to play themselves out in ways that can force reconsideration. Two uncomfortable experiences of my own as a college student in the early 1990s shocked me into recognition of the limits of my own communal narrative of suffering—and, indeed, highlighted for me that this narrative was just that: a narrative. The first was when a Polish acquaintance casually remarked that his father had been interned in Auschwitz, and I responded that I hadn't realized his family was Jewish. He replied—charitably revealing only a bit of the frustration he likely felt—that his family is not Jewish, and didn't I realize that ethnic Poles, too, were put in camps?

The second experience occurred when I began chatting with a young man selling small souvenir paintings of Krakow's historic sites. After a few minutes of pleasant banter, I asked him where he was from. He replied, "Oświęcim," which I had recently learned was the Polish name for Auschwitz. But the fact that Oświęcim is an ordinary Polish town (and one that had been more than half-Jewish before World War II) was still relatively new to me at the time. In any case, these realities didn't make a dent in the much more significant revelation that this man had grown up in *Auschwitz*. I could not hide my consternation and said something along the lines of, "Oh my gosh, that must be a *horrible* place to live." He informed me that the Polish town is not the Nazi camp, that his parents had been resettled there after the war not by their own choosing, that he enjoyed a normal youth *thank-you-very-much*, and—most discomfiting for me—asked if I was trying to shame him. This final question has stayed with me for a long time, because I think, in a way, that I was. I wanted (and was used to having) my narrative of historical suffering validated: Germans = perpetrators; Jews = victims; Poles = at best onlookers to my tragedy. I needed him to affirm my story. His response reflected my ignorance (and the more general Jewish erasure) of his.

Stephanie Rowden, an artist who accompanied me to Poland in 2008 on a project to record Jewish and Polish experiences at Krakow's annual Festival of Jewish culture, called her trip "a reality-rearranging experience." Through the stories Poles told her, she was confronted with not only her own obliviousness to Polish wartime experience, but the resistance other Jews put up against sharing in such realizations.

> To find out about the loss of life and the devastation for Poles during and after World War II was absolutely stunning. Why didn't I know this? Even learning that Auschwitz [the Nazi camp] was originally built for Poles came as a surprise. . . . I spoke to an older, highly educated American Jew visiting the festival. When I mentioned my new awareness of Polish losses during the war, the idea was kindly but clearly dismissed.

Confrontations with Poles are often opportunities to confront the limits and distortions of one's own understandings of history; sometimes they are also a spur to consideration of the larger or deeper structures—like communities, institutions, and emotions—that have shaped and contained these understandings.

Like Stephanie, Amos felt transformed by his travels. I asked him if he would ever come back to Poland. He clearly felt his hoped-for "therapy" had been efficacious, allowing him to work through what he previously experienced as a traumatized relationship to Poland. "If I come back it is another story. . . . It is to see nature. Because I think this is a beautiful country, and I have friends—non-Jewish friends—who are from Poland also. Perhaps I'll come back with them to see nature." Szifra, too, seemed changed. She sent me an unsolicited e-mail just after her return from her trip to Poland, reporting "how much more connected I feel to Poland and being Polish now."

When not constrained by the priorities and itineraries of highly ideological group travel, Jewish visits to Poland stimulate multifaceted personal and cultural reckonings, at times between Jews and Poles or within Jewish family groups. Indeed, quest travel has memorial reverberations beyond the generation that undertakes it. Despite often traveling against parental or grand-parental wishes, the contacts travelers establish and the tales they bring back can change the minds of their elders, tapping into deep wells of previously unexpressed sentiment, occasioning never-before-told stories, and activating entirely new frames of remembrance.

Sometimes it is a returning survivor who is the catalyst. Walking out of Szeroka Street in Kazimierz, an elderly man shouted excitedly across the road at me and my two American Jewish friends, "Ah! Jews!" and hurried over, his two middle-aged daughters following. He was a Jewish Holocaust survivor, originally from Lvov and now an American, and as is the norm in Kazimierz he told us his wartime story right then and there in the middle of the road. I told them about the research that brought me to Poland. The response came from one of the daughters: "How can you *bear* to live here?" As I tried to formulate an answer, a local man I know walked by and we exchanged a few words. The survivor's face lit up. "You speak *Polish!*" he declared. "My kids never learned Polish," he added, shaking his lowered head with apparent regret. The same daughter, looking away, said to the air, "He never *taught* us Polish." A moment later she turned back to me and snapped, "Why do you speak *Polish?*"

Such encounters hint at the pain and ambivalence on both dangling ends of a broken cultural link between Jewishness and Polishness. Both child and parent struggle to deal with an evocative element of identity, at once intimate and taboo: Polish language. Something that could have bound them together in intimacy binds them instead to opposite sides of a chasm. The daughter loudly rejects Polishness as a cultural category; more quietly she seems to express the loss of a family tie to a world that appears to be a source of joyful memories for her father. His decision to not teach his children Polish— presumably made for any number of emotional and practical reasons—is thrown into question for both generations.

The Mission and the Quest

I do not want to argue that the sense of trauma experienced by post-Polish Jews (a generation or two removed from the original persecution) is somehow essential, irrepressible, and thus wholly inherited. Whatever social, cultural, and emotional challenges confront these individuals find form through cultural channeling and social construction in which institutions and individuals participate.[42] Indeed, my concern is precisely to draw attention to the choices we make—and the larger power structures that influence these choices—about what to *do* with our pains, longings, and resentments; what we decide to focus on, how we evaluate it, and what lessons we take away and disseminate from both our sense of history in the abstract and from our targeted attempts to connect with the past in the present day. What kinds of narratives make space for complexity, difference, and possibility, and what kinds of travel practices lead to encounters that might nourish these stories?

As literary scholars George Rosenwald and Richard Ochberg argue,

> It is possible, though surely difficult, to enlarge the range of personal narrative. Individuals and communities may become aware of the political-cultural conditions that have led to the circumscription of discourse. If a critique of these conditions occurs widely, it may alter not only how individuals construe their own identities, but also how they talk to one another and, indirectly, the social order itself. Discourse mediates between the fate of the individual and the larger order of things.[43]

On one level, I counterpose quests to missions because missions, in both their ideologies and their formats, seemed to work against the enlargement of discourse by their powerful prefabricated structures, their narrow sense of what constitutes kinship, and their commitment to uniformity, while quests appear to allow more space for processes of becoming and encounters with difference, and discerning new kinds of resemblance, sharedness, and interconnection. But my interest in quest travelers was also sparked by the particular experiences and senses of self they themselves articulated. Many of them expressed a productive (if painful) sense of difference, a kind of memorial excess whose quality and affective force put them more easily at odds with dominant, homogenizing narratives. In this way they struck me as a kind of *avant-garde* of memory workers, complementary figures to the Polish memory activists I discuss in the next chapter. These individuals, due to their own experiences of friction, frustration, and memorial misfit, carried alternative creative resources for envisioning a broader range of cultural possibility.

Framing Jewish Poland today not as a sacred wound that is ever-bleeding but as a tale of lost love—one that includes not only love's pain and betrayals but the messiness of such relationships, shot through as they always are with honeymoons, the sense of solitude's lack, the imagination fueled by desire, and possibilities for reconciliation after rupture as well—might release us from the now-stock stories of good and evil that "perpetuate themselves by the redundant, self-certifying actions they instigate."[44] Further, just as mission travel is intertwined with broader Jewish politics, the desire of a small, perhaps growing group of Jews to reevaluate and re-narrate their relationships to Poland is a form of memory work with potential significance beyond their ranks. If new stories instigate fresh actions and these actions make possible novel storylines the insights revealed in relation to Jews and Poles may lay the groundwork for new outlooks on broader humanistic concerns and projects as well.

CHAPTER FOUR

SHABBOS GOYIM: POLISH STEWARDS OF JEWISH SPACES

One doesn't struggle with ghosts; one placates them and lures them back.
—RUTH GAY

Why would a Pole open a Jewish bookstore? Jewish visitors ask. A non-Jewish Jewish bookstore would be cause enough for suspicion (what are *they* doing with *our* culture?). But a Polish one? This combination violates the basic order of a Jewish moral universe built from grandparents' stories of Poles turning over Jews to the Nazis for vodka. Zdzisław Leś, owner of the Jarden Jewish Bookshop, recalled his inspiration for opening the shop; it had missionary and accidental aspects. "I visited this normal bookshop, in this very building, in which sat two bored women selling crime stories and third-class literature. And there was one shelf, maybe two small shelves, on which was written 'Judaica.' Ten titles! And I asked them, 'Do you know where you are?' I thought it was a scandal, and I told these women so. So I took it over, moved it next door, threw out the other 90 percent of the books, and began to increase the Judaica. And now I have about 150 titles—in practice, all of what is published in Poland. And it is the only Jewish bookshop in Poland."[1]

The books range from high culture—the newest academic works in Polish-Jewish studies—to local legends, photo albums, and Holocaust memoirs and films, some of which Zdzisław and his wife and co-owner Lucyna have published or produced themselves.[2] They also sell trinkets, such as brass kabbalistic talismans and plastic screen-prints of synagogues and barbed wire. He

wrinkled his nose at them, but shrugs, "People buy them." They stock Klezmer music CDs, Jewish figurines, a few cards, and the odd ritual object. After
Steven Spielberg chose Krakow as the location for filming *Schindler's List,*
visitor demand led them to add "Schindler's List tours" and then a companion guidebook.

The bookstore is open every day—every day except Yom Kippur, that is,
the holiest Jewish day of the year. Other "Jewish" businesses here have expanded with flash and fashion along with the boom in Jewish culture, but
the bookstore plods along at its own more considered pace. Zdzisław doesn't
have much capitalist spirit. He often dissuaded customers from his Auschwitz
tours, confiding to them, "It's really very expensive to go with us. It's much
better if you just take the bus from the main station. Here, I have the schedule
written down."

Of course, more business would mean less time for conversation and fewer
breaks to visit the closet-sized Club of Leftist Intellectuals upstairs. Zdzisław
used to direct Krakow's House of Culture, the omnipresent communist-era
center for community arts and cultural ideology, where he introduced a series
called "Meetings with Jewish Culture." There were gatherings with authors of
books, concerts of Jewish songs, and other events. Zdzisław trained as a Slavi-
cist at the university. He attributed much of his sensitivity about Jewish influences on Polish culture to his familiarity with Polish literature. He poked fun
at Polish nationalism and said that many of Poland's cultural heroes were actually Jews. He always had an example up his sleeve:

> I don't know if you know that the best Polish poet of the twentieth century was
> Jewish. Bolesław Leśmian. *And* [he was] the best master of Polish language.
> Many Polish poets in the twentieth century were Jews: Tuwim, Leśmian,
> Słonimski . . . isn't that a paradox? And some other fields, history for example,
> science. Maybe our stupid nationalists will finally understand that Polish folk-
> lore, which makes them have an orgasm, owes Jews a lot, and that their favorite
> potato pancakes are also a Jewish recipe, that our so-called folk art was also in-
> spired by Jews, and this [Polish] nation was only copying what they invented.
> So consider this: if so many Jews have done so much for Polish culture, why
> shouldn't two poor Poles like us do something for Jews?

Adopting Orphaned Memory

If in the early 1990s, as anthropologist Jack Kugelmass has noted, Jews visiting Poland were able to stage their performances of Jewish memory un-

contested as actors,[3] as the decade wore on these visitors were increasingly confronted by local Poles with their own scripts. Since the end of communism, the keepers of Jewish memory in Kazimierz, of Jewish space and culture, have been—perforce—mostly not Jewish. As Polish historian Edyta Gawron described in the early 2000s, despite the post-communist material gains made by Krakow's official Jewish community (*gmina*), it was "unsuccessful in coordination of the activities aimed at rejuvenation and restoration of Jewish religious and cultural life. Thus, the present revival of Jewish culture has taken place in Cracow thanks to non-Jews with the help of the Jews from Israel and the Diaspora."[4]

Yet few observers have taken such non-Jewish participants in Jewish revival seriously as stewards of Jewish culture, memory, or space. Despite the reliance on such individuals by many Jewish visitors to Poland, to the extent that they have garnered popular attention it has generally been as a curiosity, either as "accidental and unimportant guides to forgotten and abandoned Jewish places" or with outright cynicism.[5] As one Holocaust survivor wrote in a community newsletter, admonishing fellow Jews to open their eyes to the problem of the Polish tourist industry and Jewish patronage of it: "Poles are making money from the Jewish tragedy. . . . Polish guides, Polish cab drivers, Polish restaurants and shops filled with Jewish customers abound. We are helping to build industry in a country that allowed Hitler to build crematoriums on their land."[6] Simply put, the notion "that preservation of the Jewish heritage of Poland lies partly in Christian hands . . . strike[s] some people as preposterous at best, and, at worst, in extremely bad taste."[7] Kazimierz is often specifically criticized in foreign Jewish reportage, for both commercialism and cultural appropriation. Poles are seen to be skimming what is fashionable and marketable from Jewishness while uninterested in and unconnected to actual Jews, who are conveniently absent. The quarter is often described by foreign tourists as devoid of Jews, comprising instead an inauthentic "Disneyland."

But Kazimierz has hidden depths. These are suggested by considering it in genealogical relationship to the communist-era "Jewish memory project" that formed a part of Poland's larger struggle for democracy.[8] In the 1970s and 1980s under late communism, grassroots interest in and activities on behalf of Jews represented a form of resistance against the government, which periodically wielded antisemitism (or occasionally a strategic "philosemitism") as a political tool, but otherwise tightly censored Jewish themes.[9] This highly collaborative, dialogic memory project saw non-Jewish Poles making crucial contributions to restoring Jewish heritage, a process deeply inter-twined with Jewish de-assimilation and community revival in Poland.[10] As sociologist Iwona Irwin-Zarecka notes, "It would often be from these Catho-lic friends that a Jew brought up in silence learned some basics of Judaism and Jewish history."[11]

When I arrived in Poland in spring of 1990, the political landscape was utterly transformed. But a significant portion of the Jewish culture broker-ing activities that were to emerge over the next decade—indeed, those that were the cornerstones of Kazimierz's public re-Judaization—were informed by a contiguous cultural politics. What I offer here is a glimpse of these evolv-ing efforts as they came into contact with new social, economic, and politi-cal realities. Foreign visitors to Kazimierz, Jews in particular, are rarely at-tuned to this broader sociopolitical landscape in which the Polish brokering of Jewish culture partakes. They often wander off Szeroka Street and into the Jarden Jewish Bookshop for the first time—as I did—with a vague air of con-fusion, blinking as they leave the bright open square for the cool dimness that lies beyond the meter-thick stone walls of its rented quarters behind the Lan-dau Palace facade. They gaze up at the shelves of Jewish books, wooden Jew-ish figurines, and progressive political posters and then down at the bearded Zdzisław or Lucyna with her menorah earrings. They seem unsure of what to make of this unanticipated and unusual constellation of signs and symbols. Yet such grassroots public Jewish heritage practices, easily dismissed for their commercial veneer, have been a vital component in the struggle to return Jewish memory to Polish landscapes both physical and psychological.

In the context of European history, Jews are not accustomed to being celebrated. "Philosemitism" is seen as suspicious, and criticisms of it range from accusations of political instrumentality to psychopathology to racism and moral relativity.[12] But the skepticism and moralism surrounding even scholarly discussion of philosemitism prematurely forecloses attempts to un-derstand it. As one scholar noted, the term itself is inherently tainted; it is al-ways approached as "anti-Semitism in disguise."[13]

I learned the term philosemitism in Kazimierz, as a local category. By the mid-1990s local culture brokers were increasingly aware of the complexi-ties and sensitivities surrounding the larger global and historical contexts, on the backdrop of which their activities were being judged. As it is in much aca-demic discourse, philosemitism in Kazimierz is typically an accusation, used to assert the boundaries of appropriate non-Jewish interest in and identifica-tion with Jewishness. I heard the label occasionally flung at others; more fre-

quently it was preemptively disavowed by non-Jewish individuals to legiti-
mize their own undertakings, as in, "Look, Erica, *we* are not philosemites
here" [*my* nie jestesmy tu filosemitami].

How to understand "out group" participation in ethnic cultural continuity? Joseph Roach's theory of "surrogation" suggests that "culture repro-
duces and re-creates itself . . . as actual or perceived vacancies occur in the network of relations that constitutes the social fabric . . . through death or other
forms of departure."[14] While the actions taken to fill these vacancies may appear as imitation or appropriation, they nevertheless "hold open a place in
memory," illustrating the multicultural dialogue always at play in historical
remembering, with its attendant innovations, erasures, and conflicts over authenticity.[15] But in my efforts to capture and communicate, especially to my
fellow Jews, the moral aspect of this sort of cultural stewardship—the sense
of obligation, of duty, of custodial care I observed—I began to think of Kazimierz's non-Jewish brokers of Jewish culture as metaphorical *Shabbos goyim*.
A *Shabbos goy* [pl. *goyim*] is a Yiddish term for a non-Jew (*goy*) who is paid a
small fee to take care of practical tasks that Jews are ritually prohibited from
doing on the sabbath (*Shabbos* in Yiddish). Despite the term's ambiguousness
(suggesting deep cultural distinctions and perhaps hierarchies), in the context of Kazimierz it captures a unique kind of caretaking undertaken with respect to Jewish commitments and traditions, despite being done by non-Jews.
Shabbos goyim have responsibilities to Jewishness (and Jews have a reciprocal
need for non-Jews) that are fulfilled from a position of complementarity and
respectful collaboration that acknowledges difference.

Another example of local cross-cultural memory keeping—albeit in a
very different historical context and set of social relations—raises the possibility that cross-group stewardship of cultural heritage sites can help to
build relationships between these groups. Writing of African Americans and
Jews in Cincinnati, Ohio, "two communities which in today's Cincinnati find
few moments of vital contact," historian Karla Goldman documents how
the establishment of churches in former synagogue buildings in the 1970s
was undertaken in such a way that potential conflict over these powerfully
emotional sites has been managed so as to forge deepened respect and inter-
community connections. Goldman illustrates how "those who now occupy
these buildings have become keepers of [the Jews'] stories and oral traditions," in some cases treating them as a vicarious replacement for the absent
traces of their own material pasts, as African American neighborhoods in
Cincinnati were demolished. Indeed, "the sanctity of these buildings as syna-

gogues has been enriched by the respect and appreciation accorded to their Jewish past" by many of the new parishioners.[16]

But the *Shabbos goyim* metaphor is not just my own fancy. I heard Polish stewards of Jewish culture in Kazimierz apply it to themselves. Janusz Makuch, founding director of Krakow's annual Festival of Jewish Culture, referred to his undertakings as those of a *Shabbos goy* "not because of religious restrictions, but because there are no (or not many) local Jews left."[17] "I knock on the doors and shutters of Jews and invite them to Krakow for the festival," he said, "for they are really the ones who create it."[18] The embrace of the term—and indeed the very knowledge of it—by Kazimierz culture brokers is evidence of engagement with Jewish concepts, suggesting the search for an acceptable niche in which a non-Jew can serve Jewish cultural goals without attempting to replace Jews. The term also goes beyond the too-obvious frame of "cultural appropriation" within which Kazimierz and related social settings are frequently judged. Culture building need not be—perhaps cannot be—just an "insider" project.

Marketing Values?

Among the earlier generation of Jewish cultural stewards under communism, there was a sense that "any immediate rewards for their efforts [would be] ethically unacceptable [because] their work, after all, grew out of a deeply felt moral concern and not a cold calculation of means and ends."[19] But given Poland's systemic transformation from state socialism to "dziki kapitalizm" (unbridled [lit. "wild"] capitalism), a reappraisal of the motivations and ethics of culture brokering is in order. Local brokers were clearly aware of the suspicions and criticisms harbored by many observers of their undertakings, and seemed to be engaged in an ongoing effort to demarcate their own ethical boundaries.

When I met Krzysiek, the young editor of the short-lived magazine *Kraków, Etc.* at the Jarden Jewish Bookshop in 1999, he stated forthrightly, "I'm pro-Jewish." I gave him a quizzical look, and he continued, "Well, you know, most people are *anti*-Jewish." He went on to stress the uniqueness of Kazimierz in comparison to Prague's *Židovské město* (Jewish quarter), which he criticized as "too expensive." "Even Westerners complain," he said. He told me that people involved in the development of Kazimierz don't want it to be like Prague; "we think it's like Disneyland there."

While certainly not all brokers of Jewish heritage in Kazimierz were idealistically motivated, neither have most of their projects been singularly mercenary. Rather, as Smithsonian Folklife Festival director Richard Kurin has described culture brokering projects elsewhere, they may be better understood as representing "an honor, a responsibility, and something that can sometimes be turned to personal advantage and profit."[20] In the 1990s, key brokers took real social risks, like claiming and forging public space for Jewishness, that the few, mostly old, remaining local Jews were unable or unwilling to take, and the handful of emerging younger Jews had not yet conceived. As international Jewish tourism and local Jewish confidence have grown, these brokers have been open to, and in some cases actively courted, Jewish engagement in their endeavors.

Zdzisław—perhaps due to his ideological background—has his own sense of the appropriate limits of the capitalist enterprise. He often criticized the prices at the restaurants and expressed disdain at the refusal of the Izaak Synagogue Project (a local memory installation in the former synagogue building) to offer a student discount, as well as charging everyone to enter, including Hasidim who wanted to use the space for prayer.[21] Café Ariel (later Klezmer Hois) offered space for Jewish community events and donated food, such as challah and wine, to the older Jews who congregated there after *shul* on Shabbat. The Jarden Jewish Bookshop provided frequent support in mediating interactions between locals and visitors—whether travel-related needs (including toilets and telephones), genealogical research support, medical emergencies, or religious needs such as opening the synagogue after hours or finding an alternative place to pray, typically involving Hasidim on pilgrimage; I once stumbled upon a Hasid swaying behind the bookshelf in Zdzisław's tiny office nook. When the old Jewish men who tend the synagogue needed translators to deal with foreign visitors, Zdzisław sent over one of his shop's tour guides. Beyond a site of cultural entrepreneurship and matchmaking for endeavors in publishing, filmmaking, and the preservation of Jewish cemeteries, the bookshop also formed a kind of home base for wandering Jews, including returning Holocaust survivors like the erstwhile *meschkiach* (kosher overseer) at the typically empty Nissenbaum restaurant, who would often stop by, bearing cakes, for companionship.

Recognition of major Jewish community events is another way these stewards demonstrated deference to traditional forms of Jewish life. Both the Jarden Jewish Bookshop and Café Ariel closed their doors during the Jewish high holidays, and it was not unusual to see Wojciech Ornat (Ariel's owner) and Janusz Makuch (founder of the Festival of Jewish Culture) in synagogue on those days. Zdzisław regularly participated in the small annual "March of

Remembrance" that traces the path of deportations from Kazimierz to the ghetto across the river in Podgórze; there is a picture of him in an album on Jewish Kazimierz, laying a wreath at the fragment of the ghetto wall at 75 Lwowska Street.[22]

Accidental Activists

There is, of course, a range of moral and political commitment in the work of culture brokers, who create opportunities and spaces to bring diverse people together to represent, translate, market, or otherwise engage in dialogue around Jewish culture and heritage. The more devoted among these intermediaries captured my interest for the ways they appeared to be a force for progressive social change. Yet most of the Jewish heritage stewards I met were not driven by clear, high-minded motivations from the start. Their participation was accidental and evolving, and for some temporary. Individuals stumbled into their callings, following a variety of ambitions and inklings of what Kazimierz could be. Commitments changed due to serendipity, as opportunities arose or paths crossed. Project founders went from being entrepreneurs to serving as social enablers, event planners, and educators. Curious individuals moved, inadvertently at first, "up the ladder" from hanging out in the Jewish café to working there, developing from a bartender or salesperson into a knowledgeable tour guide, with a notable number continuing on to become graduate students, filmmakers, professors—and sometimes Jews.

Zdzisław acknowledged the role of chance in his undertaking. In 1994 I asked him whether he thought that by opening this bookstore, he had created an opportunity for Poles who had discovered Jewish roots to begin to engage with their heritage openly. He answered,

> At the time, I didn't think about it. . . . I thought only more professionally, that this kind of bookshop, it is interesting. . . . Then after some months, I observed, and now I see this problem. But no, in the beginning, no. I wasn't a genius, a prophet. [But] it is very pleasant for me, that without my knowledge or goodwill, it was created. I created this thing, [although] I didn't know all the consequences of this step.

Lucyna agreed, saying that in the beginning the bookstore "had no ideology." They were just in the right place at the right time, and their idea took off. There was "business, of course . . . and a new place for doing something. . . . [It] was a good time to start to talk about Jewish things and Jewish history." Slowly they realized that it was possible to do "something more. . . . And in this way we also teach our workers. . . . It's like, maybe, not only work, it's ideology to be here."

The work of these non-Jewish stewards to represent Jewish culture has also evolved. The dilapidated neighborhood they stepped into may have been long empty of Jews. But the end of communism and the accompanying rise of tourism meant that Jews were increasingly present and responsive to the culture brokering initiatives they encountered. The reaction on the part of Jewish tourists was not infrequently hostile, and rarely entirely favorable. Through trial and error, Kazimierz's culture brokers refined their ideas and grew into their roles. They gained increasing expertise in mediating Polish and Jewish interactions and realities—realities that have in turn evolved, in part due to the work of these "outsider" cultural agents. Despite it being unanticipated, Zdzisław has embraced the role thrust upon the bookshop. He takes no small pride in the transformation, calling the bookshop a kind of "club":

> This isn't just a place where we sell books. Because tourists come and they ask us questions. Also inhabitants of Krakow come here and we talk with them. It was even shocking for us: people who write doctoral dissertations come here. They come here for scholarly consultations. Even if we don't have [a book] they ask us where in the world it exists. The tourists . . . don't just ask about the war, the Holocaust. They think we're some sort of information center for Jews in Poland. They expect that of us.

These stewards have worked to create not musty museums of Jewish heritage, but living social space in which that heritage can be enacted and debated. Jews are seen as essential to that endeavor. Describing the evolution of his role as director of the Festival of Jewish Culture, Janusz Makuch said that he "tried more and more to feel at home in that Jewish culture . . . [but] to avoid imposing my own feelings and dreams. Instead, I looked for ideas among the Jews themselves. . . . To try to make them the true creators of this festival."[23] Eugeniusz Duda, director of Krakow's Jewish museum in Kazimierz's Old Synagogue (Stara Synagoga), told me that it was only in the late 1980s when foreign Jews began to come looking for roots that Kazimierz "started to live again." Brother Stefan, a Catholic monk and director of Kazimierz's Brother Albert soup kitchen and shelter, echoed this point. "This quarter has no soul," he told me. "Because there are no Jews who could pray here. Remu [synagogue] is just a symbol, a museum. [Except when] youth groups from Israel pray there when they visit."

But despite a sense of having risen to the occasion that the new social and economic moment thrust upon them, there is an understanding of the historically and perhaps morally temporary nature of this work. This is not simply because Kazimierz's cultural stewards anticipate going out of business, but because they understand their task as that of a placeholder, or as a form of midwifery, a responsibility fallen to them due to tragic historical circumstances. I discerned a keen sense of the limits of their undertakings for recuperating Kazimierz's Jewishness, and an awareness of the profound void they cannot hope to fill. "It is not we who should be doing this," said Joachim Russek, non-Jewish director of Kazimierz's Center for Jewish Culture. "But shall we do nothing and let this become a subject for future archaeologists?"[24]

Dialogue and Development

The historical function of Kazimierz as a Jewish space has not ceased. It is a living, changing terrain; its purposes and products cannot be domesticated by any one party and its narrative possibilities remain open. As anthropologist Cymene Howe says of queer pilgrimage to San Francisco, the city becomes a site for the elaboration of identity "through emerging discourses that, though sometimes 'essentialized,' are continually in a state of negotiation . . . between 'insiders' and 'outsiders.'"[25] If local purveyors of Jewish heritage in the quarter work to produce particular meanings, they are confronted by foreign visitors with their own interpretations. These are at turns contrary and convergent. Visiting Jews are far from reticent about their perspectives on Kazimierz's undertakings. And in light of such Jewish commentary, culture brokers have reformulated their performances of and engagements with Jewishnesses. Observing these regular dialogues complicates accusations that Kazimierz promulgates a static portrait of an idealized, ahistorical culture. The heritage landscape—as well as its stewards—are flexible, responsive, and evolving.

Krakow's Festival of Jewish Culture is a key example of evolution through dialogue. The festival was started in 1988 by a couple of Poles with a few Jewish films and an intense curiosity about the culture and issues depicted therein. Today, it is an international event that draws 25,000 people over nine days. It goes far beyond film, offering everything from Hasidic dancing and Jewish cooking to Yiddish and Hebrew lessons, lectures on religious and current political topics and world-class live music, culminating in a final outdoor concert in Kazimierz's main square that draws thousands of revelers and is simulcast nationwide on Polish television. It was through early encounters with Jewish musicians from abroad that Janusz Makuch, the festival's founding director, became "aware that [Jewish] culture was alive, and important for many people . . . that despite the Holocaust, there was a flow, a continuity of that culture," and thus that an entirely gentile Jewish cultural festival seemed inappropriate.[26] Over more than twenty years Makuch has moved away from nostalgic themes of shtetl and klezmer to include avant-garde Jewish culture and current debates on Polish-Jewish history coming out of Europe, Israel, the United States, and elsewhere. Makuch has said his aim in the festival is "to present Jewish culture—and Jews—as alive, not trapped behind a museum glass of nostalgia or archaeology." And yet he has admitted that "arriving at this attitude took some evolution."[27]

Small daily manifestations of a desire for evolution based on Jewish input also abound. This is particularly evident in Jewish tourists' interactions with Polish tour guides. Jewish tourists are not passive recipients of information and frameworks provided by Polish guides. In what historian Saidiya Hartman has described as the "personal seizure and appropriation of the narrative resources made available by tourism,"[28] visiting Jews often criticize their Polish guides, whispering to fellow travelers or openly contradicting their guides' facts or perspectives. Sometimes Jewish visitors simply commandeer the tours. Małgorzata, a twenty-one-year-old Polish guide from the Jarden Jewish Bookshop, had expected to guide Julie, a forty-three-year-old American Jewish lawyer, through Kazimierz—Julie's grandfather's birthplace. Instead Małgorzata was compelled to yield to Julie's recitation of her grandfather's memoirs, a transcript of which Julie brought along. As soon as the three of us were out of the bookshop on Szeroka Street, Julie took over. Whenever Małgorzata began to speak, Julie would interject with another story she had heard about the quarter, or ask another question, or pull something out of the family documents she brought with her and say enthusiastically, "But *look*, here it says that . . ." or "Well listen, *here* my grandfather says that . . ." and the conversation turned to her family once again. Małgorzata looked back favorably upon this exchange. "I never thought I'd meet someone with such a story!" she said, adding that she was always learning more about Kazimierz from Jewish tourists. Another guide, Marta, echoed appreciation of such "teaching" by Jewish visitors, "because sometimes they know more than I do, so sometimes they correct me. Like a few days ago, someone told me something interesting about the prayer *Sh'ma Yisroel* [Hear, Israel] that I never heard about before. It's really good."

Wojciech Ornat's Café Ariel / Klezmer Hois began designing the Jewish foods on his menu based on the family recipes of Róża Jakubowicz, the mother of the head of the Krakow Jewish community.[29] But Ornat described how his recipes have been critiqued by "Jewish grandmothers" from abroad who have informed him in no uncertain terms how a kugel, cholent, or dish of chopped liver should be made. He tinkers with the dishes accordingly. He told me,

> We're constantly having discussions with the people who come here, especially the older people, and we're constantly learning something new. In fact our menu is going to be more and more interesting because of that. It will be interesting ethnographically, because you'll get things here you won't be able to get anywhere else. Because we're going to get recipes from people who lived here, from people who remember exactly how it was made at home. . . . It's going to be really interesting in documentary terms. Culinarily and culturally interesting.

Attaining some notion of prewar Polish-Jewish authenticity is less important to Ornat than hosting a transnational Jewish culinary dialogue. He has added dishes like roasted peppers that he learned from visiting Sephardic Jews, and a Jewish visitor from New York demonstrated how to prepare *matzo brei* in the café kitchen, which a clutch of local and visiting hangers-on sampled and evaluated in a lively debate at a corner table.

While many of Kazimierz's Jewish initiatives are aimed primarily at visitors and do not target—and indeed at times irritate—the local Kazimierz denizens, some projects direct their efforts more locally. Zdzisław and Lucyna, for example, used their modest position to promote grassroots education on Jewish-Polish history through intercultural dialogue. An initiative in the mid-1990s involved sending letters to 200 schools in the Krakow area offering to organize a special tour for students around Kazimierz, culminating in a meeting with a Holocaust survivor. Only one school responded.

Jewish Geography: Shifting Terrains of "Kosher" and "Treyf"

Not all of Kazimierz's "Jewish" venues participate in the ethics I describe, and I would not designate all Jewish culture brokers there as *Shabbos goyim*. The distinctions shifted based on ever-changing social knowledge and fluctuating relationships among local actors—myself included. The quarter is constantly being remapped, with individual venues tacitly emerging as "kosher" or Jewishly acceptable, and thus patronized, versus *treyf* (unkosher), and thus spurned, distinctions generally below the radar of one-time visitors—although word does spread internationally with surprising detail. While such fault lines are usually based on an ethics of perceived Jewish community investment and relevance, the sense of "the community" is not coterminous with the local official religious communal body (*gmina*), nor is a proprietor's ethno-religious background the local measure of authenticity for patrons of Kazimierz businesses.

Intense interpersonal politicking and widespread gossip about the corruptness and ineffectualness of "really" Jewish communal projects—including the *gmina;* the communist-era holdover TSKŻ (Jewish Social-Cultural Association, known to its adherents as "the Club"); as well as foreign Jewish interventions like the Lauder Foundation's youth club or the Nissenbaum kosher restaurant—made these unattractive to many young local Jews and non-Jews alike. Some of these people also felt that certain venues made stringent demands for Jewish observance or lineage, making them forbidding or off-putting for tentative new (or newly religious) Jews, many of whom felt far more Polish than Jewish. For the motley cluster of uncertain souls exploring their connections to Jewishness in post-communist Poland, Kazimierz's Jewish cafés were often the least-threatening entry point.

I met Jonah Bookstein, a young American Jew from Detroit, in 1992. While he later became the director of the Polish branch of the Ronald Lauder Foundation and an Orthodox rabbi, at the time Jonah was a free-spirited student deeply involved in bringing Jewish social, intellectual, and ceremonial life into Kazimierz. In 1993, he and local Jew Henryk Halkowski began by organizing Shabbat dinners for young people at the low-profile TSKŻ in the center of Krakow. Then they organized a Hanukkah party and a celebration of Israeli Independence day at the proto-version of Ornat's Café Ariel. "It was just a room!" Jonah recalls, but full of "schmoozing and drinking and singing and talking" until all hours. "There were lots of guests; it was really fun. Jewish and non-Jewish both. Probably half and half."

Indeed, folklorist Eve Jochnowitz noted, "As soon as it opened, Ariel became the center of all non-ceremonial Jewish activity" in the city.[30] The café hosted a variety of Jewish ritual activities as well, including the wedding of a foreign Jewish couple in 1994. But "Ariel" as a social space was defined not only by its celebration of Jewishness, but by dialogue, negotiation, critique, and debate about Jewishness. Indeed, the café was born out of strife around the definition of Kazimierz's Jewish space. A protracted legal battle between partners in the original Ariel venue during the early days of Kazimierz's post-communist development resulted in a series of splits and expansions, culminating in a period when no fewer than three separate restaurants—in essence, one whole side of Szeroka Street's commerce—bore the name Ariel on their facades. The venues Ornat and his colleagues subsequently developed out of Ariel—Austeria, Alef, and Klezmer Hois—were long still called Ariel by locals, variously modified by "green" for the color of the façade, "left" for its spatial location vis-à-vis the original venue, "double" for the fact that it opened a second venue in the old mikveh building on the corner, or simply "good."[31] The only Ariel that remains today is an expansion of the original (the "bad," white one), an enormous complex with plaster Lions of Judah and a six-foot-high electric menorah, a venue that Jewish-identified locals over-whelmingly reject. As Jonah put it with a laugh (playing with the two mean-ings of "kosher"—the colloquial "socially acceptable" and the literal "ritually pure"), "There's a kosher and a treyf Ariel. The white one's treyf, and the green one's kosher. But you can't eat there."

Local Jew Henryk Halkowski himself was an excellent resource for map-ping a broad swath of Jewish space. He made daily rounds of Kazimierz venues in search of free newspapers, gossip, and food, and his appetites—intellectual, social, and gastronomical—superseded petty local disputes.[32] He remarked on how a given venue's responsiveness to Jewish concerns contrib-uted to its success. The non-profit Center for Jewish Culture, run by non-Jews and housed in the grandly renovated B'nei Emuna prayer house on Rabbi Meisels Street, often stood empty, the occasional visitor's footsteps echoing off its shiny stone floor, white walls, and high ceilings. Jewish tourists often reported that their most basic questions about local Jewish community life, such as the schedule for synagogue services or the possibility of a local Shab-bat dinner, were met with shrugs on the part of the young front-desk staff, or with indications that the Center was not connected to the Jewish commu-nity. Locals, on the other hand, were put off by the Center's perceived outsider orientation—that it aspired to be a fancy symbol for Western dignitaries and international academics rather than a place for local cultural engagement. It was not utterly shunned, as were venues perceived to be totally irrelevant to Jewish concerns. But its central flaw, Halkowski said, was that it had been adopted by no one. "For Poles, it's Jewish, [and] for Jews, it's Polish. No one completely identifies with it."

Ironically, the Center's director, Joachim Russek, has a staunch civic man-date for education and dialogue about Poland's Jewish heritage and to help build an open society. And yet his contention that "this Center cannot be ethnic-oriented, because we are not Jews," seemed to dim its appeal among both locals and visitors, Jews and non-Jews. In part his approach may be traced to the notion widespread when the Center was established, that there were simply no Jews left in Poland, and thus he positioned the Center as a custodian of memory. But his predilection for cultivating elite programming and audiences, and the need he seemed to feel to draw a sharp line between the Center's undertakings and those of the commercial venues on Szeroka Street, did nothing to help. His mantra that "we don't want to be a Jewish Disneyland," while echoing foreign Jewish concerns about what was happening in Kazimierz, similarly misread the commercial venues as vacuous. But the success of those venues has lain in part with their willingness to engage with the messy variety of claims on, concerns about, and desires for Jewish life, culture, and space that flowed into Kazimierz along with tourists and capital. It is precisely the balance of Jewish and non-Jewish identification that has led particular commercial venues to both thrive socially and win the passionate loyalty of both local and foreign Jews, who have favored these establishments over less-engaged venues, including officially Jewish ones.

Hybrid Physical and Social Space

Two generations of Poles and Jews have had almost no contact with each other. Even in a Poland whose Jewish community is experiencing quantum rebirth, the tiny number of Jews mean there are few sites where non-Jewish Poles may experience Jewishness or mingle with Jews doing specifically Jewish things, or where Jews can engage with Poles around questions of Poland's Jewishness. Today's gentrifying Kazimierz is just such a site. Local heritage brokers have turned the site into Jewish space of a particular kind, what Diana Pinto calls the "the crown jewel" of a pluralist democracy.[33] More than artifice or veneer, these brokers created something unique in homogenously Catholic Poland, and something different from and beyond what Krakow's tiny official local Jewish community was able or willing to provide. The venues that are comprised by this space—often listed among "Jewish sites" in guidebooks—have formed centers of gravity for a range of Jewish quests, catalyzing significant encounters and reckonings around Jewish heritage in the process.

Kazimierz is many things to many people. On the most basic level it is today perceived by local Jews as a safe space, free from widespread Polish suspicion and prejudice about Jews. Journalist Ruth Gruber noted that "the district consciously forms a sort of 'Jewish zone' where different rules from the rest of the city—or country—may apply."[34] Not only do many Polish Jews feel it to be a rare place in Poland where one can wear a *yarmulke* (skullcap) openly, as Stanisław Krajewski, another prominent figure in the Polish Jewish community, told me, but it is a place "where it feels *more* proper to wear one than not."

Jewish or non-Jewish individuals from parochial Polish settings are often reticent to be known as interested in things Jewish. Telling evidence of this can be seen in a mid-1990s brochure that was scattered in Kazimierz venues entitled *Przerwany Łańcuch* (Broken Chain); printed by the *Jewish Forum*, it advertised a confidential telephone hotline for individuals who had discovered they have Jewish roots and did not know where to turn: "Maybe you are ashamed or afraid because of your Jewish roots?"[35] A gentleman from Bochnia, a small town about twenty miles from Krakow, visited the Jarden Jewish Bookshop every month during my fieldwork to buy the magazine *Słowo Zydowskie/Dos Jidisze Wort* (The Jewish Word). Lucyna informed him that he could have a subscription delivered straight to his house; he demurred, explaining that the envelope might reveal to his antisemitic neighbors that he was receiving Jewish materials.

Kazimierz venues are also perceived as a living space in what visiting foreign Jews otherwise encounter largely as a landscape of death. Ornat told me he opened Ariel to counteract what he saw as the quarter's emptiness and sadness: "One year ago," he said in 1995, "tourists saw only death. Now, with Café Ariel, they see life." An American Jewish professor who asked me for help in arranging an educational trip in the late 1990s echoed those sentiments, telling me her group's meal and concert at Ariel "was a highlight of our trip—the first time after visiting concentration camps and cemeteries that the participants experienced Jewish life, not Jewish death."

Local Jews frequented Kazimierz in part to meet other, often foreign, Jews. And Jewish foreigners often came to Kazimierz's Jewish cafés "to see and be seen, to meet the younger members of Krakow's Jewish community."[36] The venues' liveliness and popularity made the quarter a space of identification and social networking. Foreign Jews (particularly Westerners) have been sources of information, resources, meaning, and even legitimization of Jewish identity for many—especially young—Polish Jews. Radek, a Polish Jew in his early twenties when we first met, lives in a provincial city that he describes as having no Jewish life at all. He told me that in Kazimierz "I found my real self [*odnalazłam się*] for the first time. I met the most important people in my life there. . . . And there for the first time I said prayers . . . in Remu [synagogue]." He noted the importance of visiting Kazimierz for "meet[ing] people with whom I have an emotional connection. . . . I see them each week [on Shabbat] and I know they're like me [*tacy jak ja*]. They have the same problems. I know that I'm not alone." Jacek, a local Polish Jew, got a job at Café Ariel in his mid-twenties "because if we [Jews] don't work there, who will?" The experience jolted him into a new level of comfort with his Jewishness. Laughing, he told me with incredulity how foreign Jewish customers would ask him outright if he was Jewish. "The first time I heard that question it was a shock," he said. He recalled being asked it by a table of Canadian Jews in the bustling café. "My first reaction was to look around [nervously]." After collecting himself, Jacek managed to mumble, "Yes, I am." Thrilled, the Canadians invited him out for a beer.

Sasha Pecaric, the Lauder Foundation rabbi from 1997 to 2005, would stroll through Szeroka Street with his wife and son—often with a contingent of other synagogue-goers in tow—on the eve of Shabbat, toward Klezmer Hois, which stood at the far end of the square between the synagogue and his home. They would stop to talk to anyone of interest: a visiting Holocaust survivor, a Jewish journalist, film crew, or loitering anthropologist. Popping in to Klezmer Hois was obligatory. Once when I dropped by to use the telephone in the restaurant office, the rabbi's small son, Aaron, was skipping through the entryway singing from the four Passover questions, *"Ma nishtanah halailah hazeh mikol halelos, mikol halelos."*[37] Even older members of the tiny local community, who tended to mistrust much of the new Jewishness Kazimierz had suddenly sprouted, nevertheless extended their social space to include Klezmer Hois (ever since its earlier incarnation as Ariel). Such old-timers developed the habit of visiting the café on Shabbat to enjoy the specially made challah and coffee that Ornat provided for them.

It is precisely the permeability of this space, the mutual interpenetration of Jewishness and the wider cultural scene, that makes it so lively and attractive for a broad range of people, and a site of exchange among them. Mateusz, a Polish Catholic student, was another early employee at Café Ariel. He enjoyed reading the Jewish books he was selling, listening to Jewish music performed live. And he shared the sense of excitement about the Jews he met, whom he often guided around the neighborhood and later corresponded with. These experiences allowed him to discover "very different kind[s] of life and systems." "There were a lot of American Jews, Israeli Jews, [Jews from] England, Holland, France. It was like, a lot of Jews!" he told me. "It was like, a great place to be."

An American Jewish professional deeply involved with the preservation of Jewish heritage in Poland told me he preferred to invest his energies not in Warsaw, where the Jewish community is larger but "full of weird people," but in Kazimierz, where the level of local, non-Jewish knowledge about Jewishness makes it "much more comfortable for me as a Jew." New Jews, secular Jews, tentative Jews, and Jewish-identified non-Jews can explore Jewishness openly here, through literature, discussions, casual socializing with Jews, and attendance at Jewish-themed cultural events. As Jewish community leader Konstanty Gebert expressed it, "The Jews might be here [in Warsaw] and the Jewish institutions. But the *ruach* [Hebrew, 'spirit'] is over there [in Kazimierz]."

Space for Truth-Telling, Listening, and Cultural Criticism

Many visiting Jews narrate their lives in ways that connect them to Poland. On the most basic level, one way of doing this is by telling family stories— often of trauma and silence—*in* Poland. Kazimierz is a crossroads, a way station filled with Jews in shared historical predicaments, a space of tales told and heard. The dim cafés, the cobbled alleys, the sunny patio tables with umbrellas, swirl with Jewish stories. It is a space of ingathering, a site of the re-embrace of lost, alienated, or suppressed memory and experience. A significant function of Kazimierz's Jewish space is its role as both a catalyst for, and a receptacle of, such stories. The nature of Kazimierz as a physical and social space works toward keeping these stories here, making them part of the social texture as well as recirculating them in direct and indirect ways.

Part of this process is intra-Jewish. Barry Spielman of Tel Aviv wrote of "the very special attraction" that Kazimierz's main square held for him, noting that people from all over the world "gravitated to this spot because they needed something," to "find some solace." He called Café Ariel "a sort of meeting place . . . a magnet, attracting all sorts of people," and mentioned certain locals and perennial visitors by name. "My uncle David, an Auschwitz survivor, immediately struck up a conversation" with survivor Bernard Offen, who visits Kazimierz frequently. Meanwhile, Barry's father engaged in conversation with a white-haired gentleman from Israel, also originally from Krakow. "It turned out that they actually knew each other, and they went on reminiscing for quite a while. Could this be the reason people come back here?"[38]

But Jewish-non-Jewish encounters are also of central significance. Visiting Jews often seemed drawn to tell stories of their wartime experiences, or their inherited pain, to ethnic Poles—particularly stories of pain caused by Poles. This may in part be motivated by a desire to use one's native tongue, whether for pleasure or nostalgia or to enact belonging in Poland. But telling such difficult stories may also be seen as a test of Polish empathy, engagement, and willingness to listen. In July 2011 an Australian woman in a wide-brimmed, brown felt hat walked into the bookshop with her husband in tow, and proceeded to unload a sheaf of documents and photographs onto the bookshop counter (see fig. 12). She told Lucyna that she had been smuggled out of both the Krakow ghetto and Płaszów camp as an infant during the war, and was here trying to piece together the whole story of her mother's desperate wartime maneuverings. Such abrupt entrances into the shop, and into history, are not uncommon. After asking again about the precise dates and places and studying the materials, Lucyna—who was obviously captivated by this unlikely story and with the richness of the collection before her—pulled out some maps and books to show the woman the precise locations of her mother's story and how best to get there. Lucyna suspected from details of the Jewish woman's story that there was a connection to Oskar Schindler's efforts to save Jews, so she also suggested that the woman bring her materials to the newly opened Schindler Factory Museum across the river.

The Jarden Jewish Bookshop's back room—along with Lucyna and Zdzisław themselves—are formidable local archives. Containing hard-to-find volumes, ephemera from local Jewish cultural initiatives, and documents copied from customers, the shop has become known as a hub for personal and scholarly research projects. The stories visitors tell across the counter are shared with the shop's tour guides and other local drop-in guests during long hours of chatting over coffee or while doing the store's accounting, enriching the collection of intimate, local memories the shop has accrued.

But Polish-Jewish interactions are not always pleasant. Jewish visitors at times make use of the "captive" Polish audience to curse Polish ground. One man stood in the bookshop, loudly explaining the brevity of his visit: "One day is more than enough among these *stinkende vilde chayes* (Yiddish, "stinking wild animals"). Many heritage brokers in Kazimierz have learned to allow space for this kind of reaction. Lucyna, whose Hebrew-studying shop assistant overheard an Israeli customer smearing Poles, reacted by quietly telling him as she rang up his purchases that she would be pleased to give him a ten percent discount if he stopped saying such horrible things about Poles. Describing a similarly painful encounter with an angry Jewish visitor, Agnieszka, a born-again Christian who has long been deeply involved in Jewish community life, said, "I'm just glad he told *me*," and not some "normal" Pole, who, she explained, would have immediately become defensive and fanned the flames.

Just as there are Jewish desires to tell their stories of trauma to Poles, some Poles express eagerness to unburden themselves of a memory, experience, or even an object by bestowing it on a Jew. That many non-Jewish Poles have inherited (and in some cases are emotionally invested in) "post-Jewish" (*pożydowski*) items acquired during the chaos of the war and its aftermath was amply demonstrated by the 1996 exhibit *And I Still See Their Faces,* which was assembled from an open call for photographs of Jews.[39] The stories that accompanied the over 9,000 images that were contributed from shoeboxes, drawers, and yellowing envelopes are testament to a wide, deep reservoir of Polish sentiment—pain, remorse, curiosity, desire for repair and reconnection. Cheryl Ward, an American Jew I met in Kazimierz in 2008, told me the story of visiting non-Jewish Polish friends of her in-laws in Warsaw. It came up in conversation that Cheryl was Jewish. While the conversation turned intense, "it was all *very* positive." She said the family seemed "really happy to have someone Jewish to talk to about these things that have really bothered them. . . . It was said very explicitly that Poles feel a lot of guilt for what happened during the Holocaust. . . . Their parents watched people go to their deaths, and that guilt has been passed on to the children." Cheryl felt that her presence "allowed [the family] to relieve a little bit of it." A key moment for her was when the man of the house brought out a book—a rare piece of communist-era underground literature telling the story of two girls, one Polish, one Jewish, during World War II—and presented it to her, saying, "I want you to have this." Cheryl accepted it but with some ambivalence. "He had had this book for twenty years. . . . He had known me for all of five hours at this point. I just happened to be a Jew he knew."

* * *

Kazimierz's *Shabbos goyim* tend to see themselves as a different kind of Pole. Enacting this difference helps make Kazimierz a space of cultural criticism. While the quarter's folkloric, commercial veneer may suggest frivolity, Kazimierz's singularity as a Jewish space draws individuals with a variety of serious Jewish concerns. One afternoon I arrived at the bookshop to find Zdzisław behind the counter, listening to a man in a beige trench coat talking animatedly. He seemed to have been there already for some time, and the conversation continued for some minutes after I arrived. The man's tone was emphatic, if a bit conspiratorial: the scraps I overheard touched on the poor condition of Jewish cemeteries in Poland. He mentioned antisemitism repeatedly, lowering his voice and leaning closer to Zdzisław when he did. When the man left, Zdzisław turned to me and said, "This gentleman [who was just

here] is a really fine person [*Ten Pan jest bardzo sympatycznym człowiekiem*]."
Zdzisław recounted the man's concerns and asked me if I knew that most Jewish cemeteries in Poland were destroyed after the war by Polish "barbarians"
who used the gravestones for paving and building materials, emphasizing
with distaste that even church clergy used Jewish gravestones to pave their
courtyards. I asked Zdzisław who the man was. He said he didn't really know
him—only that he was from a small town near Tarnów. I asked why the man
was telling him these things. Zdzisław replied, "It's not possible to speak to
a normal Pole about such things." The average Polish person, he said, would
just think "everything is as it should be [*wszystko w porządku*]"; they would
just be unsympathetic to the problem. "So," Zdzisław said, "he comes to talk
to me."

Workers in Poland's Jewish heritage tourism industry are a rare interface
in the meager field of vernacular Polish-Jewish relations, often drawn into
unanticipated realms of cultural contestation. An American Jewish woman
complained to Zdzisław after taking the bookshop's Schindler's List tour that
the guide, when they stopped at the nearby Płaszów concentration camp site,
had said that "*only* 20,000 Jews" had been imprisoned there.[40] The woman
was very upset by what she perceived as the guide's attempt to diminish Jewish suffering and argued with him. Later, when the guide reported what had
happened, Zdzisław chastised him. "You stupid man!" he said. "Every half-
intelligent Pole knows that the situation of Jews and Poles was incomparable.
For Jews, Płaszów was only a stopping place on the way to Auschwitz. It is not
our job to argue this [numbers] question with our customers. This is a question for historians. We must provide a service for these very sensitive people."
Despite the fact that the guide may actually have (erroneously) inflated rather
than downplayed the number of Jews interned at the Płaszów camp (and that
the Jewish visitor may have inflated it even more), Zdzisław here highlights
the distinct difference of character in the overall fates of Poles and Jews during the war—that Jews were targeted for extermination as a group. More significant, whereas in Poland a narrative of ethnic Polish wartime suffering (or
"martyrology," as it is called there) is dominant, Zdzisław sees his role as being sensitive to the primacy of the Holocaust framework for visiting Jews.

If Kazimierz's Jewish heritage stewards and brokers are not engaged in
mere commercial instrumentality, neither are they in the thrall of unthink-
ing hagiography. Anthropologist Virginia Dominguez's foremost criterion
for judging a cultural "rescue" project, which she distinguishes from what
she designates as mere "salvage," is its basis in "real love and respect for real

people."[41] To me, this includes open acknowledgment and debate of perceived points of conflict. There is no shortage of criticism of Jews or Jewish discourse among dedicated culture brokers. Indeed, fodder for such criticism often comes from Jews themselves, local or foreign, who openly voice their complaints about their co-ethnics—the locals about the foreigners, and vice versa. I heard startlingly acerbic comments from local Jews and brokers alike, often to each other. An active steward noted wryly that in terms of support and recognition, "the best thing that could happen for the community here would be a small pogrom." Local Jew Henryk Halkowski liked to quip to visitors as he passed by the foreign-Jewish owned Nissenbaum restaurant, an architectural eyesore defined by its blue steel archway, that "the only thing missing is *Arbeit Macht Frei*" (Work Sets You Free), recalling the notorious Nazi sign over the entrance to Auschwitz. And this was not the worst.

While Zdzisław sees his mandate as criticizing Polish distortions and ignorance regarding Jewishness, he and Lucyna also work to dispel misconceptions about Poland that Jews bring with them. As Lucyna told me:

> I fight sometimes with Jews [too,] because [they need to] understand [that just] as on the Polish side, [on] the Jewish side there's a kind of mythology, you know, from the years of the Second World War time, and it's not exactly the truth, what they're telling about Poles. Of course it's possible, you know, to break this. But it's a very long process; it's for generations. But somebody has to start something, anyway.

Zdzisław often lamented the lack of basic historical knowledge of many visiting Jews, telling me stories such as one about a Jewish group that called the bookshop wanting a guide to take them to Auschwitz—a Jewish guide, they specified. Zdzisław told them that there is only one "half-Jewish" guide at Auschwitz, but that he could promise them a competent guide for Auschwitz and Birkenau. "No, no," they responded, "we only want to see Auschwitz." Zdzisław was furious, telling me, "They demand a Jewish guide, but they don't even know that Birkenau is so much more important, where the vast majority of Jews died!" He said he had informed them, and that they had been surprised by the information.

For Zdzisław and Lucyna—part of whose struggle is a fight against ethnonationalism—visiting Jews' apparent fixation on Jewishness and Polishness, their desire to know who among Kazimierz's culture brokers is Jewish and who not, or wanting only a Jewish guide—could seem puzzlingly, frustratingly regressive. "Why do Jews insist on having Jewish guides at Auschwitz?"

he asked rhetorically. "They should want the best guide possible." A communist-bred atheist (although he always said if he were religious, he would choose Judaism), Zdzisław would probe me hopefully for similar sensibilities. "You just eat what tastes good, right? Not like those people who have fits about eating a little pork or whatever," he would ask. He poked fun at my occasional synagogue attendance. "Every orthodoxy is terrible" is a phrase he uttered often. But critiquing Polish culture is a more pressing cultural project. While anti-semitic views are arguably becoming less popular to publicly espouse in Poland, they are still widely tolerated, even in polite company. But not in the bookshop. As if in direct response to Konstanty Gebert's observation that "in Poland one can be an antisemite and still be seen as an upstanding person," Zdzisław often tells customers, "Antisemitism should disqualify one from being considered a cultured person."[42]

I also observed a willingness on the part of Jewish culture brokers to support critical activities that may question these brokers' own undertakings—even aside from Jarden's gracious, decade-long tolerance of my prying ethnographic presence. In July 1996, Andrew Ingall, an American Jewish graduate student participating in New York University's summer program housed in the nearby Center for Jewish Culture, sat at a table on the patio of the "good" Café Ariel on Szeroka Street.[43] On the table before him stood the accouterments of a "taste test" for "kosher vodka," a product that had gained popularity in the early post-communist years. Ingall, with the help of a colleague, called out to passersby in Polish and English asking if they wanted to participate. Ingall had commissioned a caricature of his own (Jewish) face and had affixed it as the label on a vodka bottle with the words "Żydek ['Jew-boy'] Vodka," and placed it alongside other bottles with stereotypical Jews on their labels. As part of his "performance," he had drafted a post-taste questionnaire that he hoped would provoke critical thinking around ideas of Jewish stereotypes in Poland. As agreed upon with the Ariel management, waiters not only provided the table and chairs, but hovered nearby, promptly replacing dirty glasses with fresh ones. As Ingall wrote, "The spectacle of Żydek Vodka permitted me to enter into dialogue with Jews, non-Jews, locals, and tourists alike about the exoticization and objectification of Jews in post-Holocaust, post-Communist Poland"—in other words, precisely the things of which Kazimierz venues like Café Ariel are often accused.[44]

Of course such engagements with Jews are always a negotiation of interests. Having a foreign Jew associated with one's establishment may be good for business, legitimizing a venue in the eyes of other potential customers.

I sometimes wondered if I served as a kind of mascot at Jarden, as Leopold Kozłowski, "The Last Klezmer," has become in much grander fashion at Klezmer Hois, where he performs and whose image graces its website. But if my presence made any contribution to the bookshop, it was dwarfed by all that Jarden offered me: space, information, ideas, friendship. And by giving me a local institutional framework of sorts, the bookshop legitimized my own undertakings as well. Zdzisław and Lucyna helped me to "catch" potential interviewees on their tours or visiting their store. This was at once kind, helpful, and an opportunity for them to amplify the voices of individuals whose stories or opinions they wanted me to record. "Here, interview *this* woman, Eryczko," Lucyna would often say; "she has a story you have to hear." As our relationship grew over the years, we came to understand each others' projects better and became mutually implicated in them.

"A Beautiful Pastiche": Curating Politics

While I focus on the importance of Kazimierz as a social space, aesthetics can also accomplish ideological ends. Images not only represent reality; better categorized as actions rather than descriptions, they are "as much engaged in the politics of persuasion as words."[45] If culture brokers in the quarter attempt to curate a historically Jewish atmosphere, what motivates the particular attributes of their vision? "The past that is invoked and called forth," argues heritage scholar Françoise Choay, "is not just any past: it is localized and selected to a critical end."[46] For the majority of visiting Jews, the Polish landscape serves as a mise-en-scène to recall a historical moment of destruction. Poles reach for other moments. The particular aesthetic preferred by proprietors of Kazimierz venues is bric-a-brac *fin-de-siècle*: hand-tatted lace doilies and tablecloths, faded velvet drapes, glass-front credenzas, and mismatched period furniture. While the use of Yiddish on the façades of contemporary Polish public venues itself strikes an anachronistic note, many venues go further, using purposefully flaking paint on mindfully weathered boards. Such signs echo the few authentic traces of original lettering on once-Jewish venues in the quarter, fast disappearing during my early fieldwork and today almost entirely gone. Singer, the first popular pub in post-communist Kazimierz and the one playing most subtly on the Jewish theme, is barely marked by a tiny sign so washed out one must have insider knowledge to locate it. Inside, candlelit even in daytime, the cast iron sewing machines bolted to each table evoke a cottage industry long gone.

The *façade* of the Rafapol bakery, which opened on Jozef Street in the late 2000s, is emblazoned with the large slogan "Bagels from Kazimierz." A sign on the front door shutter reads: "Bagels: From Krakow's Kazimierz, they took on the world. It's high time they found their way back to our Polish tables."[47] "Bagels" is spelled out in Yiddish on the storefront. The apocryphal notion that bagels originated in the quarter—a myth perpetuated by the beloved, once-Cracovian Jewish author Rafael Scharf—is here made more interesting by their reclamation as part of Polish national cuisine.[48]

As folklorist Barbara Kirshenblatt-Gimblett argues, heritage productions always portray a "tradition" foreign to the context in which they are presented, making them a "critical site for the production of meanings other than the 'heritage' message," including messages of reconciliation or multiculturalism.[49] If the mise-en-scène of Kazimierz venues calls forth an idealized past in Poland, its evocation in a gentrifying present-day district suggests an attempt to imagine a possible future Poland. The nostalgic aesthetic—quoting literary and cinematic representations of Poland's pluralistic past—can be read as the desire for and proposition of a pluralistic future. The "Poland" most visibly curated in Kazimierz represents the liberal side of two long-warring visions for the Polish state: the multi-ethnic, romantic notion of Commonwealth Poland, in which the worlds of Poles and Jews were "thoroughly shaken together."[50] This Poland is embodied by the celebrated literature of Adam Mickiewicz and revived in the short-lived politics of Józef Pilsudski during the interwar period; most significantly it "is inclusive of the memory of 'others' and acknowledges the wrongs done to them."[51] This vision counters an exclusive, ethno-national model of Poland, in which Pole is equated with Catholic. Put forth most forcefully by the right-wing Endecja movement led by Roman Dmowski leading into World War II, this homogenous Poland was achieved de facto in the demographic landscape after the deaths, displacements, and territorial redrawings that accompanied the war and its aftermath. The model has been described as one "not interested in the memory of 'the other' and seek[ing] to foster a vision of the past that stresses Polish suffering and the wrongs done to the Poles."[52] Kazimierz's visual argument, then, evoked by the built and preserved landscapes, is that of a "państwo" (citizen/civic) Polish nation in a country whose ascendant self-conception in the last half-century has been that of a Polish "naród" (ethno-nation).

Both models circulate in current Polish cultural and political discourse, the latter favored among conservative nationalist groups such as the League of Polish Families and outlets such as the Catholic radio station Radio Maria. The embrace of the pluralist model in Kazimierz is evident not only in the Jewish motifs, but also broader multi-ethnic themes evoked by "old Poland": cabarets feature "Gypsy"/Roma, Russian, and Ukrainian performances, and itinerant Romani bands roam the square in summer, playing for the outdoor café denizens. Even the names of Kazimierz venues suggest a multi-ethnic vision: one restaurant bears the name of the imaginary Russian shtetl Anatewka (made famous in the stage musical and film *Fiddler on the Roof*); "Austeria"—the name of the second incarnation of Café Ariel, which offered inn-like rooms for overnight rental—references the small, multi-ethnic towns of old Eastern Poland in the early years of the twentieth century depicted in the film based on Julian Stryjkowski's novel bearing that title. Indeed, the tavern style of these venues evokes Mickiewicz's epic national poem *Pan Tadeusz*, featuring Jankiel the Jewish innkeeper who "act[s] as a dedicated preserver of the Polish national tradition."[53] In drawing on this iconography, culture brokers in Kazimierz are reproducing a linkage made by their more explicitly political predecessors in the recent revolutionary movement for Polish democracy. As historian Michael Steinlauf notes, "It was no coincidence that within the pluralist worldview of Solidarity, the figure of the bearded, black-garbed Jew first emerged as the intriguing representative of a lost Polish past."[54] Indeed, there are explicit aspirations here, too; the bilingual (Polish-English) sign outside the pub Once Upon a Time in Kazimierz bears a short essay proclaiming a romantic vision of historical Polish-Jewish coexistence, stating that their décor is "symbolizing integration between two peoples [Jews and Poles] and their religions and cultures."

Heritage representations that strive for authenticity are often politically fraught because they demand that the ways that authenticity is staged be concealed, "repress[ing] what is at stake for those whose heritage is exhibited."[55] But Kazimierz venues display a conspicuous lack of concern about any hermetic authenticity to some past moment or cultural ideal. On the contrary, the anachronism and artifice of the Jewishness staged in Kazimierz is worn self-consciously, often highlighted rather than obscured. Zdzisław calls the aesthetic "post-Jewish culture," representing fragments of a destroyed world, known only secondhand by the representers, re-mixed in new configurations. The postcards for sale at Klezmer Hois trade in this sensibility. Interspersed among sepia-toned cards depicting ethnographic "Jewish types" reprinted from a historical archive are the restaurant's own line of cards depicting today's neighborhood characters. The white-maned klezmer musician

Leopold Kozłowski, the venue's main attraction, is surrounded by insets of his non-Jewish, Yiddish-singing protégés. Bearded local Jew Henryk Halkowski, a "public character" who figures repeatedly in the past two decades' worth of reportage on Kazimierz's revival (and who, thanks to the tourist industry, turned himself into what other locals jestingly call "the great *tzaddik* [wise, righteous man] of Krakow"), is pictured in his natural habitat, helping himself to a slice of cake from behind the restaurant counter (see fig. 16). The cards are done in the same muted colors and soft focus of the nostalgic ethnographic images, as if poking fun at the very idea of a "Jewish type." Both Kozłowski and Halkowski could often be found sitting, sipping their daily coffee, within a stone's throw of the postcard rack.[56]

Across the square, Once Upon a Time in Kazimierz highlights theatricality in its self-presentation. A creation of Dominik Dybek, a set designer by training who also produced the now-defunct Izaak Synagogue Project, Once Upon a Time makes use of its six original doorways to create imaginary entrances to prewar businesses: Abraham Rattner, *kupiec* (merchant); Aron Weinberg, *towary galanteryjne* (notions); Stanisław Nowak, *sklep spożywczy* (groceries); Benjamin Holcer, *stolarz* (cabinetmaker); Szymon Kac, *krawiec* (tailor); and Chajim Kohan, *skład towarów różnych* (five-and-dime). The restaurant interior is decorated with themed antiques, including a salvaged woodworking table with holes for tools and a massive, threaded wooden vice still attached; a 1913 art nouveau mirror advertising retail and wholesale cold cuts; World War I military regalia; a Jewish ritual washbasin; old musical instruments; shelves of hand-jarred pickles; and a framed portrait of local prewar Jewish bard (and carpenter) Mordechai Gebirtig. As if winking at the pub's sign boasting that these "premises . . . are fitted out exactly as they used to be," clothing and furniture also hang, in a magical realist twist, from the ceiling.

It may be argued that the use of Jewish iconography in Kazimierz's venues divests Jewish material culture of its proper historical context. But the meanings with which we invest images and objects are constantly changing, and they also keep history accessible to successive generations—particularly in a theatrical, image-saturated age. Jewish iconography marks the quarter, making it a placeholder that lures a wide array of visitors to reanimate and re-narrate these symbols within present histories. For many visitors, the curation of this Polish-Jewish space touches on deeply felt, often suppressed memories, desires, and sentiments. As one would expect from such an un-orchestrated cottage industry, there are multiple aesthetics and battles over the aesthetic choices made; no monolithic visual strategy is attempted, achieved, nor universally appreciated.

In Konstanty Gebert's assessment, "To the extent [Kazimierz] is a play act, it's grotesque and ridiculous, and at times crass and insensitive. To the extent that it's a pastiche, it's beautiful." Pastiche, in Gebert's use, recalls Claude Levi-Strauss's *bricolage,* a form of creative recycling that acknowledges brokenness. Faced with an abundance of still-meaningful fragments of past cultural formulations—but fated also with massive contextual change—borrowing in the service of innovation can be inspiring. At least someone is picking up the pieces and recalling that they once belonged to now-absent others, before moving on.

Figure 13. Singer, a popular Kazimierz youth café, 2000.

Figure 14. On offer at the café Once Upon a Time in Kazimierz, 2010.

Figure 15. Kazimierz denizen and local authority Henryk Halkowski (left) with American historian Joshua Zimmerman on the Klezmer Hois patio, 2009.

Tel./Fax (12) 411 12 45. 411 16 22
e-mail: klezmer-hois@klezmer-hois.cracow.pl
www.klezmer-hois.cracow.pl
Kraków 31 053 ul.Szeroka 6

Figure 16. Henryk Halkowski pictured on a Klezmer Hois postcard, 2001.

Figure 17. Józef's figurines, Jarden Jewish Bookshop, circa 2007.

Figure 18. Józef's special-ordered
bride and groom figurines.

Figure 19. Figurines in a market stall, Sukiennice, main square, Krakow, circa 1995.

Figure 20. Unique figurine in a Krakow jewelry shop, circa 1994.

Figure 21. Figurines, Pokropek collection, Folk Art Museum, Otrębusy, 1999.

Figure 22. Portraits of Jews counting money, Krakow, 2007.

Figure 23. Nazi and Jew (L) by Mikołaj Zagórny, (R) Prisoner by Władysław
Chajec, Pokropek collection, Folk Art Museum, Otrębusy, 1999.

Figure 24. *Cheder* (Jewish religious elementary school), Pokropek collection, Folk Art Museum, Otrębusy, 1999.

Figure 25. Cheder Café, corner of Józef and Izaak Streets, in 2010. The graffiti reads "Fascism will not enter here."

CHAPTER FIVE

TRAVELING TSCHOTSCHKES AND "POST-JEWISH" CULTURE

In times of change, controversy, ritual, or performance, people are led to examine their culture, and the coming of the tourists has a similar result.

—EDWARD BRUNER

Józef brooded over a vision he had in the early 1960s. He grew animated. "A path led to a wooden fence, and a man sat there, in a black cloak and hat. It was just before dusk, the distance between us was about twenty meters. This man just looked at me. I felt paralyzed, as if something unnatural were happening. I turned away, and then back. There was nobody. I had never seen anybody dressed like that. I was ten years old." Decades later Józef understood he had seen a Jew.

Fragments of the prewar Jewish world, physical and metaphysical, linger in the Polish landscape. Tombstone shards, crumbling synagogues, troubling or puzzling memories—in the absence of a significant Jewish community, they have been up for grabs. For a long time, few Poles shouldered their weight and ambivalence. But as we have seen, tourism, economic necessity, and a growing sense of obligation in the post-communist era are increasingly making some into keepers of Jewishness in this post-Holocaust terrain. Some excavate the Jewish histories of their towns, others subsist by ferrying Jewish visitors around the archive, cemetery, and death-camp loops. Józef makes wooden Jews.

An elfin man in jeans and a button-down shirt, Józef invited me to his home. He is a sculptor and ice cream vendor in a small Polish town. Why, I want to know, do Poles carve tiny Jewish figurines—have carved them for over a century—and why do Jewish tourists buy them? I set off in search of answers. What I found serves as a micro-ethnographic portrait of the complexities of tourist economies and the ways they mediate the central themes of this book: heritage making, cultural stewardship, and memory work in commercial contexts. The new moment in the history of these figurines also reveals links between Polish and the Jewish heritage quests spanning a range of transnational domains; these overlapping memory projects collude (wittingly or unwittingly) in ways that shape even the smallest manifestations of the Jewishness found in and around Kazimierz.

Lilliputian Jews stare out by the hundreds from shop shelves in Krakow's tourist shops. Tiny mountain-folk, Jesuses, Marys, and Devils accompany them in segregated regiments. The Jews are all men, traditionally coifed and black-cloaked. In the early post-communist 1990s I saw meaner caricatures, echoing Nazi wartime propaganda: sneering lips framing a single tooth, money-clutching fists, a nose threatening to topple the piece forward. The image seemed to grow tamer with time and tourists. Most were described by Jewish visitors during my fieldwork in the early 2000s as "melancholy," with "sad eyes," "drooping," "gaunt," "haunted" faces—"prayerful" or "resigned"—even as some played tiny violins or accordions. Through the lens of the Holocaust, these wooden Jews seem to know their fates.

The idiom has shifted with the era, the carving tradition swelled and receded, along with the lurches of politics and the demands of memory and the market. Krakow's ethnographic museum, only a five-minute walk from the center of Kazimierz, and often empty during my fieldwork except for attendants who lit the exhibits on demand, is not on Poland's Jewish tourist itinerary. Given the tendency to read all things Polish as precursors to Jewish tragedy, perhaps that's a good thing. Here, grotesque masks of Jews and little puppet Jews on sticks in elaborately decorated Christmas crèche-theaters, and a black-and-white photograph of a straw Jewish effigy—Judas the betrayer—hanging from a tree are interspersed with tall, ribboned, marsh fronds and delicate hand-painted eggs.[1] In these dim rooms, the Jew is presented in his prewar guise as an ambivalent, often-baneful character internal to the rituals of Christian Polish peasant culture.

Dorota, a curator, presented the collection of Jewish figurines for my video camera. Behind a long pane of glass, fading and worn Jews with un-

kempt locks of hair made of real fur, seem a clear proto-form of today's Jewish figurines. Made as children's toys for sale during Easter church fairs, these
Jews, also in traditional garb, seesaw, swing, frolic with the devil, or sway in
whatever way squeezes the most amusement out of their moving parts.[2]

Speaking from a prepared script, Dorota recited the museum's perspective on the figurines and their function in Polish culture. The Jew, she stated,
is a figure of supernatural mediation in the Polish peasants' worldview, and
thus his prominence in their traditional cycle of ritual. Jews were one group
among others who appeared in the peasant realm on the border zone between
the local and the outer world. They were traveling merchants who read books
and did not work the land, flickering curiously in and out of the peasants'
field of vision. This imbued them with a mystery and a power that the peasants tried to harness at harvest time, to "breathe new life into the whole of nature." The seesaws, Dorota told me, are symbolic of the growth of plants.

Traditional ethnographic museums have long treated culture as something that governs "primitive" society, separate from the contemporary political and social realities of those who look at culture under museum glass.
Dorota rejected my suggestion that antisemitism could be a theme worth
considering in relation to the figurines. When I asked her about the multi-
tudes of figurines sold today just a few blocks away in the tourist shops—if
perhaps they represent the emergence of a new Polish-Jewish border zone—
she looked at me quizzically. "Those are just souvenirs."

How to understand today's Jewish figurines? Are they Poland's version
of black-faced lawn ornaments or tobacco-store Indians—forms now widely
disavowed as racist by the North American educated elite? To whose needs,
whose longings do they speak? The figurines are hard to pin down. They gape
blankly across tabletops in Krakow's Polish-run Jewish cafés at dining Jewish tourists (who may buy them). They idle between the salt and pepper shakers in the occasional Polish kitchen and pose on the curio shelf in a progressive Warsaw journalist's apartment. They begin intercontinental trips from
shiny cases in hotel lobbies and airport duty-free shops. They have even wandered as far as Ann Arbor, Michigan, where they balance precariously along
the molding in a popular Polish restaurant.

Other scholars have produced detailed and fruitful formal, iconographic,
and sociological analyses of Polish-made Jewish figurines. Folklorist Olga
Goldberg-Mulkiewicz makes the point that there can be no discussion of
"the" stereotype of the Jew in Polish culture but that various stereotypes—
both negative and positive—have circulated both simultaneously and in dif-

ferent periods and sectors of society, in dialogue with various individual and institutional interlocutors.[3] Building on her work, I shift attention to networks of meaning and social relations associated with the creation and circulation of the figurines. This approach illustrates the dialogues that are catalyzed by and shape their production and meaning. Closely following the travels of souvenir Jewish figurines as they pass through a dynamic system of commerce illuminates how the market partakes in, and influences the creation of, cultural meanings through the commodity form.

Understanding the significance and circulation mechanisms of commercial, touristic cultural forms is particularly important when considering Jewish culture in present-day Poland, because so many manifestations of Jewishness in Poland today exist under the direct or indirect influence of the Jewish heritage tourist industry. Whether such cultural expressions and products are Jewish (or rather post-Jewish, or Polish, or something else), or indeed whether they are positive, nefarious, or captured by any of a range of other definitions, claims, or disavowals, is a subject of ongoing debate among diverse individuals.

Yet despite how varied, conflicting, or ambivalent its associated meanings, a broad, grounded perspective reveals in Poland's Jewish heritage industry a domain of shared cultural relevance that connects Poles and Jews in far-flung sites. The connections suggest a complexity of sentiment and shifting cultural identifications erased by narratives and studies that, a priori, take Polishness and Jewishness as antagonistic—or even discrete—entities. The late twentieth century reemergence of Jewish figurines in Polish popular culture expresses in part an identification many Poles feel with Jewishness, and a need to grapple with the loss of a part of the Polish world that the Jewish Holocaust represented for Poles. Goldberg-Mulkiewicz's work on an earlier reemergence of the figurine form is suggestive of this view. She discussed how the war ended both the living presence of a Jewish community in Poland and the organic, ritualistic, and magical functions of Jewish figures as presented in the museum. Thus Poland's postwar, secular Jewish figurine tradition is—due to the circumstances of its birth—memorial in character. Emphasizing that some figurines depict German wartime mistreatment of Jews, thus representing Polish recognition of Jewish suffering, Goldberg-Mulkiewicz views what she sees as an occasional tendency to antisemitic caricature in some figurines as anomalous, and attributable to the lingering influence of Nazi propaganda. Alina Cała, conversely, places the onus of what she interprets as anti-Jewish imagery in Polish folk expression more squarely on Polish culture.[4]

The sudden emergence in the early 2000s of Jewish figurines with gold coins—along with a proliferation shortly thereafter of small, framed paintings of bearded older Jews counting money by candlelight—suggests the need to re-open the discussion. It seems worth considering both the endurance and the renewal of the figurines' "magical" functions. Jews' association with prosperity and abundance would seem to stretch back to the late 1800s, as evidenced by the museum's life-size wooden *ul*, or beehive, shaped like a Jew.[5]

Yet a dialogical look at the Jewish figurine market is a useful reminder that for the last twenty years the figurines have existed between worlds, in a globalizing milieu in which not only Poles but foreign Jews and others take part. Jews, too, stereotype and essentialize Jewishness, and producers and purchasers of diverse backgrounds are implicated in what Goldberg-Mulkiewicz described as a market-induced engagement with non-controversial, ahistorical themes in the figurines' forms.[6]

* * *

Based on her observations in an Israeli tourist shop, Shelly Shenhav-Keller suggests that the "purchase of [a] souvenir becomes the legitimate framework in which to ponder, debate, expose, and declare one's position in regard to the question of identity."[7] This conception is also useful in the Polish case. But attention to the meaning of Polish-made Jewish figurines to their creators makes clear that their production can also provide a context for such identity work. The creation and commercial circulation of symbols of Jewishness can further animate the social and cultural processes of which they are artifacts. Taken as a functioning whole, the trade in Jewish figurines, from maker through seller to buyer, not only reflects identity struggles but produces them, in part in the form of contact and debate and cultural exchange among Poles, Jews, and others as they confront, in overlapping fashion, to imagine the Polish-Jewish past, and try to find a place for that past in the present.

Józef's kitchen shelves teemed with wooden figurines, some the size of chess pieces, some a foot tall. Mostly they depict Jews. They seemed to have stepped out from *Fiddler on the Roof*: peddlers, musicians, and worshippers with gray-green faces, a color that Józef said "symbolizes the epoch that is gone." I scanned the room to see bas-relief plaques on the walls, including a kneeling prisoner in striped uniform, a series of camp numbers hanging in the air around him. The words "Auschwitz-Birkenau" arced across the top.

In other contexts such a constellation of icons would connote Jewish suffering; in Poland, such images almost always reference Catholic Polish martyrs.
Scenes from the Christian Passion defined the living room and the ice cream
shop. Bookshelves displayed miniature washerwomen, plowmen, and pack
animals carrying harvest fruits. The stairwell swam with fantastical, neon-
bright fish.

Józef unearthed a photo album from a jumble of papers on the couch. He
flipped it open to a picture of his sister-in-law. "She was a Jew. A *wonderful*
person," he said. Her family was killed in the Holocaust. She died of cancer a
few years ago. Next, Józef's wife laid a prewar picture of a grade-school class
on the table in front of me, perhaps to connect with me by showing sympathetic proximity to other Jews. "My mother's girlfriends, all Jews," she said,
pointing to dark-haired girls.

Józef talked, his brow furrowed. He filled pauses with apologetic, tight-
lipped smiles. He has brown hair and close-set eyes. The lids drooped slightly,
as did his shoulders, wearily, as he sat. He was forty-seven when we spoke. He
had carved wood since an army friend showed him how twenty-odd years
ago. But Józef began carving Jews only about ten years earlier. His brother-in-
law, director of a regional museum, asked him to make some Jewish figurines,
a growing trend. Józef discovered later that his early attempts were full of
"mistakes," such as uncovered heads. He had worked from "a feeling inside"
about how Jews should look. Then communism waned. Jewish films ran on
TV. Jewish books became available. He pointed to an album of old photos and
the *Encyclopaedia of Jewish Religion and Tradition*. His accuracy improved.
He began to include a *minyan, tsitsis,* Shabbat candles. He said he wanted to
avoid offending potential customers.

By the mid-1980s, Poles could finally read I. B. Singer's novels depicting
shtetl life. Singer spent his early years in Bilgoray, not far from Józef's home—
familiar country. Józef was fascinated by the stories. "So Jewish and so Polish alike," he gushed. Older local folks told Józef that in 1942 the Germans
rounded up his town's Jews, shot most, and trucked the rest away. "Something
exists and then vanishes without any trace," he said, adding softly, "Sometimes I feel devastated when I think about it." Józef, though quiet, has a taste
for drama. Poverty captivates him, as does struggle. "Happiness is boring,"
he said. "Sadness is deep; a person can find so much in it." After eight years of
carving Jews, Józef began reading about the Holocaust. Filtered through Catholicism, the theme shows up in his work in fiery red and orange colors that
leap from the rough-hewn tops of his more recent pieces. He showed me a *Pietà,* a

strong Jew holding another, collapsed in his arms. "People around here know so little about Judaism," Józef said. "Christianity *came from* Judaism."

Although each carver I spoke with during my research cited unique inspiration and denied any knowledge of a larger tradition or of other carvers, it is useful to consider Jewish figurines in the context of the larger tradition of Polish folk carving. The theme of national suffering in Polish culture—including the common trope of Poland as the "Christ of nations"—finds expression in the copious *Pietàs* and *Chrystus frasobliwy* (Christ in distress) figures that appear in the genre. The Jewish past and Jewish tragedy, too, is Polonized, or made relevant to Polish self-conception, through the sculptural form. Indeed, it has been a central stumbling block in Polish-Jewish relations that Western Jews and Poles have had mutually exclusive views of Auschwitz; to most Jews it is the preeminent symbol of the Holocaust, but to Poles it represents their own national martyrdom. The problem can be seen vividly in Edward Kolacz's description of his recently completed carving illustrating a concentration camp crematorium scene: "It depicts children, pitiably thin, who bid farewell to the world and life with a primitive cross of wire."[8] Whether a scene depicting Polish suffering, or a scene depicting Jewish suffering, or both, the cross indicates that the scene is subsumed into the framework of a Christian response to that suffering. Regardless of the identity of those who populate the scene, it would likely not be accepted by most Jews as a Jewish scene or memorial, as the presence of the cross violates mainstream Jewish cultural sensibilities. Beyond the Holocaust, too, Jews play roles in Polish folk culture in ways that share little with Jewishness as understood by most Jews. As journalist Konstanty Gebert writes, "The Abrahams, Jacobs, and Moseses presented in folk art are figures from Christian iconography, not Jewish. This is not surprising, since Jewish religious iconography simply doesn't exist, and the Polish countryside would have had no contact with secular versions. There remains, however, the fact that Moses descending with the tablets of the commandments directly in front of a church, or a dreaming Jacob, by whose side lies the holy Bible with a cross on the cover, makes a strange enough impression."[9]

Jewish figurines are Józef's main business. "I won't pretend they're not," he offered amiably. But he said he feels a mysterious connection with the Jewish world, a "supernatural level of life." Isaac Singer helped him comprehend that, too. Józef half-joked that he chose to live in his town because of "something in the air . . . maybe because of its Jewish inhabitants," and that he carves "for the needs of my heart" as well as for money.

Józef's heart was carved by a childhood that mostly confined him to bed with intense bouts of strep throat and other illnesses. He read a lot about far-away places—including works of Karl May, creator of the mythic American West for a generation of Europeans. "I lived in my own world, and this developed my imagination. Sometimes illness is useful. Sometimes I think God arranged this." Early on he sculpted the head of an American Indian "with a little Egyptian influence," he mused. A later statuette shows a thick-lipped African woman, and then a "Yoruba village" with grass huts. Still, he laughed, "The farthest I've ever been is Warsaw!"

* * *

Linden branches, soon to be cut into figurine-sized pieces, leaned along the interior walls of Józef's bunker-like workshop. Pale light washed in through a long window. He had left his rough workbench strewn with carving tools, wood shavings, a tin with paintbrushes. On the floor lay a clutter of wood, cans of thinner and paint, unfinished plaques, and sculptures. Józef set a pair of glasses low on his nose. He chose an eight-by-three-inch rectangle of wood and penciled a rough outline, following the bough's natural curve. He chiseled out the basic form. When he carves, Józef said he thinks of the Vistula River, fishing, mushroom picking. Gripping the block between his knees—a small scalpel held between his lips and another in one hand, a thick rubber thimble covering his thumb—he peeled the wood like an apple. An arm quickly emerged, holding a book. A long nose became visible. A beard. Finally pupil-less, vacant eyes.

* * *

With postwar modernization, Polish folk traditions waned. But a new form of sculpture arose, encouraged (and remunerated) by the newly communist state energetically reviving and reforming national culture on a working-people's aesthetic. The Jews, so recently and suddenly wrenched from the Polish landscape—itself ravaged and in need of restoration—reappeared in wooden form, remembered by witnesses to this lost world.

A September 1999 exhibit of Jewish figurines outside Warsaw revealed a broader conception of Jewishness than one sees in the tourist shops. Many were creations of an older generation of carvers depicting their personal experiences with real individuals. Jews in modern clothes. Industrialists, doctors, teachers, pupils, farmers.[10] Even a Jewish hunter, shotgun and dog complementing beard and cloak. A wedding. And the Nazi occupation. The best of this category are truly moving, testifying to the pain with which some neighbors must have watched others being taken to their deaths—or at least to the pain experienced upon recollection. A uniformed SS man marches a baggage-laden Jew along, a pistol to his head, titled "Polish Jew 1939" (see fig. 23). "Last Embrace Before Parting" shows carver Wacław Czerwiński's Jewish couple "saying goodbye because in the ghetto they are going to be separated and certainly will never see each other again."[11] Adam Zegadło, a carver who did "fieldwork"—visiting synagogues to better understand the Jews he depicts—stated simply, "I make these woodcarvings in honor of their memory. . . . It is my aim not to let the traces of this ancient culture sink into oblivion."[12]

Zdzisław and his assistant, Janina, a graduate student in Polish-Jewish history, stood on either side of the sales counter in the Jarden Jewish Bookshop. Together they wrapped a shoebox full of Józef's Jewish figurines in brown paper, securing it with packing tape. Zdzisław completed the job by imprinting the package with his company stamp and carefully writing the mailing address with a fat, black marker. Destination: Cornwall, Vermont. The box was going to an American couple who saw a musician figurine on a recent visit and commissioned Józef to make a whole orchestra.

Zdzisław "discovered" Józef and his sculptures in the late 1970s when the former directed the local House of Culture, the omnipresent, communist-era community arts and propaganda center, performance and exhibit space, and shelter for local artists, all dedicated to the aesthetic uplift of the proletariat. Zdzisław had heard of Józef's work, visited him, and decided to organize an exhibition. Years later, when Zdzisław opened his Jewish bookshop, he decided to sell Józef's sculptures as well. Since then, Józef, in collaboration with Zdzisław as his critic and muse, has specialized in the Jewish figurines. Zdzisław makes efforts to educate tourists aesthetically, as well as to monitor their taste. He carries a few figurines by "lesser" carvers as a "negative background" against which he believes Józef's artistry will shine. He shows me the roughly cut foils, turning one over in his hands. "They're standard, without character. They all have the same face, the same expressions, the same hands, they're static. They're sort of lightly caricatured. They have no *life* in them. With Józef every one is different. Look at the placement of the hands," he offers, pointing at a Józef figurine. "It looks almost like he's thinking. Sometimes you even see a sense of humor. You see character in them."

For Zdzisław the figurines are a key example of the "post-Jewish" genre, because they depict both a world that no longer exists in Poland and one that Józef knows only second-hand. Józef gets reading materials from Zdzisław's shop; in addition to the historical albums, I saw a copy of *Midrasz*, the lively Warsaw-based magazine on contemporary Jewish life and culture, on a table in Józef's home. Zdzisław acts as a reference librarian for Józef's questions on Jewish culture. "He asked me about a Jewish wedding. . . . He asked me what a *khupe* [wedding canopy] looks like . . . so I gave him a picture," Zdzisław told me. Zdzisław visits Józef often to pick up orders, sometimes to critique Józef's creations. "He doesn't like it," Zdzisław says, "but it's good for him."

Zdzisław arranged a new shipment of Józef's figurines for display. He picked them out of a cardboard box he held against his hip, piled high with the black-cloaked sculptures: there was a group of ten men, one *tallis* (prayer shawl, plural *taleysim*) encircling them all. A man clutching a goose. More klezmorim [musicians]. A man holding a kindled *menorah* before him. Zdzisław placed some next to a pile of loosely crocheted *yarmulkes*. "Very nice, right? Aesthetic. Even the hands." He set a row of them across a top shelf in front of a painting of the old synagogue that stands at the other end of the square outside. A fiddler. A merchant with a sack. A rare couple embracing a row of children. They came alive against the backdrop.

Zdzisław admitted that Józef traffics in stereotypes. "But tourists think in similar stereotypes to Józef," Zdzisław said. "Józef's stereotypes fulfill the expectations of the tourists." And Zdzisław has developed a keen sense of tourist expectations, of the desire on the part of visiting Jews for a particular legend; he thinks they would feel most happy if Józef were an old man—perhaps even an old Jew—chiseling out his own memories.

During the summer, Zdzisław can barely keep Józef's figurines on the shelves. According to Zdzisław, they are snapped up by "very educated" people, university professors, businessmen, and, of course, tourists—fifty of Józef's for every one of the other carvers. "That's the most optimistic part of it. The tourists themselves, almost intuitively, know, feel, and choose the more interesting ones. They have an aesthetic taste. Either innate, or learned. But they have it."

Józef speculated about why Jewish and German tourists buy his figurines (nostalgia and guilt, respectively). Poles, he said, buy them as amulets, to ensure financial success. Some complained to him later that business isn't going any better. Józef suggested harder work. He himself works ten hours a day, carving. One figurine takes two to four hours. He makes about 300 a year, enough to finance a large addition on his small house. He would make more if Zdzisław had his way, but in the warm months Józef dons a white smock and soda jerk's twin-peaked cap and dispenses ice cream to local passers-by.

For Józef, imagination is tempered by marketability. At home, he has wooden Jewish women in lilac and sky blue, with red skirts and white shawls, green and yellow details, and children. But the legions of figurines he sells are old men in black. Józef's Jewish world has color, passion, possibility. The buyers' world, it often seems, has only sorrow.

*　*　*

Despite the popularity of wooden Jews among Jewish tourists, against the background of recent Polish-Jewish history, the stylized wooden Jews can also rankle their animate counterparts. Some Jews abhor the figurines, claiming they can "see the antisemitism" in them. Zvi Engel, a seventeen-year-old student at Hebrew Academy in Montreal, described the figurines he saw in Krakow during a high school trip to Poland with distaste, as "beggars in long black coats, with big noses, big ears."[13] Photographs I took and showed to a Polish-born Jewish man in Boston elicited rage: "Something must be done to *stop* this," he demanded. He later told me he wrote a letter to the Pope to complain and request intervention. Eric Schwimmer, a secular American Jew who grew up in an Orthodox household, was "vehemently opposed" to the figurines because he felt Jews buy them out of guilt and nostalgia for their lost connections to Jewishness. He also balked at what he saw as the inherent suggestion that traditional Jewishness—as depicted by the figurines—is dead and gone, existing only as a tourist trinket. Even Jews who do buy figurines can be extremely ambivalent, both fascinated and repelled; some make the purchase to bring evidence of Polish antisemitism home from their trips.

But Józef and the Jarden Jewish Bookshop keep albums for customer comments, and they are full of admiration and gratitude. An American Jewish woman who had ordered a set of *klezmer* musicians wrote about showing the figurines to her father, who found them happily reminiscent of "the world of his ancestors, which he has denied any knowledge of." The woman praised Józef for having, in the faces of the figurines, "exactly evoked the expressions of their souls," and thanked him "for so tastefully bringing back a small part of our past."

It makes sense that someone who dedicates himself to a craft cares how consumers respond to his products. Goldberg-Mulkiewicz recounted the story of a carver whose Jewish figurine ended up in a New York shop window and was seen by a former inhabitant of the carver's town. The man was so affected by the image from the world of his lost childhood that he wrote to thank the carver, who was himself moved "immensely and [thus] convinced . . . of the legitimacy of his chosen path."[14]

I have had my own range of emotion to grapple with throughout my research. Even when my requests to visit carvers were most graciously indulged, sometimes the weight of history, the poverty of wooden miniatures where flesh and blood used to be, could be blinding. The first figurine-carver I interviewed—before I meet Józef—was as suspicious of me as I was of him. What I learned didn't ease my mind. A tiny Jewish head, wearing a fur-trimmed hat, rolled across the lace tablecloth in his Krakow apartment. It was stopped by a pack of Marlboros. The gaze pointed toward a disjoined arm. Its miniature hand clutched a curling scrap of parchment lined with painstak-ingly flourished Hebrew letters. Assembled, it stood about five inches tall on springed legs. I touched it. It *shokled*, rocking in the characteristic gesture of Jewish prayer. In the 1960s the carver discovered a Torah scroll hidden in the rafters of his father's house. He was vague on details, wary of my questions. Not an uncommon find in postwar Poland, the scroll was perhaps stashed there during the war by a doomed Jewish neighbor in an eleventh-hour act of hope or resistance, aided (or not) by the Polish homeowner; it may also have been come by nefariously. Over the years, the carver clipped small squares from the parchment and put them in the hands of his sculptures. He was not the only one to use this method, though many carvers had turned to photo-copying by the 2000s, perhaps due to waning source materials. This carver said he stopped recently after Jewish tourists told him he was doing some-thing sacrilegious. Figurines in his personal collection still hold the original Hebrew texts, often upside down. He chuckles. "I can never remember which way they go."

* * *

Tracking Polish Jewish figurines took me to White Plains, New York, to the home of Alisa Bernstein, an American Jew. Her white house was bounded by a white picket fence and a small yard scattered with plastic tricycles and cow-shaped planters. Jutting above the front porch, three flags—American, Canadian, and Israeli—flapped in the winter wind. Alisa and her husband David, a rabbi, ran an Israeli-American organization that creates classroom-based educational programs that teach tolerance to Israeli and Palestinian youths and ultimately bring them together to meet, play, and make art.

Bernstein, a petite, smiling woman in her mid-forties, with curly red hair and a black sweat suit, invited me into her home, introducing me to its vari-ous residents over the course of the afternoon. Bernstein's children—one Chi-nese, one white, both adopted and now Jewish—sat on the living room floor, mesmerized by *Star Trek* playing on a widescreen TV. The dining room table was being set for brunch with bagels and lox, cream cheese, onions, and tomatoes. The director of Rabbi Bernstein's Palestinian partner-organization in Gaza was visiting, and as the conversation switched into Hebrew, I wandered through the house. Almost every surface bore a sign of Jewishness. In the living room, a Disney "Happy Hanukkah" wall hanging showed Pluto, Mickey, Goofy, and the gang playing with a *dreydel* (Hanukkah spinning top). An enormous cloth "Shalom" draped along the wall in the hallway. A scroll of the Ten Commandments hung around the corner. A ceramic *shtetl* scene sat on a dining room sideboard, a capped fiddler perched on the eaves of a thatch-roofed house while a dancing Tevya, arms aloft, whirled in the front yard next to a woman hawking geese from a cart. Nearby stood a matched set of salt and pepper shakers in the image of a Jewish man and woman.

In the living room, I found a wall of ethnic dolls stacked in their original plastic packaging. Mostly Barbies: Native American Barbie, Asian Barbie with her fan, African Queen Barbie with striped gown and elaborate beaded neck rings. Also a New York Yankees Barbie and a couple of Barbies in bikinis, as well as a miniature Liz Taylor in Cleopatra Barbie garb. Other dolls include an Aunt Jemima figure with a polka-dotted headscarf and curlers and a small porcelain Japanese doll wearing a kimono.

Bernstein didn't "believe in" Barbies ("too whitebread") until the arrival of her Bosnian foster daughter, who collected them. The spectrum of the dolls' colors and ethnicities echoed the jumble of international visitors who had set up camp throughout the Bernstein home ("We have an open-door policy," she said). Finally I spotted what I came for. On top of a white cabinet filled with dishes, among menorahs, kosher wine, a *dreydel,* and other ritual Judaica, stood two of the Polish Jewish figurines. With striped, fringed *taleysim* hanging over their shoulders, they are the rare, older, rocking type, their necks (attached with springs) letting their heads nod into the torn scraps of Hebrew prayer book in their hands.

After brunch, Bernstein told me of her five years of East European travel, guiding Jewish heritage travel tours, sometimes for Holocaust survivors, often visiting the sites of Nazi camps. We finally touched on the topic of the figurines. "I'd *love* to find out anything about the people who made these," she began. "The real significance for me, and why I was so drawn to them—aside from the fact that you're so starved for anything Jewish in Poland, so when you see something, you *freak out*—was that I felt that they were a symbol, just sitting there, that Judaism would never die no matter what happened. That here in the midst of all this destruction that you saw, with few Jews left, that sitting in a market were these dolls. . . . That's really what it is for me. That no matter how many times you try to put the Jews down, they pop up somewhere."

* * *

In Poland, "a guest in the home is God in the home," and in Józef's small town in 2000, an American Jew sat high in the hierarchy of guests. Back in his kitchen, his wife supplied endless, steaming food: eggs and ham, pierogi glistening with fat, sweet tea and cake. In the afternoon, local dignitaries and relatives dropped by to meet me. Each added his two cents about Jews and Poland—always emphatically rosy about the past, vaguely defensive about the present. Some brew of curiosity, economics, history, and conscience made me an honor, an opportunity, maybe vaguely suspicious. None of this dampened Józef's overwhelming generosity and goodwill. (I came back months later with a three-person film crew. Rather than send us to a hotel, the family gave up their own beds—fold-down couches in the kitchen and living room—and camped out together in an attic room.) Still, a final guest trumped me.

Józef's wife, who had been running errands, returned in a commotion with their teenage son and daughter (who had earlier shown me small watercolor Jewish scenes she had painted). They speedily groomed themselves and then the house. The local priest blustered in moments later to give an annual blessing. I watch from the kitchen, accompanied by my wooden co-religionists. The priest pulled a *surplice* over street clothes and sprinkled holy water on the family, who stood in the living room with lowered heads. Everyone chanted, surrounded by Józef's own rustic crucifixes, madonnas, and popes. The priest held out a cross. Each kissed it. Amidst parting pleasantries, the priest accepted the money the family offered and then hurried out again.

Near the end of my visit, Józef disappeared. He returned holding a small wooden sculpture. Jesus *frasobliwy*—in distress at the state of the world, crowned with thorns, lost in melancholy under a tree. Józef wanted to give it to me. He hoped it won't offend me. He looked at the floor as he stressed that I shouldn't think of the gift as a religious gesture. He wants me to have it because, he said, unlike the Jewish figures, "it's something of *ours*."

* * *

American Jews who travel to Poland, purchase Jewish figurines, and display them in our homes reveal a symbolic, iconographic (and thus, according to some, "un-Jewish") aspect of Jewishness. For Max Rogers (the Hasidic Londoner we met in chapter 2), Jewishness is an encompassing matter of daily practice.[15] A small and sprightly man, he dresses as his community demands:

white shirt, long black jacket and pants, black *yarmulke* under a black fedora, long beard, *peyes,* and *tsitsis* (all of which he tucks and pins demurely and in-geniously away while traveling among non-Jews). He looks like one of Józef's figurines.

Though Rogers rejected any attachment to Poland (his parents came from a small Polish town), I often caught him musing about the lilt of the Polish language, how he wished he could speak it, how it reminded him of his mother. He listened intently to the Poles around him, straining to recog-nize a word or two. Rogers was one of the few Jewish visitors to Krakow who took almost as much interest in Jewish figurines as I did. He simply admired Józef's work—which he first encountered in the Jarden Jewish Bookshop—and couldn't stop talking about it. But an item of Orthodox Jewish tradition—the Third Commandment, barring graven images—forbids him from keep-ing a figurine in his home. So he negotiated with Józef to commission an acceptable piece: a landscape, a shtetl scene, a bas-relief without people or animals.

Rogers had some business in the area the day I travel to meet Józef, so we rode together from Krakow and he dropped me off at Józef's home for my interview with the carver. On the drive home, after plaintively urging me not to eat the chicken Józef's wife packed for me (not kosher), Rogers tilted his head toward the sculpture I was carrying and complained, to no one in particular, "Look, when she leaves, she gets a present; when I leave, nothing!" I replied that I don't think he would want the piece Józef gave me. I showed him the statue of the pensive Jesus—an image replicated in crossroad chapels throughout the Polish countryside. Rogers surprised me by saying, "Why wouldn't I want this?" I answered, "Because it's Jesus Christ." Rogers balks, "*Where* is Jesus Christ? For me this is a Jewish man, sitting, thinking—*beautiful.*" I laughed, but insisted again that it is Jesus. Rogers demanded, "From where you think it's Jesus Christ?" I was intrigued that his world could be so insular that he wouldn't recognize a figure of Jesus. I said, for one thing, that the man who made it told me it was Jesus Christ. Rogers rolled his eyes and said, "Ahh! He sees what he *wants.* I see what I want. He can tell you this is *Hitler,* but it doesn't *make* it Hitler." I chuckled again at what struck me as surprising role-reversal: the subject telling the anthropologist that meaning is culturally contextual.

Rogers clarified with one of his frequent *midrashim:* "If a bad man writes a Torah, it must be burned. Why? You might think, well, the words are the same, the Torah is holy, right? But where does writing come from?" He gestured as if he were writing and pointed first to his head, then down to his arm, his hand, and finally settled on the imaginary page before him. "Even the name of God written by a bad man isn't holy." But Rogers went on to explain that this understanding of intention and creation only applies to the Torah. For other things we make—art, for example—the intention doesn't matter. Rogers can see a beautiful Jewish man in Józef's Jesus sculpture, and that's sufficient.

As an afterthought, though, Rogers added that if there were a cross on the sculpture, it would be a different story. It would be a problem because a cross is a symbol of Christianity, which Jews must avoid. "If *everyone* knows this is Jesus," he added for clarification, pointing to the sculpture, "then it would be different." I told him again—with our driver and our mutual Polish friend supporting me—that everyone does know it's Jesus. I pointed to the crown of thorns, the characteristic pensive pose, the fact that identical statues dot country roads in much of Europe. "Oh," he said reflectively, handing the figure back to me. "Then it's not for me."

* * *

Viewing only the Polish side, we might revisit the ethnographic museum's explanation of the image of the Jew in Polish culture and find it newly useful: Jews have suddenly reemerged at the border of Polish experience after a generation of almost total absence, a new kind of liminal figure flickering in and out: as pilgrims, tourists, businesspeople, as well as potential reclaimers of property in towns and cities across Poland. (As a local friend told me, "If you show up in a small Polish town and start taking photos of a building, people assume you're a Jew.") This might help explain the emergence of the genre of coin-holding or coin-counting figurines, described above. The longstanding European association of Jews with money (as merchants, tax collectors, and financiers), combined with a more general aura associated with cultural difference, makes these figurines favorite good-luck charms for Poles seeking fortune in business in this newly capitalist society.[16]

Globalization and mass production have led to both a standardization of the figurines' form in the tourist economy, as well as new styles, materials, and sources. Jewish production of Jewish figurines is now a part of the Polish market. Folklorist Shifra Epstein notes that figurines of Hasidim have been produced in Israel since the establishment of the state, and the largest producer—a single company making over thirty-five different styles—today exports these to shops in the United States and Europe, including Krakow.[17] She also describes the emergence of a particular genre of figurine out of Jewish-Ukrainian dialogue: a nested matrushka doll of the deceased Hasidic spiritual leader Rav Odesser. It was commissioned from a local artist by the owner of the souvenir shop in the Israeli-run compound built for the Brazlaver Hasidim on their annual pilgrimages to the grave of Rabbi Nachman in Uman (south of Kiev). Such pockets of renewed creativity on the "high end" of the market serve a variety of Jewish self-imaginations: in 2008 I photographed a pair of Jewish partisans, male and female, cloaked and booted for the wintry woods, each carrying a satchel and World War II–style rifle, special ordered from Józef by a sympathetic non-Jew from Texas.

Making, purchasing, and displaying Polish-made Jewish figurines, then, is a means of engaging with the Polish-Jewish past and present, and with conceptions of self and other, for Poles, Jews, and others. These figurines, like much "Jewish heritage" in contemporary Poland, are being shaped and reshaped in a slow-motion memorial dialogue. Both producing and purchasing them can signal the desire to enlarge as well as to delimit the self. Despite their particularly ambivalent status, these figurines comprise a unique form of Jewish heritage production. As the congealed representation of multidirectional memorial impulses, they also travel widely, carrying messages and sparking conversations wherever Polish-Jewish heritage is a meaningful, living force.

CHAPTER SIX

JEWISH LIKE AN ADJECTIVE:
EXPANDING THE COLLECTIVE SELF

The first casualty of conflict is identity and . . . redefining identity is a fundamental step toward reconciliation.
—ANTIJE KROG

In mid-summer 2000, Michał, a middle-aged Cracovian translator, traveler, and practitioner of Buddhism, came walking into Szeroka Street unshaven, disheveled, and distracted. I was sitting at the patio of the Nissenbaum restaurant with a couple of American Jewish friends. When I first met Michał the previous autumn, he told me he had simply been "pulled to Jewishness" in recent years. Today he apologized for his long absence from Kazimierz and said he "didn't have the guts to come." An American Jewish Holocaust survivor who had become a public presence in the quarter had apparently accused Michał of "pretending to be Jewish." Michał told me of how timidly he had approached both the head of Krakow's formal Jewish community, Tadeusz Jakubowicz, at Remu synagogue, and then Lauder Foundation rabbi and youth club director Sasha Pecaric. He said they had both accepted him "as I am: not Jewish, uncircumcised, ignorant." His story suggests that not only is Jewishness enacted in a range of ways in Poland, but a spectrum of variously identified Poles have found spaces to participate in it—although not entirely free from social risk, particularly from within normative (i.e. non-Polish) Jewish ranks. "All I can be accused of," Michał lamented, his voice cracking, "is going to synagogue, wearing a yarmulke, and saying 'shabbat shalom.'"

Proprietors of Jewish-themed establishments in Kazimierz (as well as most regular customers) tend to be Poles, many of whom have a sense of being caretakers of Jewish heritage in the absence of a robust local Jewish community. But at times the line between being an outsider custodian of Jewishness—what I have called a Shabbos goy—and being an insider to Jewishness is blurred. The result is that many of the "non-Jewish Poles" involved in Jewish cultural production in Kazimierz are not quite as "non-Jewish" as they seem at first glance. Whether due to their own experience and self-representation or the attribution of others, they fall between conventional categories of "Jew" and "Pole." I describe these individuals as "Jewish-identified."

If late-communist-era expressions of interest in things Jewish often signified democratic aspirations and opposition to the government, the trend of Poles identifying with Jewishness since 1989, in the first two decades after communism's fall, is a phenomenon that must be reassessed in its new social, economic, and political context. "Subject positions," after all, "are always also political stances, placing an actor in [both] an historical tradition and a present-oriented field of power and interest."[1] Expressions of affinity for Jewishness in Kazimierz illuminate how the pursuit of pluralism has extended into and has in turn been shaped by the new commercial environment. While the official battle for basic democratic institutions and laws in Poland has largely been won, Jewishness remains a potent tool in the post-communist era for building pluralistic civic culture. The role of Jewishness in resistance against communist-era erasures has made way, in an era of Poland's national self-reimagination and economic transformation, for its role in resisting a narrow, homogenous, mono-ethnic conception of the nation.

The popularity of an ethno-national understanding of Polishness in which Polishness is equated with Catholicism (and Jewishness as thus un-Polish) has been a central problem for Polish-Jewish relations and notions of shared heritage.[2] It can be argued that the naturalization of this exclusive conception of Polishness constricted the "universe of obligation" that Christian Poles inhabited and influenced how they acted toward their Jewish fellow citizens during the Nazi occupation.[3] Kazimierz, as a Polish Jewish space, is a place where broader conceptions of Polishness are promulgated. Rather than only providing space for Jews as a significant "other" in Poland (which they also do), some Kazimierz heritage brokers actively call into question rigid notions of Polishness and Jewishness altogether. This makes the site uniquely conducive for exploring a range of identifications with Jewishness, many of which are motivated by progressive cultural politics. It is a place where otherwise contradictory identities can be reconciled.

There are two interconnected functions of identification as they play out in relation to Jewish memory work in Poland. A claim to a Jewish identity (whether or not one has actual Jewish ancestry) can be a memorial gesture—that is, an attempt to publicly mark and remember historical Jewish presence in the Polish social landscape, in itself a form of historical justice. Yet such identification does not imply only a backward glance. Identifying with Jewishness as a Pole means confronting the deeply ambivalent relationship between Polishness and Jewishness that exists in both ethnic communities today. Claiming Jewishness as a legitimate way of being Polish means expanding both Polish and Jewish national self-conception based on "more inclusive principles of present day affiliation."[4] This suggests a process of grappling not only with the past, but with forces at play in the present day that would constrain the range of possible public identities.[5] Such identification, then, implies a commitment to multiple truths: about historical wrongs, present-day cultural constraints, and evolving individual and collective subjectivities.

Productive Encounters with Difference

The sense of ethnic boundaries—of memory, of representation, of identity—is a central challenge confronting those who participate in the Kazimierz phenomenon. Who owns the Jewish past, Jewish culture, the right to mourn Jewishness lost, the right to act Jewish, to feel Jewish, to define Jewish, to be Jewish? These questions are a matter of daily concern in the quarter. The answers some local people are formulating have implications for both Polish national and Jewish communal debates about history and identity, as well as intergroup allegiance, individual agency, and the possibility of change. They also form a unique barometer of the core challenges and the "state of play" of Polish-Jewish relations and the potential for reconciliation. A rare site of ongoing, face-to-face interaction among Poles and Jews (both foreign and increasingly Polish ones), these interactions reveal the desires, challenges, and possibilities that exist for imagining a shared Polish-Jewish heritage.

Among those who do Jewish cultural work in Kazimierz, tour guides form a kind of "front line" in relation to Jewish visitors. In attempting to enact new allegiances with Jewishness, they confront significant challenges from the foreign Jewish side—most basically a Jewish incredulity toward positive Polish engagement with Jewishness. For many Jewish visitors, the mere participation of non-Jewish Poles in brokering Jewish culture is distasteful. As recounted by Polish tour guides (and corroborated in interactions I witnessed), foreign Jewish visitors often evince a sense of ownership of Jewish heritage and history in Poland and a suspicion of ethnic Poles attempting to interpret this heritage in ways that may conflict with the collective memory of Poland that foreign, mostly Western, Jews bring with them.

Janina, a tour guide for the Jarden Jewish Bookshop who went on to earn a doctorate in Polish Jewish history in the United States, told me with a laugh that the question of when and why she started to be interested in Jewish history "is a question I've heard a hundred times" from Jewish tourists. Some Jews, she noted, "don't really listen to me, they don't treat [as] serious what I'm saying . . . because I'm not Jewish." Similarly, Marta, an ethnology student and one of Janina's fellow guides, told me:

> Basically there is a difference between Jewish and non-Jewish [tourists]. . . . I think non-Jewish tourists, they basically listen to me, whatever I tell them. They believe it. . . . And [with] Jewish tourists . . . very often, especially people from Israel, and America, Jewish people, they're very anti-Polish. And the only thing they "know" [she gestures quotation marks in the air] about Poland, or they think they know, is Polish antisemitism, and those Poles collaborating with Nazis through the whole war.

But beyond either the common accusation of crass, mercenary self-interest (that Poles are now profiting from Jewish tragedy toward which they were inadequately empathetic in the first place), or dismissal of the idea that a Pole could interpret Jewish heritage and history in a sympathetic manner (even championing a "Jewish perspective"), there is a particular kind of discomfort caused by the confusion that occurs when Poles step into what is seen as ethnically Jewish territory. There is a deep and widespread sense among visiting Jews that only Jews should do "Jewish things," as revealed by a comment made by a thirty-five-year-old Californian, a convert to Judaism and the daughter-in-law of a Polish Holocaust survivor. Referring to wooden figurines of Jews traditionally made by non-Jews in Poland, she said, "Did you see the figurines? The little, mournful-looking fiddlers with long sad faces and beards? It's just sick! These people are dead, were killed! And you want to buy a little statuette? It makes my stomach turn! I mean, *unless there's some Jewish person making these in some artistic way.*"

The way Jews attempt to identify who is Jewish in this foreign social milieu diverges not only from halakhic (Jewish religious) definitions, but also from broader Israeli or American Jewish notions of authentic Jewishness under the banner of either descent or religious observance. Kazimierz's rarefied environment, however, reveals other underlying logics by which American Jews often assume the identities of their fellow Jews. These are based on outward signs—whether phenotypical, sartorial, or behavioral. In other contexts the inner and the outer may correlate more closely. But in Poland we see clearly how the shift from Jewishness as a shared, "unconscious culture" to its circulation as self-conscious "heritage" opens previously taken-for-granted connections between Jewish ancestry and Jewish behavior (and between non-Jewish ancestry and non-Jewish behavior) to unexpected new combinations.[6]

In Kazimierz I spoke with Josh and Danny, two twenty-something American Jewish brothers. I asked them if they had visited any Jewish businesses. They mentioned the Jarden Jewish Bookshop we had just left, but I told them the owners were not Jewish. Josh seemed a bit dismayed and said, "Well, we saw a Klezmer band—they were Jewish." The conversation continued:

> **Danny:** Presumably one of them was. I don't know about the other ones.
> **Josh** [to his brother]: What, the band?
> **Danny:** Yeah, I mean I think the bass player was, but I don't know about the rest of them.
> **Josh:** Really? I thought they were all Jewish.
> **Danny:** Well, he didn't say he was.
> **Erica:** Why do you think they were Jewish?
> **Josh:** Because they were wearing traditional . . . Jewish-specific clothing . . . Huh.
> **Danny:** The guy with the beard was certainly Jewish. But I don't know about the other ones.

I asked which band they saw. When they mentioned the popular local band "Kroke," I told them none of its members are Jewish. Danny responded that he had had suspicions because the accordion player had "looked very . . . Nordic." I asked them if they had met any Polish Jews at all during their trip. Suddenly more tentative, Josh said, "We talked to the guy who wouldn't let us into the synagogue." But Danny interrupted him. "We don't know that he was Jewish," Danny said. "We could assume, but we don't know." Josh said, "I think he had a kippah [skullcap] on."

The failure of external markers in this environment to align with some notion of a deeper essence (that usually has not and often cannot be articulated) is part of what makes Kazimierz's observable Jewish activity suspect to outsiders. The anxiety this creates is suggested by journalist Ruth Gruber, who noted that some individuals deeply interested in Jewishness in Poland "go so far as to wear Stars of David around their necks, assume Jewish-sounding names, attend synagogue, send their children to Jewish schools, and follow kosher dietary laws, in addition to championing Jewish causes."[7] Since Gruber does not espouse halakha (Jewish religious law) as her yardstick for Jewish authenticity, she seems to be relying on a common sensibility that undertaking such apparently Jewish actions is not what qualifies one as really Jewish.

Yet the encounters visitors have with locals engaged in non-normative performances of Jewishness may also prompt reconsideration of received understandings of Jewishness, Polishness, and antisemitism, as well as epistemological reflection about the sources of one's own knowledge. Being confronted with Poles positively engaged with Jewish heritage can be a "reality-rearranging" experience for Jewish visitors.[8] Visiting Jews are often taken aback—whether they are pleased, angry, or ambivalent—by non-Jewish tour guides or shop employees deeply involved with and educated in Jewish ritual, history, and even languages (not infrequently to an extent greater than the visiting Jews to whom they cater). As an American Jewish lawyer involved with Jewish initiatives in Kazimierz told me, "There, some Gentiles know so much about Jewish traditions that they're almost part of the community."

An exchange between an American Jewish mother and daughter I interviewed in Kazimierz illustrates how the encounter with heritage brokers can provoke deep questions:

> **Mother:** We definitely keep asking, and we keep saying to ourselves, "Do you think she's Jewish? Do you think the proprietor of that place is Jewish?" Every time we go in anywhere—we've sort of learned now that the answer is no. But particularly our first few days here [we kept wondering], "Is our guide Jewish? Can you tell if he's Jewish? Does he have a Jewish name? Would he have said something already?"
>
> **Daughter:** But then again, what does it mean to be Jewish? That he doesn't self-identify as a Jew? I still think he could have had a Jewish grandparent but just wasn't telling us. So it's clearly . . . identity isn't very clear. . . . We have a

much more complex view as a result of this trip, wouldn't you say that? Of Polish history, of Polish-Jewish relations. Much more complex. And I think we found it stunning that a young woman like Janina [their non-Jewish tour guide] would be so interested.

Jewishness in today's Poland is found in unexpected places, stubbornly refusing to reveal itself where and how convention would have it. There are Polish people who feel a deep connection to Jewishness they feel is important to express—despite the skepticism with which their feelings are often met (by fellow Poles and visiting foreign Jews alike). But the fact that a Pole who by conventional definitions is not Jewish can also pass as Jewish in the eyes of an American Jewish tourist suggests that these visiting Jews recognize something familiar, something Jewish, in these Polish efforts. Some of these moments—of misrecognition, of blurring, of recognition—can help transform meanings of Jewishness that conflict into meanings that connect. As Larry, an American Jew visiting Krakow's Festival of Jewish Culture in 2008, mused:

> You wonder, maybe there is some sort of gilgul . . . a reincarnation. Who knows? I mean there's so much in this place, so who knows if these people haven't gotten certain sparks of different souls who once were here? I mean it's a kabbalistic idea. This place retains its Jewish character to such a tremendous extent, and yet you have all of these people who aren't Jewish who are connected—who are definitely connected. So who knows?

Truths of Jewish Identity in Contemporary Poland

The question of Jewish identity in post-Holocaust Europe, and perhaps especially in Poland, is tortured and often tangled. Given the profound wartime pressures that demanded life-or-death choices to conceal, assert, attribute, or resist Jewish identities, as well as the traumatic postwar legacies and political pressures, how could individual identifications with respect to Jewishness not be influenced in the process, leaving palimpsests far richer than the conventional, seemingly unitary, and history-less identity categories of "Pole" and "Jew" seem to proclaim?

The number of Polish Jews who survived the war was small (about ten percent of the three and a half million prewar population) and many Poles have mixed heritage that in many cases is just now coming to light.[9] Community leader Stanisław Krajewski names some of Poland's varieties of Jewish identity, noting "marginally Jewish Jews," "non-halakhic Jews," and "Catholics of Jewish origin."[10] One of the more striking—although by no means unique—cases is Catholic priest Romuald Weksler-Waszkinel, who changed his name in 1992 from Romuald Waszkinel. Not until twelve years after his entrance into the priesthood did his Catholic mother Emilia Waszkinel reveal to him that he had been born to the Jewish couple Yaacov and Batya Weksler, and was adopted by Emilia and her husband Piotr, just before his Jewish birth parents were deported to the Vilna ghetto. A shelf in his home displays a scale and a samovar that belonged to his biological parents, along with a picture of his adoptive parents, a set of tefillin, a Hanukkah menorah, and the framed Herew prayer Sh'ma Yisroel—along with a picture of Jesus Christ, bleeding on the cross.[11] Despite deep and abiding stereotypes, intolerance, and essentialism regarding Jews in Poland, the logic of Jewish identity allows for the existence of particular types of hybrid or non-normative Jewishnesses that the hegemonic—the non-Polish—Jewish world does not. As Weksler-Waszkinel put it, "I can be a Jew in Poland, but as a priest, I cannot be a Jew in Israel."[12]

My goal is not to define Jewishness in Poland. It is rather to expand our field of vision, to explore what richness and realities are overlooked if we predetermine what we mean by "Jewish" before we begin looking for it. Many observers of the "Jewish scene" in Poland—following Ruth Gruber—have suggested that European non-Jewish interest in Jews has produced a "virtual" Jewish world on a continent with few "real" Jews. But this argument depends on the most basic essentialism: the existence of "real Jewishness" in a definable, stable, authentic form. My interest is rather how such imported (generally American or Israeli) templates erase local manifestations of Jewishness. What is considered really Jewish and what is not in different times and places? Who has the rights and resources to propagate their views on the matter? How are ethnic groups and cultures formed and sustained, and how are they reestablished in the wake of decimation? To gain insight into these questions requires us to discard notions of identity as static; we must think instead of identification as an ongoing process upon which forces of memory, intercultural relations, politics, resources, and emotion bear heavily. This is not a claim of infinite flexibility, nor a simple valorization of postmodern play. Rather, it is a way to recognize that even in core Jewish community sites, what binds members is as much a shifting set of shared issues of concern as any essential characteristics or boundaries.[13] Many key leaders in today's Polish Jewish community began not so long ago as "completely assimilated, non-Jewish Jews," their budding community dismissed by the remnants of the prewar community as "a fraud."[14] If many such "Jews" were drawn to Jewishness for the new social, cultural, moral, and spiritual domains it opened for them, is it such a surprise that in a radically transforming, democratizing society, such ethnic minority concerns are being embraced by individuals who possess no Jewish descent at all?

* * *

Kazimierz is a place to which many Jewish-identified people gravitate, offering as it does a conducive atmosphere for exploring Jewishness. The quarter draws category-defying individuals, people "sort of on the edge between being Jewish and not-Jewish," as Jarden Jewish Bookshop owner Zdzisław Leś designated himself and his wife, Lucyna. Such in-between, Jewish-identified individuals find unique ways to represent their sense of self. Marta, an employee in the bookshop and a tour guide to Jewish Kazimierz, had dyed-black hair and a large tattoo bearing the Hebrew word "Chai" (life)—a common Jewish talisman—on her right shoulder.[15] She told me,

> The first question [tourists] ask me is if I'm Jewish. And recently, since I wear [the] Chai [tattoo], they usually don't ask me this question anymore. They think that I'm Jewish, they figure it out from my Chai. So instead they say, "Since you're Jewish, what are you doing here? Why didn't you move to Israel or America? Why are you still here? What is your family doing, and how did they survive the war?" And then I really don't know what to answer. Because sometimes I'm so sorry for them, because they're so sure that I'm Jewish, so sometimes I just don't want to tell them, "You know, listen, it's not that simple, I'm not really Jewish." I try to get out of this question somehow, because I feel like they would feel, kind of like hurt if I told them I'm not Jewish.

Marta suggests that if she were to tell visitors she's not Jewish, they might perceive her as having cheated them, somehow falsifying her identity. But she also implies that such an answer would be inadequate. Disavowing Jewishness altogether would fail to capture the complexity of her situation and her longstanding involvement with Jewishness. "It's not that simple," she says.

> It's been probably half of my life—I'm twenty-three—that I remember I've been interested in that. And I remember my biggest dream was going to Israel and learning Hebrew, for the longest time. And there was always this something that was pulling me to Judaism and Jews, and there was always this deep feel-

ing inside of me that I couldn't explain. And I finally managed to go to Israel when I was nineteen, and right before I was going there, really it was maybe two days before that, my grandmother, my mother's mother, she told me, "Oh, you know, it could be interesting for you, I never told you that before because I thought it was nothing important, but since you're going to Israel, I guess it could be interesting for you, but you see your grandfather was Jewish."

Marta later converted to Judaism, made aliya (immigrated to Israel) to marry, and settled with her husband in an Orthodox enclave in Jerusalem.

Working at the high-traffic Jewish bookshop, Marta, Zdzisław, and Lucyna were often called upon to articulate their identities. The sense of self and Jewishness they express has been subject to the ongoing scrutiny and feedback of foreign Jewish visitors. While the typical criticism casts them as appropriating or faking Jewishness, I was taken aback at a recent conference to have an Israeli professor familiar with the bookshop tell me with some agitation that, on the contrary, Zdzisław tries to *hide* his own Jewishness from the public—to pass, in effect, as an ethnic Pole running a Jewish bookshop. If tracking such foreign Jewish confusion and criticism tells us something about dominant mainstream frameworks of Jewish identification and sensitivities to the breaching of these in the Polish context, tracing out the functions and flows of Jewishness in Poland—and particularly in Kazimierz—reveals a logic of identification different from either mainstream Jewish or Polish notions of group belonging.

Brother Stefan is a Catholic monk and was the director of a shelter and soup kitchen in Kazimierz during my fieldwork. He initiated multiple Jewish-related initiatives, including introductions to Jewish culture with specialists for homeless people at his shelter, field trips for them to Kazimierz synagogues, and films about the Holocaust. Behind the shelter he also created a rare "green space" in the quarter for children to play. In its center he installed a small bronze statue of Janusz Korczak, the renowned Polish Jewish orphanage director who voluntarily went to his death at Treblinka so as not to abandon his young charges, standing alongside Brother Albert, the "Cracovian Mother Teresa" after whom the shelter is named; a figure of a girl playing with a ball is nestled between them. In 2000 Stefan opened the small storefront Café Ester—his own Jewish commercial initiative—next to the shelter, although it closed again just a few months later for lack of customers.

I met Stefan through his mother, a woman with whom I struck up a conversation on a city bus in Tel Aviv some months earlier when I noticed her reading a Polish magazine. When she was thirty, she found out that her father had been Jewish. We sat in a café where she told me her story. When she had finished, she suggested I contact her son when I returned to Krakow. Stefan's father, she told me, had also been Jewish. When we met in the office of his Kazimierz shelter, Stefan expressed his felt identity over tea:

We don't feel like Jews, but rather Jewish. Like an adjective. I feel my mother has a lot of Jewishness in her, but she isn't a Jew. Jewishness . . . it's different from being a Jew.

We feel an atmosphere, the problems of Jewishness. We feel near, a closeness. As a boy I had an intuitive feeling of connection to Jewishness. It felt like something mine. I read a lot about it. But we grew up Catholic. This can be a dilemma, but also a synthesis. The situation in Poland made many people creative. . . .

Many people involved in the development of Kazimierz have Jewish roots but can't say this aloud because of the intolerant atmosphere [in Poland]. So they work on Kazimierz's development as a way of doing something Jewish. . . .

American Jews have to understand that Polish conditions are different. To be a Catholic doesn't mean to lose one's Jewishness. . . .

[Such people] also carry Jewishness. Such people are also chosen. They feel themselves chosen as Jews. Their hearts are Jewish. . . .

In normal conditions, my family should have lost our Jewishness. But my grandmother spoke well of Jews. And [said] that we are different, even though we're Catholic. So something must be there. It's a very mystical phenomenon. One cannot scorn this phenomenon. In Poland there are 1% real Jews, and 99% of these others. A lot of these others developed Catholic culture in Poland—but in a very special way, original, with something of Jewishness. Tuwim, Słonimski, Lechoń [classic Polish authors of Jewish descent]—they were Jews, but built, contributed to Catholic culture. [Film director] Agnieszka Holland in the U.S. is a Jew, but also Catholic. Daniel Rufeisen, a Carmelite priest in Israel, wanted to invent Jewish rites within the Catholic liturgy. . . .

I think Polish Jews have a special task. If they survived so much—the Holocaust, Communism—it can't be for nothing. Somehow Kazimierz exists in that current. Maybe thus there is the conflict [with] American Jews—with their need for speed, for effectiveness. People here have a different pace. Another way. American Jews want to give money, push a button, and see results. I know Polish Jews who gather with their families on Saturday. No Torah. They don't even say it's Shabbat. But it's important.

Brother Stefan suggests a grammar of identity in which the kind of Jewishness he possesses, comprising feelings of closeness to and engagement with
the "problems of Jewishness," has the function of an adjective, profoundly inflecting his sense of Polish self. He also suggests that engaging with the revitalization of Kazimierz—a place so intensely coded as Jewish—is itself a way
of being Jewish.

One might argue that these are "safe" examples of identification with
Jewishness—both for my argument and for the social world these individuals
inhabit. For one thing, both Marta and Brother Stefan invoke descent as the
basis for their identifications with Jewishness, a claim to which mainstream
Jewish communities would be somewhat sympathetic.[16] But what about those
non-Jews who do not or cannot make even that claim? Here I would stress it is
the claim to Jewishness, and not the drop of Jewish "blood" that may or may
not course through one's veins, that is significant in Poland's contemporary
national-cultural landscape. Such a claim is a sign of Jewish engagement, concern, and a foray on the part of individual Poles into (if not always a full embrace of) their own internal pluralism, an important step that may underlie
the building of a robust culture of pluralism on a national scale.

Indeed, it is examples to the contrary—when Poles who have been identified with Jewishness attempt to disavow the "taint" of Jewish blood—that
seem doomed to fail. In the Polish context, imputing Jewishness to someone
or claiming it for oneself has proven extraordinarily effective to socially define someone as such. Despite their lack of Jewish self-identification, individuals known to have Jewish origin are often cast as "Jews" out of suspicion
and for purposes of delegitimization. The Jewish ancestry of Adam Michnik, editor-in-chief of the left-leaning Gazeta Wyborcza, makes that paper
"the Jewish paper," just as the Jewish origins of key members of the hated
postwar communist security forces result in their still widely being decried
as "Żydokomuna," or agents of a mythic Jewish-communist alliance. A somewhat dated if high-profile instance of the power of Jewishness as a stigma
even in cases in which no Jewish ancestry is present took place during Poland's first free elections in 1990. Despite presidential candidate Tadeusz
Mazowiecki's formal documentation of Catholic baptismal certification going back twelve generations, his opponent, Lech Wałęsa—in what political
scientist David Ost describes as a neoliberal populist attempt to transform
economic anger into nationalist political power—intimated that Mazowiecki,
along with his supporters, was hiding Jewish ancestry behind a Polish name.[17]
The very suggestion was enough to sway the voting public, and Mazowiecki

was forced out of the race. The episode illustrates a popular joke: while anti-semitism elsewhere functions on the logic of "if something is Jewish, it's bad," in Poland the equation is that "if something is bad, it's Jewish."

Brother Stefan's suggestion that American Jews are intolerant of, or simply do not recognize, the subtleties of Jewishness in Poland is apt. An expansive definition of "Jewish" operates not only among antisemites in today's Poland, but also in the inner sancta of Poland's Jewish community institutions, where a kind of "don't ask, don't tell" policy has prevailed. Local Polish Jews acknowledge the constitutive role of "Jewish identified" individuals, including a variety of curious non-Jews and not-quite-Jews, in the flourishing of Jewish culture, community, and discourse. The Polish Jewish magazine Midrasz, launched in 1997 by journalist and community leader Konstanty Gebert, bills itself as serving "Polish Jews, active in the existing communal organizations, non-Jewish Poles interested in things Jewish," and "Poles of Jewish origin, who have relatively recently become aware of their Jewishness, and are exploring it, or considering that possibility."[18] Krakow's new Jewish Community Center (JCC) has, in addition to its own Facebook page, a page established by a group calling itself—in a tongue-in-cheek reappropriation of a derisive Jewish term for a non-Jewish woman—the Shiksa's Club, "for all the shiksas around the JCC and their allies."[19] The clash of this local logic with that employed by many visiting foreign Jews, for whom ethnic Polishness, in contrast, appears to have the power to taint, can be confusing and painful for the Jewish-identified individuals caught in between.

Vicarious Identity as Cultural Critique

Despite the painful recent history of identity categories in Poland—which for Jews included persecution, hiding, dissimulation, and forced adoption—one cannot reduce the current complexity of Jewish identities and practices of identification with Jewishness to this history's detritus. Rather, Jewish identification in contemporary Poland is best understood as a way of coming to terms with history, a site of active cultural agency and creativity, involving memory and emotion, ethics and aspirational politics. Jewish-identified Poles in Kazimierz do not identify themselves as Jewish in conventional terms. But they clearly identify with Jewishness in a variety of ways that deserve attention. Indeed, in the confusion and consternation they at times create—whether intentionally or accidentally—such Poles can function as a form of social pedagogy and cultural critique. This notion derives in part from Naomi Seidman's provocative concept of a "politics of vicarious identity," which recognizes that

expressions of ethnicity can take unexpected forms, most specifically in asserting the self by "resisting a straightforward identity politics in exchange for
participation in the struggle of 'someone else.'"[20] Poles who identify with or
pass as Jewish work more or less explicitly against both the racist distortions
of identity once enforced by the Nazis and the ethno-national constraints still
placed on identity by both Polish national and Jewish communal mythology
today. These individuals use "strategic provisionality (rather than . . . strategic essentialism)" to disrupt entrenched notions of what difference is—and
what forms it can take.[21]

While some Jewish-identified Poles may fully pass as Jewish, and thus
only on occasion educate visitors that their assumptions about Polishness and
Jewishness need revision, other people actively "represent" as Jewish, publicly
asserting that they are Jewish as a means of cultural protest against exclusivist
Polish nationalism and antisemitism. Jewish bookshop owner Zdzisław, told
me he gave his son the middle name David (a conspicuously Jewish name)
for this reason, and once sarcastically retorted in the bookshop that he himself is Żydokomuna (a longstanding slur for "Jewish-Communist") to a priest
who had presumed both Zdzisław's Jewish ethnicity and an accompanying
religious conviction.[22] Similarly, Krzysztof Czyżewski, the founding director
of the Pogranicze (Borderlands) Foundation in Sejny, Poland, told the audience at a Jewish conference that, on principle, he does not deny it when Polish people ask him if he is Jewish.[23] He added that he would not, of course,
claim this identity among Jews. In these cases, "passing" is clearly being used
to make a point. As Judith Butler suggests of drag, a blatant yet purposely
flawed cross-identification "is an example that is meant to establish that 'reality' is not as fixed as we generally assume it to be."[24] The anxiety such dem-
onstrations can provoke among individuals invested in the purity of particular categories was made visible by the response to Czyżewski's comment
by a rabbi in the conference audience, who demanded that identities be more
discrete. He began in Yiddish (a choice that was itself an assertion of boundaries), "Vos, bistu meshuge gevorn?" (Have you gone crazy, or what?). The
rabbi continued that just as he does not want synagogues—another component of Jewish heritage discussed at the conference—to lose their identity, he
does not want people to mix their identities. "I want people to be comfortable
in their identities. I am comfortable with who I am, and I want you to be comfortable with who you are," he said.

In addition to subtle interventions into people's understandings of the
forms Jewishness can take and where it might reside, identification with Jew-

ishness is also expressed in protesting against the kind of everyday antisemitism common in Polish life.[25] Agnieszka, another Jewish-identified Pole and a born-again Christian who is deeply involved in Jewish community life, recounted an activist moment in the following incident:

> There is a shop on the corner, a milk shop. And a man came, he was just before me, and he said to this woman [shouting], "And all these things are because of Jewish people!" You know, "It is horrible that Jewish people are doing this and this and this!" And he was complaining to this sprzedawczeni [saleslady] . . . about the prices . . . that the price of butter was growing. . . . Stupid things! Which it usually is . . . in blaming Jews. . . .
>
> And then I said, "Panie! Ma pan cos preczwiko Żydom?!" I told him, "Hey! Do you have anything against Jews?" And he was so terrified, you know? That he was just silent, and the woman who was selling was also—you know, there was just a silence. They didn't say anything. [Maybe] they do have something [against Jews], or they have nothing. But I was so angry, you know, uch. . . . I left this shop, and I didn't even realize what I did. But then I was proud, you know! What is this, you know? What, am I going to tell them nothing? Because of that, because there was such a silence, so many people died.

Agnieszka represents Poles who are demanding recognition of Jewishness as a legitimate way of being Polish if Poland is to be a democratic polity. Once she told a saleslady from whom we were buying strawberries, who made an offhand comment blaming Jews for the bad parking situation on her street, that the woman had just sold her strawberries to a couple of Jews (meaning us), and suggested to her that she might want to reconsider her stupid opinion. By such occasional stepping into a Jewish subject position, some of those who take it as their task to represent Jewish culture—in Kazimierz and beyond—are also "representing for" Jews, in the sense of "speaking for (and as one of) those commonly left unrepresented in public forums."[26]

Navigating Polish Shame

In the postsocialist era Poles have been confronted with previously suppressed aspects of their nation's history concerning Jews. They have been scrutinized particularly by Israel and the American Jewish establishment for their willingness and ability to re-reckon their collective rachunek sumienia (bill of conscience), and to revise their national self-image accordingly. But if demands to bear witness to history have an impact on (national) self-conception, perhaps the inverse is also true—that one's self-conception guides and constrains one's latitude to bear witness. As historian John Gillis suggests, "The core meaning of any individual or group identity, namely, a sense of sameness over time and space, is sustained by remembering; and what is remembered is defined by the assumed identity."[27] If one's own sense of self affects one's ability to witness (and if the identity ascribed to a person by others determines their willingness to accept one's witnessing), then a central problem in both coming to terms with Poland's difficult wartime past and Polish-Jewish reconciliation are the narrow categories in which one's identity—and thus one's orientation to the past—is so often presumed to fit.

This problematic is illustrated in a widely republished meditation by Adam Michnik, Polish dissident, journalist, parliamentarian, and current editor of Gazeta Wyborcza, one of Poland's major daily newspapers, addressing the revelations in the early 2000s about the Polish wartime slaughter of Jews at Jedwabne.

> By coincidence I am a Pole with Jewish roots. Almost my whole family was devoured by the Holocaust. My relatives could have perished in Jedwabne. Some of them were Communists or relatives of Communists, some were craftsmen, some merchants, perhaps some rabbis. But all were Jews, according to the Nuremberg laws of the Third Reich. All of them could have been herded into that barn, which was set on fire by Polish criminals. I do not feel guilty for those murdered, but I do feel responsible. Not that they were murdered—I could not have stopped that. I feel guilty that after they died they were murdered again, denied a decent burial, denied tears, denied truth about this hideous crime, and that for decades a lie was repeated. . . .
>
> Writing these words, I feel a specific schizophrenia: I am a Pole, and my shame about the Jedwabne murder is a Polish shame. At the same time, I know that if I had been there in Jedwabne, I would have been killed as a Jew. Who am I, then, as I write these words? Thanks to nature, I am a man, and I am responsible to other people for what I do and what I do not do. Thanks to my choice, I am a Pole, and I am responsible to the world for the evil inflicted by my countrymen. I do so out of my free will, by my own choice, and by the deep urging of my conscience. But I am also a Jew who feels a deep brotherhood with those who were murdered as Jews.[28]

Michnik does not hide the difficulty of witnessing he faces due to the fluidity, the time-sensitive nature, and resulting historical discontinuity in the ascribed aspect of Jewish identity. He is a Pole by his own choosing, presumably through a combination of self-identification, his maintenance of Polish citizenship, and his lack of embrace of a Jewish identity, in his daily life. Yet he feels a "brotherhood" with Jews—even that he is a Jew—by virtue of the Jewish identity he would have been ascribed by the Nazis. Perhaps such recognition of the shifting circumstances that help make us who we are is a form of witness itself: to the injustices of history perpetrated by those who would remove choice.

But of course even (perhaps especially) categorical identities one "chooses," since they are not individual but always social formations, can in turn generate formidable emotional constraints to bearing witness to the suffering one's own group perpetrates against others. I asked Lucyna, the non-Jewish co-owner of the Jarden Jewish Bookshop, how she feels when visiting the ruins of Polish Jewish cemeteries that she helps Max Rogers, the Hasidic Jew from London, restore. Her response eloquently expresses the bonds imposed by social identities:

> Oh, it's a very difficult question.... Inside I feel a mixture of feelings, because I'm very sorry for everything that happened. And I know why mostly these cemeteries are looking like this. Not because of the Second World War time, and German occupation here. They look like that because of everything that happened after the war [at the hands of Polish people].
>
> But this is from one side. On the second side, because of my knowledge I understand what happened, and how it worked, that it looks like this now. That World War II completely destroyed people's morality. Jewish life [wasn't worth] anything. And people got used to [the fact] that Jews could be killed anytime and that Jewish property doesn't belong to [Jews]. It belongs to Germans and the rest for Poles.
>
> I think for people who were born after the war, it's very difficult to understand what the wartime meant. How people lived. Especially in Poland, you know. Where if you wanted to help a Jew, you should be very strong.... It was a big responsibility to help a Jew to survive. It was like a game, gambling, you know. You play not only on your life, but on the life of your neighbors, your family. It was a big responsibility. And I don't think people can understand what heroes these [Polish] people were who were trying to help Jewish people. And even nowadays, you know. How many people like them can you find? It's impossible. People are rather afraid, they are cowards.
>
> And this is the second feeling that I have. I'm mostly sorry because I'm looking at Max's face. I'm trying to understand what he is feeling, exactly. What I could feel if it happened to a cemetery where my parents' graves are.

[handwritten marginalia: emulating Polish sympathizers]

And this is very difficult even to describe. This is the very sad part of this work. Because as a Pole I'm trying to find an excuse. As a human sometimes I cannot find any excuse. This is very difficult.

It is this kind of witnessing that Jews demand from individual Poles, the only kind that will be taken as faithful and thus fulfilling: Polish acceptance of some responsibility for the fate of the Jews during and after the war, a Polish statement that, as Jan Błonski plainly put it, "Yes, we are guilty."[29] And yet precisely at issue is the content of that "we." Historian Brian Porter offers a framework in which the attempt to blur identity categories between "Poles" and "Jews" can indeed be central to a Polish "apology" for historical wrongs against Jews:

> For Poles to say, even with the most heartfelt sorrow, "we did it," might sound very nice, and indeed this is probably an important part of any process of historical reconciliation. But ultimately the apology needs to go something like this: "We did it, because the very conception of ourselves that pervaded Poland in the interwar and war years drew sharp lines around 'us' and 'you,' and made it impossible for us to perceive you as neighbors and compatriots, and equally impossible for you to view us in this way. Instead we saw you—and you saw us—as aliens, and at best we watched silently as you were killed, at worst participated in the killing. But we recognize that these self-conceptualizations, these cultural forms of identity, are mutable—that they arose in a specific time, under specific circumstances—and we are working to change them. We recognize that these forms of identity are not the only ones available to us. They never were. And we are working towards a new fluidity of identity, which will allow us to start to blur the lines between 'us' and 'you,' to recognize that in many ways 'you' are also 'us.'"[30]

Jewish rejection of Jewish-identified Poles—and thus a Jewish attempt to constrain or impose identity categories on Poles—may make Jews appear regressive, and indeed as if they were almost perversely embracing the ossified identity categories under which they suffered in the past. Yet such rejection must be understood against the backdrop of a seminal event of identification—the Holocaust—during which the boundaries were inflexible, utterly imposed from without, and determined who would live and who would die. Auschwitz, it has been said, "reactivated an archaic concept" of Jewish peoplehood, a "byproduct of massive persecution."[31] Furthermore, Jews today live with a consciousness of the centuries prior to the Holocaust, throughout which Jewish identity was not only not chosen, but inflicted by outsiders with particular force and narrowness—and too often with cruelty, humiliation, and persecution. In Poland in particular, Jewish attempts to become Polish, to blur identity when they desired, were, when at all possible, available only at the total resignation from one's Jewishness. The ability to assume and cast off identities at will is an unevenly distributed privilege. Socially stigmatized identities are often impossible to shake. Thus it is not surprising that skepticism reigns among Jews at what is perceived to be an outsider's luxury of fair-weather dabbling in Jewishness.

Still, Jews also experience and perform their Jewishness according to the social and political context in which they find themselves. And if the right to self-definition is centrally at issue (for Jews as well as for everyone else), Jewish employment of racialist logic of identity as the measure of a person's "true" Jewishness—using the question "If you had been in Europe during the war, would you have been killed?" as a measure of Jewish authenticity—seems a particularly cruel irony of history.

Encounters in Kazimierz cut productively into the problem from both sides. They plant seeds of self-scrutiny in non-Jewish Poles, and lead visiting Jews to confront their own national mythologies as well. Many of Kazimierz's culture brokers have actively sought to engage with Jewish concerns—including Jewish concerns about what these culture brokers themselves do. And Jewish visitors to Kazimierz, confronted with Polish engagements with Jewishness, respond not only with concern, but also with potentially transformative recognitions. These take forms ranging from Jews acknowledging that they share with Poles the self-identity as victims of Nazi persecution, to realizing that some Jews live happily, safely, and voluntarily in Poland, feeling themselves to be Poles as much as Jews.

A final explanation of the lure of Jewishness for contemporary Poles comes from Anna, a twenty-three-year-old Polish woman who had been studying religious practice and participating intensively in the Lauder Foundation Jewish Youth Club in Kazimierz. She had begun by pursuing a degree in Jewish religion and culture at university but became convinced that her interest and identification were not only intellectual, but spiritual as well. Anna told me she felt "80 percent certain that I'm Jewish, but the papers were burned. . . . I can't document it." Thus, she felt compelled to convert. Despite pursuing the most traditionally enshrined trajectory for identification with Jewishness—namely the halakhic procedures for conversion to Judaism—

Anna's self-explanation seemed to center on precisely the escapist motivation that troubles scholars considering the appropriate limits to philosemitic empathy and identification. As Anna told me, "There is a wise saying: A Jew after World War II said if Christians died in gas chambers, he would have felt morally compelled to convert to Christianity. I feel most strongly that I'm not on the side that was bad."

It seems that Anna, in her relation to her Jewish ancestry (whether real or imagined), has made the opposite choice from the one Adam Michnik felt morally compelled to make. She seeks to escape, rather than embrace, a "Polish shame" in exchange for a kind of Jewish valor. The talk and behavior of some Polish "new Jews" I observed—whose cultivation of newfound Jewishness was accompanied by finding fault in everything Polish—seems to reflect this desired exchange. In making it, they reinforce the widespread identification of Jewishness as a kind of anti-Polishness.

"Empathy," we are told, "is not complete identification, the unconditional 'sympathy' in which, no matter how noble the intention, the subject is usually lost—replaced by the sympathetic doctor himself, who unconsciously appropriates the subject's voice and attributes."[32] Empathy, rather, is a form of "attention and respect" accompanied by an "awareness that another's tragic experience may never become our own."[33] Perhaps in this historical context, Polish conversions to Judaism constitute, via total incorporation, a more troublesome "refusal of loss" than do the other, more ambivalent identifications that are common in Kazimierz.[34] As Butler suggests, when a particular set of identifications is "threatened by the violence of public erasure . . . the decision to counter that violence must be careful not to reinstall another in its place . . . to [instead] make use of a category that can be called into question, made to account for what it excludes."[35]

Polish antisemitism, like every antisemitism, is deeply based in rejection and desire, in the anxious attempt to delineate the borders that separate self from other. To the extent that "new Jews"—or any Jews—attempt to reject Polishness in pursuit of some idealized, pure Jewishness, they set the stage to replicate what has been perpetrated against them in the past. It is the opposite of what I understood the late Cracovian Jew Rafael Scharf to have meant when he advised Jews to embrace the accusation of "dual loyalty" that has been so often flung at them—indeed, he said, we should even multiply those identifications, for these allow the bounds of one's empathy for others to expand. Ultimately, it is when the bookshop owner Lucyna steps temporarily outside the bounds of her Polishness—indeed, outside of any category smaller than the one that contains us all—that she seems able to bear unambiguous witness.

As is illustrated by the reticence of many Christian Poles who helped Jews during the war (or even some who attempt to memorialize Jewish suffering today) to be identified and celebrated for their actions in front of their neighbors, once a Pole has allied herself with Jewishness in some way—blood or no blood—she is already suspect, her Polishness tainted by ambivalent difference. Again, the presence of "actual" Jewish blood is not the key factor in a person being marked by Jewishness. Jewish identification in Poland is a risk for all who engage in it.

Extreme trauma, historian Dominick LaCapra recognizes, may "exceed existing modes . . . of mourning," and the ghosts such trauma produces "are not entirely 'owned' as 'one's own' by any individual or group. If they haunt a house (a nation, a group), they come to disturb all who live in . . . that house."[36] In Kazimierz the need for bearing witness to the tragedies of others comes face to face with what anthropologist Jonathan Boyarin calls "our terrifying bleedings into each other."[37] Whatever else may be said about Kazimierz, in important ways it should be recognized as the product of a Polish desire to bear witness to Poland's own Jewishness, through what critic bell hooks describes as a "cultural space where boundaries can be transgressed, where new and alternative relationships can be formed."[38]

TOWARD A POLISH-JEWISH
MILIEU DE MÉMOIRE

Cultural tourism becomes simply life-enhancing rather than life-consuming,
not a spectacle but an experience, because real people still live it and share it
with real people who interpret it. We are able to experience reciprocity and feel
enriched by it.

—STUART HANNABUSS

A Shifting Ecology of Jewishness

Locating ethnography in time is a perennial problem for anthropologists. Despite the sense that we are describing current cultural problematics, the "ethnographic present" is already over by the time we sit down to write. Especially
in social settings defined by rapid global flows like tourism, the challenge is to
capture the emergence, historicity, and dynamism of the cultural formations
we document and in whose change we participate. This book, in particular,
was written, and is being read, in a very different moment than when many
of the situations it describes took place. In the 1990s and early 2000s, Poland
was just rediscovering its Jewishness publicly. Catapulted into the orbit of the
West, Poles were suddenly faced with entirely new discourses about (and for
some, encounters with) cultural difference. Most of my fieldwork took place
before the country was gripped by the polarizing debate that would soon
be provoked by historical scholarship regarding Polish complicity in crimes
against Jews, set off by the publication in 2001 of Jan Gross's *Neighbors*.

From a Jewish perspective, Europe was still a site of old, rather than new, antisemitism, with Poland its symbolic epicenter. While old myths have certainly persevered among both groups, the decade-plus after the fall of communism also saw the first popular opportunities for Jews and Poles to experience (and for an older generation, reexperience) each other as living realities rather than. Equally significant was the range of unexpected new actors that emerged, social agents who have taken up Poland's Jewish heritage as a key domain of cultural and ethical transformation. Whether in the form of shop owners, festival organizers, tour guides, or souvenir figurine carvers (as well as their consumers, local and foreign visitors on a variety of journeys), these actors have been at best overlooked as agents of change, and often vocally dismissed or derided. In this book I have tried to sketch out the evolving, perhaps ephemeral environment that they have inhabited, and in important ways created: a new ecosystem that has developed atop—and because of—the Jewish void left by the Holocaust.

By the time I did my "official fieldwork" in the late 1990s, a range of global flows were making inroads, further complicating the seeming boundaries of time and space. These were visible if I stepped back and looked beyond the lovingly curated tableau of antique Judaica that Mateusz had curated in the apartment described in my prologue. On his Ikea dining room table, Mateusz had left me three video store membership cards and nine pages of handwritten directions for how to use the eco-friendly Italian washer/dryer and Japanese TV/VCR with hundreds of cable channels. There were also other nostalgias in the mix: a communist-era "Polski-Fiat" placard recalling the tiny, once ubiquitous *maluch,* or "little one," car, from an auto manufacturer that disappeared in 1992; a massive oak credenza filled with feather bedding from Mateusz's grandmother's prewar home in Lwów; and a variety of antique bric-a-brac: a wooden radio-box; art-deco tins and glass bottles with faded labels; 1920s golf shoes and a pair of rusted pinking shears. From still farther afield, a Native American dream catcher hung on the bedroom wall, and a hand-held African drum and Australian Aboriginal boomerang sat nearby.

Just as in Mateusz's home, continuing economic development in Kazimierz had also begun to obscure the particularly Jewish quality that was the primary theme of interest for early investigators and investors in the neighborhood. With the exception of Szeroka Street, Kazimierz's character has been incrementally flattened to that of a hip, bustling, youthful quarter, described to me during a visit in early 2004 as the *de rigueur* weekend jaunt for Warsaw's nouveau riche. In summer 2011 a chic Varsovian curator focusing on Holocaust memory told me that her crowd now eschewed the "folkloric" Kazimierz and its Festival of Jewish Culture as passé. In any case, the new leisure class that fills the quarter's cafés is as likely to expand their cultural horizons by eating sushi or chimichangas as *czulent* (Jewish stew traditionally served on Shabbat).

Yet if the first blush of interest in and development around Jewish culture seemed to have peaked by the end of my formal research, if the quarter's Jewishness is today partially eclipsed by the more general commercial hubbub, interest in things Jewish has also been normalized. Already in the mid-2000s the Poles I met in the Jarden Jewish Bookshop were less distinguishable from the foreigners, not only in that they all wore the latest European fashions, but by the uninhibited, matter-of-fact way the former browsed for Jewish books, as if the topic were self-evident and unremarkable for locals—a posture strikingly different from the diffident, ambivalent, or even paranoid forays of ten years previous.

Kazimierz's forms of Jewishness have also continued to deepen and proliferate, extending new tendrils through the quarter, intertwining with each other and allied cultural projects. A certificate of *kashruth,* signed by Krakow's Israeli Orthodox rabbi, Boaz Pash, for a local Polish Jew's ice cream brand, hangs in the window of a local sweets shop; the treat is also available in a cart rolling daily in the nearby square, labeled "Lody Koszerny" (kosher ice cream) in a Hebraicized Polish font. Pash has also led joint Shabbat services with the tiny new progressive Beit Krakow community, run out of the Galicja Jewish museum by the Russian-born Reform rabbi Tanya Segal. The museum itself now does more local family outreach, sponsoring "Saturday mornings with Jewish Culture," Yiddish classes, and *Krav Maga* (Israeli martial arts) workshops. In 2011 the Hasidic Chabad Lubavitch group, which has since 2007 rented the Izaak synagogue for its services, pre-school, and kosher shop, opened the first fully kosher restaurant in the quarter, The Olive Tree, a few doors down.

The Jagiellonian University's Jewish Studies Department has moved into Kazimierz, across the way from the Festival of Jewish Culture's new (since 2007) Middle Eastern–style Cheder Café on Jozef Street. The latter is a cultural center in its own right, hosting a range of literary events, live music (from Tunisian to German), and political discussions with groups like the joint Israeli-Palestinian military and police alliance Combatants for Peace, which is working to end Middle East violence.[1] The city's ethnographic museum, situated just blocks away and home to a fascinating collection of Jewish figurines and costumes employed in Polish folk rituals, has begun a major physical and conceptual transformation. Long a musty, dim, outdated edifice (as described in chapter 5), the museum's collaboration with the Festival of Jewish Culture in the summer of 2011 brought two shows, "Jews on Vinyl" (showcasing Jews in mid-twentieth-century music, sponsored by the trendy, youth-oriented, U.S.-based Idelsohn Society) and "Matzevoth for Everyday Use" (a Polish photo project depicting scavenged Jewish tombstones that have been used by Poles as building materials). These developments suggest the museum, too, may become part of the quarter's vital, increasingly transnational "Jewish space," contributing to Polish engagements with Jewish culture and debates around the Jewish past. My overall impression at this writing is one of surprising vibrancy; examining a tourist brochure on activities in Krakow in summer 2011, the ratio of Jewish to other initiatives would suggest that the city has a Jewish population the size of New York.

Reclaiming Jewish Poland—with and without Jews

The changing times, discourses, and culture—and not least different perspectives—scuttle easy attempts to sum up the atmosphere. Poland's Jewish developments, and Jewish assessments of these, are unevenly dispersed. Talking to Jews who are involved in and enthused about the pockets of Jewish renaissance, one may hear that times have simply changed. As one avid Jewish commentator on post-communist Jewish Eastern Europe said to me, "To see EU Poland as a cesspool of Jewish hatred is like being determined to shove yourself into a coat that no longer fits." Yet the gap between the complex reality of Poland's multifarious, creative engagements with Jewishness and the mainstream Western Jewish world's vision of Poland is still striking.

Since the mid-1990s, almost annual variations on the same irony-tinged story appeared in the *New York Times,* the *International Herald Tribune,* the *Guardian, Le Monde,* and the *Forward,* skeptical of Poland's new Jewishness. The titles framed the emerging situation as Jewish Revival/Jewish Culture/Jewish Disneyland/Jewish Discovery/Philosemitism . . . *without Jews.* If the new kinds of Jewishness cropping up in these sites are still largely invisible, there has been a slow awakening to the status of such spaces as crucial environments of memory and reconciliation, and perhaps even a kind of renaissance in which foreign Jews themselves would want to participate. A 2009 article in the new American Jewish magazine *Tablet* observed that Krakow's Festival of Jewish Culture "has provided a critical public space for its audience to grapple with the stains of their history"; the author also lamented that the festival is such a "well-kept secret" in the United States, convinced that young Jews would flock to it if they only knew.[2] As this knowledge spreads, and as Jews begin to take a second look at Poland, I hope this book will help draw attention not just to the relative institutional latecomers described above, but also to the avant-garde of non-Jews who stepped into the pre-fad gap. These Poles adopted and nurtured the fragments of Jewishness they found and helped the few local Jews reconnect with and reconstruct a sense of living Polish Jewish heritage when Western Jews rejected the possibility of such a thing.

Complex obstacles to "knowing" also endure. A mythic Poland remains highly relevant to global Jewish constructions of self. The country still serves overwhelmingly as a stage for projections and reenactments of tragic Jewish history that too often engage in what former Knesset speaker Avraham Burg describes as a "coercing of emotions" around the threat of antisemitism, rather than a resource for creative culture-building and dialogue around shared humanity.[3] The divergent constructions of Jewishness attendant to these stances are tied to broader global politics, making the Jewish relationship to Poland a kind of backstage to the main stage of the Israel-Palestine conflict. The connection is made clear in a 2006 blog post entitled "Reflections on Poland" on the Moreshet Jewish heritage travel seminar website, written by a young Jew named Marc Spund during the Israeli war with Lebanon that summer: "If anyone has the temerity to question why Israel is at war, I invite them to spend a week in Poland as we did."[4]

Jews remain central, as well, to Polish self-conceptualization, and amidst the post-communist struggles at national reinvention there seems to be a degree of success in overcoming the image of Jews as suspicious outsiders and integrating them into the national narrative. According to historian Joanna Michlic, since 1995 "a more assertive domestic culture of civic and pluralistic nationalism and the pressure of international Western opinion" have pushed Polish national identity away from its previous principles of ethnic nationalism.[5] At a grassroots level, one increasingly hears of former citizens honored as both Jews and Poles in one breath, as Polish foreign minister Radosław Sikorski did of Warsaw Ghetto fighter Simcha Rotem at the unveiling of a new monument to the ghetto uprising.[6] Poland's chief rabbi Michael Schudrich, an American import, recounted, "I get these calls from town X saying: 'We feel an obligation to perpetuate the memory of the Jews who once lived here.' It used to be: 'What can be done to clean *your* cemetery.' Now it's: 'What can be done to clean *our* cemetery.'"[7]

If the image of Jews is changing in Poland, it is in part the result of difficult, complex, dedicated work across many domains of culture and education. Polish historiography in relation to Jews is being rewritten, educational programs for teachers are being administered, new monuments and memorials (to the Holocaust as well as the 1968 expulsions) are being erected, and new museums are being built—like the Schindler Factory Museum—that speak about the Polish and Jewish wartime fates in a shared frame. Avant-garde artists have been developing a new genre of memorial provocations—touching on the ambivalent historical connections between Jews and Poland—that are critical and playful, embodied and participatory.[8] And at the grassroots level there is an astounding number of initiatives. While some—like Grodzka's Gate in Lublin and the Borderlands Foundation in Sejny—are well known, in 2010 I heard presentations by teachers from provincial towns across Poland who have ongoing exchange programs that have been running for fifteen years, in collaboration with students and teachers from Poland, Israel, and Germany. Polish prisoners now work in a program called *Tikkun* (Hebrew for "repair") to clean Jewish cemeteries, while receiving lectures on Poland's and Israel's Jewish history, organized as part of their rehabilitation.[9] Ceremonial public Hanukkah menorah lightings now take place outdoors in downtown Warsaw, with multiple Jewish denominations and the city's mayor in attendance; in 2010 the president of Poland hosted a Hanukkah program at his home.

But attention should also be paid to the role of active "rebranding" campaigns on both the Polish and foreign Jewish sides of the equation, which have attempted to change the discourse about Poland vis-à-vis Jews. The Polish government has made a programmatic effort to change the country's image in the eyes of the Jewish world, through diplomacy and artistic and cultural collaborations. Major initiatives have ranged from the 1995 establishment of the unique post of ambassador to the Jewish Diaspora, to the significant financial support for the Museum of the History of Polish Jews, to the 2008–2009 Israel-Poland Year that supported the development of a number of powerful artistic projects and exchange programs.

Lobbying on the Jewish side has been rarer. The American Jewish Committee's co-sponsorship of the book project *Difficult Questions in Polish Jewish Dialogue* and their support of the Warsaw-based Forum for Dialogue among Nations, which runs small annual trips for American Jewish leaders to see a different side of Poland, is a notable exception. The San Francisco–based Taube foundation is singular in its championing of Poland as a site of

Jewish renewal. That Taube would run ads with the tag line "Jewish Culture is Alive and Well . . . in Poland," and—given that heterosexual courtship is a domain of major identity activism in the American Jewish community—advertise a "Jewish singles" trip to "romantic Krakow" is provocative. Along with the new Krakow Jewish Community Center's bold choice of "Never Better" as the center's slogan (speaking back at the familiar Holocaust-oriented watchword "Never Again"), these are plainly interventionist choices, signaling a call for a shift in attention from a focus only on Europe's Jewish wound at the expense of the fascinating processes of healing.

The Regulation of Jewishness and the Fate of "Jewish Space"

There is so much that feels triumphant in the reestablishment of institutions in Poland for "core" Jewish communal life, culture, and practice. In the shadow of the hundreds of such institutions that existed in the city before the war that were dissipated as their members were annihilated, how could there not be? Yet my aim is for this process of reconstruction to be recognized as something more complicated—and in my opinion, more hopeful—than the reestablishment of a terrain for Jewish cultural performance, production, and community building *ex nihilo,* an imported Jewish life raft thrown from Israel or the United States into an abject sea in which a few Jews may still be adrift. Such a view would erase two decades of creative caretaking and cultivation of Jewishness by local actors, Jews and non-Jews alike.[10]

Further, I want to draw attention to the ways in which the institutionalization of local Jewishness in Kazimierz also "formats" it—to use anthropologist Andrew Shryock's term. Jewishness must be legible to foreign observers to enable its acceptability to and smooth integration into dominant transnational channels of Jewish communal knowledge and practice.[11] Such cultural formatting always entails both gains and losses, unevenly distributed across diverse landscapes of stakeholders. Kazimierz is a unique and fragile social ecology. Claims made on behalf of "the community" mask a range of dissent, fissures, and silencing. The creation of more spaces explicitly for Jews has implications for the quarter's character as a "Jewish space" in Diana Pinto's visionary sense: broader than a Jewish community, an agora where Jews and non-Jews can engage around issues of Jewishness, an exemplary marker of a pluralist democracy.[12]

Existing amidst the broader cultural flows in the first twenty years after the end of communism in Poland, in relation to Jewishness, Kazimierz constituted something like what Hakim Bey has called a "Temporary Autonomous Zone" (TAZ): a space ignored or not yet mapped by the institutional powers that be, giving rise to dreams of and experiments with the kind of "free culture" that crops up in situations of "cracks and vacancies" in structures of authority.[13] Like a TAZ, Kazimierz's cultural anarchy and even the impermanence of many of its institutions seemed a key component of its Jewish creativity and freedom, existing for a time beyond the constraints of definition. It was a space where fragments of earlier Jewish formations, destroyed or diminished by the Holocaust and communism, were being lured into the half-light of sudden, unsure openness, by a collection of Jews and non-Jews with various, often overlapping claims on them: personal, political, entrepreneurial. There was a frontier sensibility through the 1990s, where anyone with gumption could stake a claim.

Against the bleak backdrop of still-dilapidated Kazimierz, each new space felt like a haven, avant-garde, significant, and up for fierce debate. Topics ranged from religion, history, and klezmer music, to Jewish and Polish identity, antisemitism and sexual orientation, tourism and Hollywood. They were hashed out in candle-lit cafés and apartments in the quarter, often late at night, interspersed with music and merry-making. Who was in and who was out of this rag-tag band of Jewish seekers depended not on ancestry but on commitment and vision and who just kept showing up. There were artists, musicians, business owners, students and intellectuals, locals and tourists and ex-pats. They spoke Polish and Russian and English and French and German; some were learning Yiddish and Hebrew. Foreign Jewish visitors were sought-after emissaries, bringing coveted knowledge and resources. Everyone had a story; all seemed important.

If the accretion of memorial and commercial projects has in part normalized Jewishness in Kazimierz—both empowering and reducing it to one of many new cultural options Poles are exploring—transnational forces have also had a disciplining effect on local Jewishness itself.[14] Perhaps the biggest change has been the opening in 2008 of Krakow's Jewish Community Center, part of a larger international association of such centers in Europe, North and South America, and Israel. Housed on Miodowa Street next to the Tempel Synagogue, in a purpose-built four-story building (the funds for which were donated by Britain's Prince Charles), the JCC is directed by young American Jew, Jonathan Orenstein. The building's very ambiance is evidence of a page being turned in Krakow's Jewish life. The room housing the "senior club"— the space for the older generation of Krakow Jews—has a timeworn décor, with sentimental, dark, melancholy artworks referencing prewar themes and wartime experience that captures the sensibility of those who grew up in the long shadow of the Holocaust (an aesthetic it shares with the Jewish-themed cafés in the surrounding quarter). The rest of the building is exploding with light and color. Comics and graphics, buttons and tote bags and T-shirts, photos and posters with sexual innuendoes, and the new Warsaw Jewish arts and literature magazine *Cwiszn* (Yiddish for "in between") pepper the hallways, the lobby, the street-facing windows. There are no security guards or metal detectors, just a smiling young volunteer—occasionally—behind the welcome counter.

It takes a certain amount of courage for someone newly exploring Jewishness to cross the threshold of a shiny new building labeled "Jewish Community Center"—somewhat more, presumably, than a potential consumer entering a commercial enterprise like a "Jewish Bookshop" or "Jewish Café." This new entryway into Jewishness thus also serves as a new boundary, with a filtering effect on Jewish participation in the city. In addition to contact information, the JCC membership form asks prospective members to check a box indicating their Jewish pedigree (family branch and generation, conversion, or none).[15] While Orenstein confers discretionary membership on those non-Jews who he feels have made significant contributions to local Jewish life, one prominent non-Jewish broker of Jewish culture in the quarter told me he refused the offer of free membership because he protests this form of ethnic labeling.

Further, while new institutions like the JCC or Chabad may be seen by some as evidence that the "tiny local Jewish community . . . has begun to stake its own, more confident, public claim in delineating the parameters of the Krakow Jewish universe," there are important questions to be asked about what constitutes "the community," and if the influences attempting to determine new parameters for Jewishness are truly local.[16] These newly "official" Jewish spaces are in large part constituted by impressive Western-funded facades, foreign leaders, and imported standards of Jewishness—standards that are themselves not only not universally accepted but are in bitter conflict with each other. The Polish rabbinate is affected by decisions by the Israeli (Orthodox) religious establishment, and the latter's recent, controversial tightening of conversion criteria has implications for prospective Polish converts. Definitions of Jewish authenticity are further complicated by questions of power and resources, and an intra-community battle has been raging over the Polish state's recent recognition of a second "official" religious community with a progressive agenda, alongside the Orthodox.[17] A key question, then, is whether the shifting focus of Jewish activity in Kazimierz toward these essentially transnational mainstream Jewish institutions will mean that some local individuals with non-normative (i.e., non-*halakhic*, non-religious, non-genetic, or non-ethnic) affiliations to Jewishness—which means, in essence, most Polish Jews—may be told or may feel they don't belong.

Perhaps more significant, will those deemed "real Jews," who are told they do belong—people who five or ten or fifteen years ago could be found debating issues of Jewish concern in Café Ariel or the Jarden Jewish Bookshop—less frequently enrich this larger civic space with their presence, evacuating its connection to "core" Jewish concerns entirely? The emergence of a more segregated landscape of diversity, where each "culture" gets its own separate terrain, may diminish the space where each person's internal plurality—along with significant intergroup encounters, reckonings, and reconciliations—can be explored. I find myself wondering about the fate of the "in-between" subject positions, social forms and processes that emerged and found a kind of haven in Kazimierz, those I sketched out in the preceding chapters. What about hybrid social space? And expansive, multifarious, ethically (as opposed to ethnically) motivated identifications? Will fluid categories become newly fixed? Will spontaneous, face-to-face encounters and difficult conversations across ethnic differences be regulated, burdened with an official framework, or diminished? Will the intermingling of the entrepreneurial and the ethical disengage? And what will be the consequences of whatever changes do come to pass, across the social spectrum: for dedicated caretakers of Jewishness, individuals on Jewish quests, those with hybrid senses of self, as well as for those local Jews and would-be Jews who may flourish in strong, normative community structures?

As forms of core Jewish "regulation" encroach, Kazimierz's uniqueness appears nonetheless to be inflecting these imports. JCC director Jonathan Orenstein—an American ex-pat whose many years in Krakow have afforded him an expansive view of the local Jewish ecosystem—prizes openness and inclusiveness for all JCC comers, regardless of their background or level of Jewish commitment. He understands the JCC's constituency not as Jews per se, but the "Jewish-identified." He has tapped into the energy and excitement of this "frontier" community and its many hangers-on, forging a model for young Jewish community that he believes Jewish leaders in the West would be wise to follow. Under his direction the JCC has put special emphasis on the Jewish notion of *tikkun olam* (humanity's responsibility in working in partnership with the creator to repair the world) through participation in broader—or other groups'—struggles. The JCC currently runs a women's group and an HIV-positive support group; is involved in the greater Polish movement for the protection of animals; and has co-sponsored a "Poland Diversity Tour" workshop encouraging allegiance with other minorities. In addition, in May 2011 over twenty JCC members marched in the somewhat embattled "Equality March" (Marsz Równości), Krakow's equivalent of a gay pride parade, under a large banner bearing a rainbow Star of David and proclaiming "Jews for Tolerance."

Pluralism is embedded in the Krakow JCC's mission. Its brochure states that the JCC's purpose is to "engage with Jews and non-Jews from all backgrounds," and a recent article in the English-language *Krakow Post* echoed this message, stressing that the institution is "not a place that welcomes only Jews, or offers only information and activities related to Jewish culture and religion."[18] Openness is also a public relations strategy; along with the American Joint Distribution Committee the JCC recently sponsored "7@nite," a nighttime visit to Kazimierz's synagogues, which were outfitted with DJs on the *bimas* (synagogue pulpits), art workshops, and a rock concert (as well as lectures on the fundamentals of Judaism) until early morning. An astounding 5,000 people attended, including 500 who began the evening with a *havdalah* ceremony (marking the end of Shabbat) on the roof of the JCC.

If the JCC is thus the new center of Jewish gravity in Krakow, it appears that the current leadership is attempting to institutionalize openness, to retain some "Jewish space" *within* a space for Jews. Under his direction, the JCC is both strengthening its own "official" Jewish mandate and contributing energy to "para-Jewish" endeavors whose interests it shares: the Jewish bookshops, cafés, museums, and festivals. Many of these latter institutions, despite being run by either self-defined non-Jews or not-quite-Jews, are being recognized not only as fellow travelers and crucial allies to work with, but also as Jewish cultural innovators and invigorators to learn from. Indeed, the lesson is drawing interest beyond Krakow: Robert Gądek, deputy director of Krakow's Festival of Jewish Culture, recounted to me with a sense of pleasant surprise that he was the only non-Jew invited to present at the first European Seminar on Creativity and Innovation in Jewish Culture in France in July 2011, an event sponsored by the European Association of Jewish Community Centers, the American Jewish Joint Distribution Committee, and the Jewish Federation of France, and "addressed to Directors of JCCs, Cultural departments of Jewish communities . . . lay leaders in charge of culture, etc."[19] But again, mainstream Western Jewish institutions are coming late to recognizing and valuing such forms and actors in the domain of Jewish culture, long embraced by the non-Jewish stewards of Kazimierz as a Jewish space.

What will Kazimierz be in twenty more years? The quarter's most important social work may be behind it. How its very particular forms of Jewishness will evolve, what it will contribute to local Jewish and civic life and to Poland's and Europe's self-imaginings as the Holocaust recedes in time, as well as how it will be looked upon from more dominant Jewish geographical centers are unanswerable questions. But the neighborhood's most recent past makes a strong case for attending not only to past tragedy but to future possibility.

Reconciling Jewish Spaces: *Milieux de Mémoire* and Possibilities of Pluralism

I have worked to trace and make visible the painful reverberations of the Holocaust not usually captured in public memorialization of the event: how it continues to touch not only those who experienced it, but also those who grew up in its shadow; and that its echoes influence the ways individuals and groups marked by it interact with each other. Given these unseen realities, I wanted to show others what I saw in Kazimierz: how a difficult heritage site can function simultaneously as an archive and a touchstone of memory, as well as a site of *possibility* for both intergroup and intergenerational rehumanization and reconciliation. Such possibility involves interpersonal exchanges and the construction of new categories of human belonging that transcend rather than perpetuate the violent patterns and wounds of the past, offering instead aspirations for interconnection, justice, and repair.

There are real battles for the maintenance of inclusive democracy in the Polish and Jewish worlds, for visions of the nation that prize equal citizenship for all and the protection of minority rights. Just as there are two Polands—an inward-looking, ethno-nationalist camp, and the more expansive, multiculturalist, civic-nationalist one—there is a growing schism in the Jewish world between those whose own narrative of victimhood trumps all other concerns and those whose commitment to inclusive liberalism is forcing them to reconsider pillars of contemporary Jewish belonging (particularly Zionism) whose dominant forms increasingly conflict with more universal values.[20] Particular, divergent visions of the past, as we know, are prized weapons in these battles.

If scholars should not—as one historian recently protested—"be concerned first and foremost with their role as reconcilers,"[21] neither should reconciliation be pitted against scholarship, even if that scholarship dredges up truly terrifying, enraging facts. A middle ground, it seems, can be found, one that doesn't demand that all parties embrace a single representation of a shared past, but helps members of the groups in conflict "enter into the minds of different members of the other group . . . to clarify for them the conditions under which each group's images of the other were formed, and to explain why certain actions by members of one group were interpreted by members of the other as they were."[22] Reconciliation as an experience and a process of coming to terms with the past does not, in any case, happen according to top-down policies or scholars' rational ideals. It has its own social and emotional logic, and a messy vitality, some of whose character and potential I have tried to document in this book.

The Jewish past is present in Poland, and in Kazimierz, in unique ways, making it a special place for Jewish and Polish regeneration and redefinition, of return and release from traumatic repetition, a site of potentially "conciliatory heritage."[23] Jewish space there harbors key ingredients of a *milieu de mémoire*—a social, evolving, embodied environment of memory (which Pierre Nora dismissed as a bygone form)—because fragments of the material, social, cultural, and perhaps psychological heritage of an earlier, disrupted reality gravitate there. But Kazimierz's potential *milieu* is unique, because the heritage of the past—Jewish knowledge, familiarity, commitment, and pain—is distributed not along mono-ethnic lines but has been more broadly dispersed. "You have all of these people who aren't Jewish," as Larry, the American Jewish visitor to Kazimierz observed, "who are connected, who are *definitely* connected."

In Kazimierz, forays into Jewish heritage can transcend pre-fabricated, escapist itineraries. The quarter offers new entryways into a painful and ambivalent heritage-scape, full of foreboding foreignness, and fraught with anger, anxiety, guilt, and fear. Kazimierz has a special magnetism, and its Jewish spaces remain a hub for cultural seekers. On any day of the week in the Jarden Jewish Bookshop one might encounter the following: A British man inquiring, "Primo Levi—you got that in English?" A young, brown-skinned French Jew with *peyes* trying on a black velvet *yarmulke* with uneven gold glitter trim exclaiming, "I love these *kippot* here—I've never seen anything like this anywhere!" A strapping Polish security guard pointing to the glass case above the counter and explaining to another guard, "This is a *mezuzah*."

These visits enable groups separated by past conflict and present geography to "revisit" both each other and remains of their earlier selves that have not traveled well. They keep dialogues open and intimate aspects of history accessible for ongoing identity projects. And they enable us to know ourselves through and with others, by experiment and error, mimesis and differentiation. This need not be narcissism, in which the "other" is merely a static prop for use by the self. It can be a site of real, intersubjective intimacy, a way to engage with one another's perspectives. Such self-constructing interactions among Poles and Jews also reveal the very constructedness of identities themselves, of our own agency in the process of construction. They offer the opportunity to revalue discarded aspects of our cultural and historical selves when we notice others valuing them.

*   *   *

If this book began with a look at the Jewish cultural challenges, motivations, and rewards of attempts to loosen the boundaries of Jewish identity, it has tried to attend equally to parallel struggles on the Polish cultural side. In Kazimierz I saw both Poles and Jews pushing against unitary, permanent, and separate identities that would join us by "blood." Poles were acknowledging their own Jewishness, holding space for difference in their own history. And Jews were embracing a more fluid, more fully diasporic sense of self, acknowledging the intimate ways they have been shaped by the broader cultural environments in which they have sojourned. These two notions of pluralism are differently grounded—one refers to the boundaries of (Jewish) ethnic space, and the other pertains to the openness of (Polish) national space. Yet Poland's (and perhaps larger Europe's) Jewish spaces are reminders of pluralistic ways of being, and unique sites in which different configurations of belonging meaningfully overlap.

Pluralism is not just a pretty slogan about loving thy neighbors. Rather, it begins by recognizing our own individual multiplicities, the many fault lines that run through each of us. If more Poles accepted their own internal plurality, if identification with Jewishness among Poles, whether based on descent or affinity, didn't taint, but rather was celebrated, perhaps the identity-based injustices of the past could be more easily acknowledged, addressed, and transcended. Those individuals who experience their own inner difference in pressing ways may be at the forefront of a shift, and change may come from their efforts to find and create spaces to be themselves. We might ask, then: What broader cultural and political implications does Jewish space, or even an altered Jewish-Polish relationship, have? What does it say about the possibilities for felt experiences of community and belonging for a wider range of people in this globalizing world? To what extent may we see emergence of broad solidarities as opposed to new boundaries or deepened essentialisms?

The boundary-crossing cultural identifications in Kazimierz are deeply embedded in a specific Polish-Jewish memorial frame, and I have observed the limits of its transferability. A Jewish man I know who is highly sensitive to the complexities of Poland's Jewish history and decries the ignorant and inflammatory ways Jews and Poles can talk about their shared history can nevertheless casually say that he feels offended when Arabs walk the streets of Tel Aviv as if they belong there, and that the great mosque in Jaffa should have been destroyed when the State of Israel was established. And after showing me the tidy local Jewish cemetery, whose renovation he had overseen in collaboration with American Jewish funders, the mayor of a small Polish town turned to me convivially and said that it was particularly important for Jews and Poles to embrace shared Judeo-Christian traditions now that "we" have a new enemy in Europe in the form of Islam. This discourse was echoed by a Polish diplomat at a recent conference on Polish-Jewish relations, who said that one reason Poland and Israel had developed such a strong allegiance in recent years was due to the lack of a significant Muslim or Arab population in Poland that would be naturally hostile to Israel and Jews.

If Poles (or other Europeans) use the idea of Jews only to further stabilize a new sense of embattled (if slightly expanded) "us," then the potential of Jewish space backfires, incorporating Jews into a new exclusionary hierarchy. But there are suggestions that broader inclusiveness is indeed being forged within Poland's new landscape of difference. Repeated encounters with other "others"—aside from Jews—during my fieldwork in Kazimierz suggest that if Jewish space has been Poland's first acceptable space for public expression of difference, it has drawn different kinds of difference into its orbit. Leaders of Poland's Jewish community affirmed to me that the high proportion of homosexuals participating in Jewish activities is a kind of "open secret" in the community. The notable presence of gay men in leadership positions in Kazimierz's "Jewish" venues is mirrored in the way Krakow's gay venues have presented clear affinities to Jewish causes, and during my fieldwork, following flows of young people involved in Jewish renewal in the quarter landed me more than once in Krakow's gay nightclubs. These latter spaces were the only non-explicitly Jewish public sites in which I ever saw *yarmulkes* worn, and casual talk there suggested sympathy to Jewish causes (perhaps in part because these clubs were targets of periodic neo-Nazi harassment).[24] As new "others" continue to arrive or emerge in still Poland, they may find Jewish space an attractive haven—as it seems to have been for Marysia, an Afro-Polish (and physically handicapped) young woman, and Witek Ngo The, the child of Vietnamese immigrants, both of whom recently worked as volunteers for Kazimierz's annual Festival of Jewish Culture.[25]

Western Europe is still seen as the continent's progressive half, having done due diligence vis-à-vis the Holocaust in contrast to a backward, ossified East. This view is being unsettled.[26] The vibrancy and grassroots impulses of many of Poland's initiatives may represent a leading edge in the reintegration and renaissance of Jewish heritage in Europe. Questions may be posed regarding how well Western Europe has really dealt with racism. Western complacency, self-congratulation, or even guilt fatigue may dovetail dangerously with a superficial embrace of (mostly absent) Jews in ways that strengthen xenophobia toward today's much more present others.[27]

On the other hand, while Poland may be unique in twenty-first-century Europe as a place where calls for more Jewish and Holocaust memory are still the dominant progressive stance, there are murmurs of Western political frames encroaching. These are most visible in foreigners' projects that have used Poland to stage their own critiques of the broader politics of Holocaust commemoration. There have been complex cultural interventions in the form of installations and performances by Israeli artists like Yael Bartana, who built a mock kibbutz on the site of the Warsaw Ghetto and founded the "Jewish Renaissance Movement in Poland," and the group Public Movement, which led a "counter-march" at the Warsaw Ghetto uprising memorial, critically mirroring nationalistic Israeli youth missions but wearing unmarked white outfits and fictional flags of no nation. More straightforward political statements were made by left-wing Israeli activists and conscientious objectors, who spray-painted "Free Gaza" and "Liberate all the ghettos" in Hebrew on a remnant of the Warsaw Ghetto wall.[28]

Countries across Europe are struggling with increasing ethnic diversity, debating the shape and bounds of the pluralisms they espouse and the problems that arise when ideals of liberal universalism bump up against group particularities. In Poland—a still largely ethnically and religiously homogenous country—the struggle is grounded much more in the past than in the present. This means that Poles can take managed risks—like exploring Jewishness in places like Kazimierz—without having to immediately face the consequences of having "difference" next-door. While it is easy to dismiss such manageable forays into otherness, in examining the question of how pluralism works it is worth considering what spaces for such "experimental" experiences of pluralism can do.

"Jewish space" is not a panacea. What it makes possible for some (through blurring, innovation, and exchange) will certainly threaten others (who prize longstanding cultural configurations and boundaries). What one celebrates as hybridization is for another dilution or corruption of sacred, embattled traditions, or even a threat to the group's survival. An entirely fluid play of shifting identifications is clearly utopian. Nor should every form of emerging Jewishness in Poland necessarily be celebrated. Yet loss—even overwhelming loss—does not leave only void or abjection, but also lays the groundwork for new growth. And the shades and gradations and admixtures of Polishness and Jewishness I encountered in Kazimierz suggested a variety of investments in cultural memory and continuity existing beyond those enshrined in dominant discourses and sanctioned by powerful institutions and interest groups.

What value might these have? "Core" Jewish institutions may benefit from proximity to such broader Jewish spaces. Even the most seemingly dense, narrow, exclusive sites in the landscape of Jewishness give to and take from the larger cultural atmosphere. Indeed, formations of core and periphery shift and change with the constant traffic of individuals moving back and forth among them. With their allegiances and understandings of multiple worlds, "in-between" people can act as brokers and messengers, agents of integration in a landscape of proliferating differences. Thus populated, civic space can be a medium for cultural dialogue, for learning from difference, for recognizing similarity, and for evolution in conversation with others. Minority heritage as a product, process, and space can make alternative cultural models more widely accessible. Cultural blurrings and cross-fertilizations will only increase as the global movement of people and ideas escalates. The untapped possibility of heritage sites, then, is as sites of perpetual return and reanimation, and the multiplication and remixing of identifications. In the other direction—ethnic retrenching, exclusion, attempts at purification—lie the horrors of the last century.

Postscript

Ethnography is not going to change the world. But if in its modern disciplinary guise it contributed to mythic certainties about bounded cultures with reified essences, in today's postmodern moment it can offer the gifts of unsettlement, of difficult questions, of new confrontations with comfortable cultural, historical, and memorial tropes. Such disquiet can lead to anxiety and retrenchment. But the suggestion of new perspectives is also the stuff of possibility, the first step toward change.

I met a Jewish woman in Montreal who recently returned from visiting Poland with her parents; they had been born there and fled during the Holocaust. I was introduced to her as someone who wrote about Poland, and the woman began telling me of her experiences: not only how emotionally heavy the trip had been, but particularly how bizarre it was that Poles were celebrating Jewish culture in the form of cafés, figurines, and klezmer. We had quickly gotten past the state-level issues of property restitution, monument building, Holocaust education, and the culture of the Catholic Church. But as with so many people I spoke to, on the issue of the Jewish heritage tourist industry she was impassioned in her denunciation. I nodded, said I understood how she might have felt, that I had experienced similar emotions myself. Weary of trying to confront this depth of feeling with my own particular pedagogical project of seeing possibility, I added only that I had spent some time researching this issue and had discovered it was "complicated." "Complicated?!" she retorted. "What's complicated? It's just weird." I added that Poles were also working through the difficult past, and that some of these "superficial" forms she had noticed were part of a much deeper process of coming to terms with history in the present. She seemed unconvinced, and I finally said that part of the problem was that nothing that Poles could ever do would make up for our feelings of loss. "After all, what are they supposed to do?" I said. She shrugged and looked at me a bit suspiciously, and we went our separate ways.

The friend who had introduced us died tragically a few weeks later, and the woman and I met again, this time at his memorial service. Standing in line to offer our condolences to the man's parents, the woman turned to me and said that she had been thinking about something I had said, which she couldn't get out of her head. Her manner was less judgmental this time, more thoughtful. "What *are* the Poles supposed to do?" she reported having suddenly asked herself. She told me that the question continued to percolate, and she was no longer so sure she knew the answer.

*   *   *

Part of my concern in this book has been what is and is not habitually seen, and how new framings can expand our fields of vision. I want, then, to acknowledge a final frame which of necessity will remain mostly empty, existing alongside the Jewish-oriented ones. My engagement with Kazimierz followed—in typical ethnographic form—certain social tributaries, primarily Jewish ones. Yet while Kazimierz functions as a touchstone for so many projects of Jewish identification, many of its local inhabitants experience it mostly in much more mundane frames.

Walking through the New ("Jewish") Square market on winter mornings, among vendors of fruits and knick-knacks tending their bags and blankets of wares, I would watch the old Polish men sitting on overturned buckets, clutching pigeons between their worn gloves, their white breath rising in clouds in the frozen air. I wrote notes to myself to remember these "other" experiences, the ones missed by visitors who step into a familiar story of absent Jewishness they have brought along for the ride. As Polish Jewish community leader Konstanty Gebert told me at the end of a long interview about Jewish Kazimierz,

> One question we haven't been asking is, so what happened in between [the prewar Jewish Kazimierz and the current revival/gentrification]? I mean, people *have* been living in Kazimierz for fifty years, right? They have nothing to do with the Jews. It was *their* district for fifty years. Now, are we in any way interested in *their* authenticity, and what *their* experience of Kazimierz was? . . . Is *that* an element of the Kazimierz experience?

This layer of hard, everyday reality in Kazimierz forms, at most, a vague backdrop for the Jewish encounter many visitors to the quarter seek, as well as for the Polish culture brokers involved in helping to provide the sought-after experience. Despite these non-Jewish inhabitants' physical centrality to the quarter—the hordes of tourists pass directly beneath their windows—their lives go on outside of most discussions of Kazimierz as Jewish space. And yet they cannot avoid being touched by its developments. On a walking tour with an American Jewish family whose father tried to locate his boyhood apartment, we entered a broken-up courtyard. A construction worker with a surly stance eyed us. He was covered in plaster dust, with his work gloves and a wheelbarrow at his side. His worn T-shirt read, "Mitchell's Bar Mitzvah—We had a great time." Telling his story, I concede, is a job for another ethnographer.

PROLOGUE

1. Malinowski (1922: 18–19) coined the term "the imponderabilia of actual life" to describe "a series of phenomena of great importance which cannot possibly be recorded by questioning or computing documents, but have to be observed in their full actuality."

INTRODUCTION

1. The numbers are difficult to establish, given the range of definitions of Jewishness and the ongoing proliferation of Jewish-themed organizations. According to the 2011 Annual Statistical Yearbook of Poland, there are 3,023 registered members of Jewish associations, but this count includes only the Social-Cultural Society of Jews in Poland, the Association of Jewish Combatants and Victims of the Second World War, the "Children of the Holocaust" Association, and the Association of the Jewish Historical Institute in Poland (2011: 204). The Union of Jewish Religious Communities would add at least another 1,000. The International Religious Freedom Report for 2011 put out by the U.S. Department of State Bureau of Democracy, Human Rights, and Labor notes that Poland's Jewish organizations estimated their actual numbers to be 20,000. Bilewicz and Wójcik (2010) state that "in the 2002 census, only 1,055 Polish citizens declared Jewish ethnicity; however, the local Jewish community estimates the number of its members as 5,000–10,000" (citing Cordell and Dybczynski [2005]).

2. A 2003 survey by the London-based Institute for Jewish Policy Research counted 196 individual events including seven Jewish cultural festi-

vals (Gruber [2003: 359–60]). New initiatives have taken place in every subsequent year.

3. Pinto (2002: 251).

4. Engel (2009: 921).

5. Lehrer (2012).

6. Shamir grew up in Poland, and his father was murdered by Poles during World War II. He made his controversial statement in 1989, when he was prime minister. Schneerson—himself born and raised in Poland—until his death in 1994 presided over the Chabad sect, organizers and financiers of Jewish religious and educational missions whose goal is a presence in all parts of the world where there are Jews. The Rebbe is popularly thought to have made a ruling against establishing a Chabad branch in Poland (e.g., Gebert and Datner [2011: 16]). Although there is some debate in the Lubavitch community both regarding the original proscription and why it was overridden (see, e.g., "Chabad in Poland" and comments on the article), Chabad established centers in Warsaw in 2005 and in Krakow in 2007.

7. Ury (2000: 214).

8. Stein (2008).

9. Jewish life was, of course, reborn earlier, in an efflorescence that lasted from 1945 until 1968. See for example Aleksiun (2002), Berendt (2006), and Berendt (2009). I am referring here to the more recent rebirth that struck outsiders as particularly incredible.

10. Scholars such as Gross (2001), Snyder (2010), Bartov (2008), Grabowski (2011, 2003), and Engelking-Boni (2003) have highlighted new spaces of annihilation, secrets, betrayals, and usurpations that are coming to define the complexity of the Holocaust in Eastern Europe.

11. The phrase "vanishing diaspora" is from Wasserstein (1996). The handful of ethnographies on European Jewry published over the last two decades provide an alternate view (Borneman and Peck [1995], Boyarin [1991], Buckser [2003], Bunzl [2004], Goluboff [2003]), as do newly assertive indigenous voices that have been translated (on Poland, see Krajewski [2006], Gebert [2008]). See also Ruth Gruber (2002).

12. Krajewski (2006).

13. Meng (2010: 47). See also Meng (2011: chap. 2), Auerbach (2011), Kichelewski (2008: 178–81), Shore (1998: 44–61).

14. Irwin-Zarecka (1989: 35), Aleksiun (2004).

15. I am not sure why or how some Poles picked me out as Jewish. Friends usually pooh-poohed the notion that I stuck out visually. And yet I also heard

that I had "that special Semitic" look. While humans undoubtedly rely in part on phenotype in categorizing people, it is rarely decontextualized. Other markers such as (in this case) my Western clothes, camera, interest in Jewish subjects or sites, or obvious unfamiliarity with my surrounds surely play a role, as does exposure to gossip or media reports about Jewish travel to Poland.

16. The significance of these characteristics for fieldwork has been discussed (respectively) by Marcus (1995), Gupta and Ferguson (1997), and Bruner (2005a).

17. Exceptions include Shryock (2004), Kurin (1997), Clifford (1988).

18. Clifford (1986: 117).

19. Zamlers were an integral part of Jewish ethnography at its inception, recruited by major research projects in the area of the Russian Pale of Settlement spearheaded by the famous S. Ansky expedition as well as the YIVO (Yiddish Scientific Institute) in Vilna, from the early 1910s through the 1930s.

20. The concept of "virtual Jewishness" was coined by Ruth Gruber (2002). For my critique of the notion see Lehrer (2013).

21. Shryock (1997: 5).

22. Cf. Holsey (2008).

23. Nora (1989: 7–25).

24. Scheper-Hughes and Bourgois (2004). See also Minow (1998).

25. Halpern and Weinstein (2004: 305).

26. See for example Pinto (2008).

27. See for example Tunbridge and Ashworth (1996), Macdonald (2006, 2009), and Meskell (2002).

28. Breglia (2006: 3). Notable exceptions are Breglia (2006) and Macdonald (2006, 2009).

29. Breglia (2006:11).

30. See Malkii (1995).

31. Of course, even positive identifications with an "other" can uphold a dominant symbolic order, and there were certainly moments of patronizing, essentializing identification during my research.

32. On Anglo-Americans "playing Indian," see Deloria (1998); on Germans doing "ethnic drag" (as "a sophisticated orchestration of forgetting") see Sieg (2002); for discussions of American blackface that offer a spectrum of liberatory implications, see Lott (1995), Lhamon (1998), and Harrison-Kahan (2011).

33. Irwin-Zarecka (1989) uses this term for the limitations on reincorporating Jewish memory in late communist Poland.

34. See Irwin-Zarecka (1989: 5) and Steinlauf (1997).

35. See Gebert (1994a: 161–67). This dialogic quality continues to be a significant factor in Jewish heritage development and interpretation, from the central role Israeli and North American Jewish experts play in the developing Museum of the History of Polish Jews to foreign Jewish participation in the evolution of Krakow's Festival of Jewish Culture. My focus here is on the grassroots level.

36. Irwin-Zarecka (1989: 90–91).

37. I use "heritage brokers" following Kurin's "culture brokers," which he uses to describe individuals who bring audiences together and represent, translate, negotiate, or exchange representations or definitions of culture or cultural goods among them. Kurin (1997: 19).

38. See Bunzl (2005: 499–508). Feldman (2001) has also noted how an interest in Jewish heritage served the cause of racism against immigrants.

39. Rothberg (2008: 23).

40. They include Virginia Dominguez's notion of "love" in ethnography (1993), Julie Ellison (2009: 9, 11, 13; 2011, 2012) and Ronit Avni's discussions of "hope" in critical scholarship and activism (2006), Hirokazu Miyazaki's elaboration of "hope as a method" (2004), and Paul Farmer's "hermeneutics of generosity" (1992: 235, 243, 250, 263). See also Behar (1997).

41. Todorov (2001).

42. Maddocks (1984).

43. I am aware of Wendy Brown's powerful critique of discourses of tolerance—that the notion does not affirm but only conditionally permits fundamentally unwanted others, while making the "tolerant" society appear superior to "less civilized" cultures and thus underwriting Western imperialism (2006). My usage here is practice-oriented, regarding individual ground-level acts of respect, empathy, compassion, and acceptance.

44. Cohen and Kennedy (2004: 36–37).

45. Jolanta Drzewiecka, in her compelling discussion of the rhetorical construction of Polish and Jewish memory and identities, claims a similar analytical politics, noting that she "strategically chose to concentrate [her] critique on the Polish side—the side [she] is more intimately connected with" (2010: 290).

46. Portelli (1997: 68). He is quoting Passerini (1988).

47. After my main fieldwork ended, I began a series of public interventions into Jewish heritage tourism in Kazimierz with the help of local culture brokers. For one example see www.conversationmaps.org/odpowiedz.

48. Marcus (1997).

49. Hirsch (1995: 82).

50. The quotation is from Michael Walzer, cited in Green (2000: 3).

51. Steinlauf (1997: 109).

52. These have been described most accessibly by Jan Gross in his widely read books *Neighbors* (2001), *Fear* (2006), and *Golden Harvest* (2012). On postwar pogroms see also below, chapter 1, note 10.

53. Antisemitic publications were also found in the church-basement bookshop Antyk in Warsaw's Plac Grzybowski, but after a public outcry in the press it was closed in 2007.

54. On state-sponsored scholarship, and the way it is empowered and resourced to influence the Polish citizenry, see Grabowski (2008: 253–270). On recent Polish diplomatic reaction to new historical scholarship, see Frommer (2011).

55. Blobaum (2005: 18).

56. Bilewicz and Krzeminski (2010: 234–43).

57. Gebert and Datner (2011: 29). The late right-wing president Lech Kaczynski personally phoned the chief rabbi of Poland, Michael Shudrich, to apologize when Shudrich was verbally abused by a young man shouting "Poland for the Poles!" in May 2006.

58. Gebert (2006).

59. For an inventory of Poland's favorable diplomatic actions toward the Jewish world, see Taube (2006).

60. I heard him use this phrase during Krakow's Festival of Jewish Culture in June 2008. See also Ulman (2007).

61. For an analysis of the status and student reception of Holocaust education in Poland, see Milerski (2010). On the current state of Jewish studies in Poland, see Wodziński (2011).

62. Barry Spielman, an American-Israeli Jewish visitor to Poland, noted his internal debate about "the very serious question of whether there is a need to go back to Poland, whether it is a good or bad thing for me and my family, and for Jews in general" (2000: 69), citing an article arguing against Jewish travel to Poland as a transgression of the commandment of "not returning to Egypt" (2000: 68; cited with permission).

63. A *Shabbos goy* is a non-Jewish individual (*goy;* plural: *goyim*) who regularly assists a Jew or Jewish organization by performing tasks on the sabbath (*Shabbos*) that are forbidden to Jews by Jewish law.

64. The theme of non-Jews (including Palestinians, American blacks, and Latin Americans) as bearers of Jewish memory and shapers of Jewish experience has been explored recently in literature, films, and plays by Danae Elon, Ruth Behar, Elizabeth Rosner, and Tony Kushner.

65. *Halakha,* or Jewish law, reckons Jewishness through the mother. These Polish "new Jews" often have but one Jewish grandparent, if any.

1. MAKING SENSE OF PLACE

1. Kugelmass and Orla-Bukowska (1998) anticipate a number of the issues I discuss here.

2. Halkowski (2003: 108).

3. For a concise, detailed overview of the history of Jewish Kazimierz, see Tighe (2001).

4. Just as Jews were long barred from purchasing houses in Christian areas, in 1564 they were awarded the privilege "*de non tolerandis Christianis,*" enabling them to block Christians from buying property in the Jewish area.

5. The most significant of these is the "Mappa," an Ashkenazic commentary by Rabbi Moses Isserles (commonly known by his acronym, "Rema" or "Remu") on Joseph Caro's Sephardic legal code *Shulkhan Aruch,* which is still the primary reference for Jewish legal questions in the Orthodox community in the present day.

6. Moses Isserles's grave in the Remu cemetery draws Jewish pilgrims from around the world, especially on the holiday of Lag ba'Omer, a date midway between Passover and Shavu'ot and the anniversary of Isserles's death.

7. Duda (1999).

8. Malecki (1997: 95).

9. The larger municipal district of Krakow had a prewar Jewish population of 250,000.

10. For information on anti-Jewish violence perpetrated by Poles in the postwar years, see Cichopek (2003), Gross (2006), Kersten (1992), and Szaynok (1992). On the later, March 1968 anti-Jewish campaign sponsored by the Polish communist government, see Steinlauf (1997: 75–88) and Stola (2000).

11. Irwin-Zarecka (1989); Meng (2011).

12. Shaw and Karmowska (2003: 13). See also Cameron and Zuziak (1994). The one tangible outcome was the establishment of the Kazimierz Local Of-

fice, a kind of NGO/community organization that advocated for improved quality of life for the neighborhood's residents, coordinated the creation of green spaces, and published a quarterly newsletter, *Praktyczny Kazimierz* (Practical Kazimierz), for residents (with an occasional special issue in English for tourists). Written by local people, it discussed issues of local concern, the quarter's Jewish heritage among them. The office closed in 2003. For a discussion of the Action Plan's conception and brief life, see Murzyn (2004: 261–62).

13. Murzyn (2006: 120).

14. Murzyn (2006: 168).

15. Urban economist Monika Murzyn-Kupisz noted that in 2003 over one-fifth of Kazimierz plots (or 22 percent of its surface area) had unclear ownership status, which fell to 16 percent by 2005 (Murzyn [2006: 166]).

16. For a detailed survey of Kazimierz's revitalization experience from 1989 to 2004, see Murzyn (2006).

17. Kapralski (2011: 183). It should be noted, however, that Kapralski himself critiques the emergence of spaces in Poland that represent Jews in the framework of multiculturalism, while the framework of the Holocaust is significantly less visible in the Polish landscape.

18. Global Volunteers Poland (1994).

19. Some tourist literature may exacerbate this problem. The mid-2000s municipal brochure "Three Days in Krakow" states, misleadingly, that "having regained their property, heirs of former inhabitants immediately took to renovation. Today, beautifully restored buildings stand in close vicinity to those devastated, whose number luckily continues to diminish" (8).

20. Anatewka was the name of the fictional Russian Jewish shtetl depicted in the Broadway musical and Hollywood film *Fiddler on the Roof.* Noah's Ark café moved to Jacob Street in summer 2011.

21. On the most recent developments in the quarter from an urban planning and economics perspective, see Murzyn-Kupisz (2012).

22. Dov Ber Maisels became chief rabbi of Krakow in 1832. He supported the cause of Polish independence, actively aiding multiple uprisings and working to convince Jews to share his views. Berek Joselewicz (1764–1809) was a Jewish Polish merchant and a colonel of the Polish Army during the Kościuszko Uprising. He commanded the first Jewish military formation in modern history.

23. Quoted in Hayden (2005: 87).

24. The former term is from Kowalska (1992: 369), the latter from Kugelmass (1995: 395). The older generation of Jews in Poland has been discussed

briefly by Kowalska (1992) and Misak (1999) and depicted in the popular photographic volumes *Remnants: The Last Jews of Poland* (Niezabitowska and Tomaszewski [1986]) and *Out of the Shadows* (Serotta [1991]).

25. Baruma (1997); Gebert (1994a, 1994b, 1997, 1999a, 1999b, 2001, 2002, 2008); Gebert, Kobus, and Olej-Kobus (2009); and scores more, including almost any issue of *Midrasz*, the journal Gebert founded; Krajewski (2006); Mayer (2002); Ronen (1999); Rosenson (1996, 1997). See Czyżewski's "Borderland" organization website: www.pogranicze.sejny.pl; Jagielski (1997). See also Bergman and Jagielski (1996); Jagielski and Pasieczny (1995); Krajewska (1993, 1983); Krajewski (1997); Wiśniewski, Elliott, and Elliott (1998).

26. See Gebert and Datner (2011) and www.tskz.pl.

27. The American funds are listed on the Center for Jewish Culture's website as coming from the Congress of the United States of America, provided through the Polish-American Joint Commission for Humanitarian Assistance in Warsaw.

28. In 1995 it separated from Kino Grafitti and became the Festival of Jewish Culture Association.

29. During the off-season, in addition to the occasional one-off musical event, for many years the festival has supported what began as an organic, spontaneous, local, annual "March of Remembrance" from Kazimierz to the Płaszów Nazi camp memorial, with participants stopping at significant Holocaust-related sites for speeches, readings of historical excerpts and psalms, and recitations of *Kaddish* (the Jewish mourners' prayer) at the former camp site. At the outset it involved mostly private citizens involved in Jewish cultural activities who felt moved to commemorate the victims of the Krakow ghetto; today it involves a few hundred people (increasingly including local Jewish and Christian clergy and visiting Israelis) and is underwritten by the local authorities. It remains the only formal ceremony commemorating the liquidation of the ghetto and the murdered Jews of Krakow. Photographs from the 2011 March of Remembrance can be viewed on the festival's website, fkz.pl/index.php?pl=galerie&nrg=150&lang= (accessed January 19, 2012).

30. Just under 50 percent of the festival's budget comes from foreign Jewish sources, while 40 percent comes from Polish local and state authorities, and a lesser amount from Polish local and national business circles. Robert Gądek, festival manager, personal communication, January 18, 2012.

31. Zubrzycki (2006); Huener (2004).

32. Such institutional kinship also exists at the grassroots level: Marek, the owner of Noah's Ark, began as a waiter at Café Ariel before opening his

own restaurant. It also ties the "official" Jewish community to "para-Jewish" cultural sites: Dominick Dybek (former son-in-law of Tadeusz Jakubowicz, head of Krakow's Jewish religious community) began as the local leader of the Lauder Foundation youth club, then orchestrated the multimedia Izaak Synagogue Project, and in 2003 opened the elaborately designed Jewish-style café Once Upon a Time in Kazimierz on Szeroka Street.The endogamy extends beyond the world of Jewish heritage venues into the city's broader cultural fabric: Krzysztof Gierat, a co-founder of the festival with Makuch, was briefly vice-mayor of Krakow in the early 1990s and is today the artistic director of the Krakow Film Festival; Zdzisław Leś, owner of the Jarden Jewish Bookshop, is the former director of the city's renowned House of Culture.

33. It is frequently the case that these unsanctioned individuals, as well as some individuals who work for and benefit from the official community, are not Jewish.

34. With the exception of local public characters, whose identities are impossible to obscure, I use pseudonyms.

35. The Klezmer Hois website shows photos of their former guests, including film directors Roman Polanski, Andrzej Wajda, and Steven Spielberg (and the star actors from the cast of Schindler's List), as well as Prince Charles of Great Britain.

36. Excellent discussions of these identity management projects can be found in Frank (1997), Glick (1982), Kirshenblatt-Gimblett (1995 and 1998, esp. chap. 2, "Exhibiting Jews"), and Dominguez (1993). Examples where Jewish ethnographers have made their personal, cultural, or memorial projects explicit include Bahloul (1996), Behar (1995, 1996, 1997), Boyarin (1996), Meyerhoff (1979), and Zborowski and Herzog (1952).

37. For discussions of salvage ethnography, see Gruber (1970) and Clifford (1989).

38. Marcus and Fischer (1986: 167).

39. For a brief description of Sasak's project see Kapralski (2011: 186).

2. THE MISSION

The epigraph is from Metzger (1992: 11).

1. Gazeta Wyborcza (2000).

2. For a consideration of the meanings of antisemitic graffiti in the city of Łódź, Poland, see Sinnreich (2004).

3. While there have been numerous one-time initiatives, the group City Space (przestrzenmiasta.pl) initiated a long-term project in 2008 to engage

private individuals in photographing antisemitic and racist graffiti (and other threats to ethnicity, race, religion, beliefs, or sexual orientation) and posting the photos on a map on the project website, so the group can clean up the offending writing. The project is funded by the Polish Stefan Batory Foundation, founded in 1988 in cooperation with Polish democratic opposition leaders, part of American philanthropist George Soros's Open Society Foundation network.

4. Pinto (2008: 25).

5. Kugelmass (1992).

6. On these developments, see Aviv and Shneer (2005: 53–56). For full-length studies of Jewish identity travel to Israel, see Habib (2004) and Kelner (2010).

7. Aviv and Shneer (2005: 52).

8. This "crisis of continuity" was spurred in part by a demographic study of American Jews that suggested declining group cohesion and commitment to Jewish religious practice, particularly among youth. See Kosmin et al. (1991).

9. Kosmin et al. (1991: 61).

10. The percentage estimate is from Alex Danzig, consultant to the Israeli Ministry of Education, personal communication in 2000. Yaron Karol Becker of the Polish Institute in Tel Aviv stated that approximately 30,000 Israeli youth went to Poland in 2006, a number corroborated by Jacek Olejnik of the Polish embassy in Israel (formerly of the Israeli embassy in Poland) in October 2010 (personal communication). Alon Simhayoff, cultural attaché at the Israeli embassy in Warsaw since 2008, states that there were 200 participants in 1988, 24,000 in 2008, and 27,000 in 2009 (2010: 182).

11. Green (2002). The website of the Auschwitz museum estimates that out of 1,405,000 visitors in 2011, there were 62,000 Israelis. Presumably some portion of the other nationalities are also Jewish (particularly of the 52,000 coming from the United States). See en.auschwitz.org/m/index.php?option=com _content&task=view&id=953&Itemid=7 (accessed August 25, 2011).

12. See Lehrer (2012).

13. See Lehrer (2010).

14. Aviv and Shneer (2005: 52).

15. Between its founding in 2000 and the summer of 2011, Birthright Israel had taken over 260,000 young Jews from fifty-two countries on these free trips. The organization's website states that "Taglit-Birthright Israel is a unique, historical partnership between the people of Israel through their

government, local Jewish communities (North American Jewish Federations; Keren Hayesod [the central fundraising organization for the State of Israel]; and The Jewish Agency for Israel), and leading Jewish philanthropists" (Taglit-Birthright Israel).

16. Kelner (2010).

17. Feldman (2008: xviii, 20, 26).

18. Kelner notes that on Birthright trips, any counternarratives are "addressed at the level of discourse only," while the preferred Israeli state narratives are more powerfully communicated through embodied practice (2010: xix). Both Stier (2003) and Feldman (2008) describe how what Stier calls "gaps and ruptures in the persuasive process" (Stier 2003: 185) of the trips they studied do not interfere with the overall influence of the ritual.

19. The Montreal firm InfoFeedback Survey Services Inc., which was contracted to carry out research, queried participants from trips between 2000 and 2008 and based their conclusions on 231 participant responses from the 2004–2008 trips. See InfoFeedback Survey Services Inc. (2010) and Lungen (2010).

20. Feldman (2008; 2005); Kugelmass (1995); Sheramy (2007); and Stier (2003).

21. Carol Kidron (2003) discusses the conscious cultivation of Holocaust-based identity among children and grandchildren of survivors. More popular writers like Michael Lerner (2003) and Avraham Burg (2008a) address the cultural costs of "traumatic repetition" of Holocaust memory.

22. The two institutional models are not only similar but are interconnected. Despite being a mostly diaspora-populated program, MOTL has been run since its inception by a combination of Israeli and North American administrators and educators. Between 1988 and 1992 MOTL maintained offices in Jerusalem, Tel Aviv, New York, and Miami, and since 1995 the program has been run out of international headquarters in New York in coordination with an office in Tel Aviv. Sheramy (2007).

23. Stier (2003: 151).

24. Stier (2003: 150).

25. Weissman (2004).

26. Sheramy (2007: 307).

27. Sheramy (2007: 314).

28. Stier (2003: 189) and Feldman (2008: 62–63) discuss this embodied manipulation in the context of the MOTL and the Israeli Ministry of Education tours, respectively.

29. Aviv and Shneer (2005: 62).

30. The first quote is cited in Sheramy (2007: 318). The second is from page 5 of "Guidelines and Handbook for Delegation Heads, Group Leaders, Madrichim, and Students"; published in 1994, the booklet was given to me by the Tel Aviv MOTL office for use during the trip when I was hired as a guide in 2000.

31. Bruner (2005: 1–2).

32. Feldman (2005: 232) notes the silencing of Polish guides by Israeli tour organizers more generally.

33. March of the Living (1994: 2–3).

34. Sheramy (2007).

35. Feldman (2005: 242) and (2008: 23).

36. Bruner (2005: 24).

37. Percy (1975: 47).

38. Kugelmass (1992: 428).

39. Feldman (2005: 224); Stier (2003: 165). A recent news article described how one Israeli high school student had her grandfather's Auschwitz number tattooed onto her own arm after her class trip to Poland (Rudoren 2012).

40. Bauman (2001: 12, 14).

41. *Gazeta Wyborcza* (2000).

42. In 2012, Krakow's local Jews spoke explicitly back at the March of the Living, in a form of a large banner that was hung between the gateposts of Krakow's Jewish Community Center when the March was in town, which read, in all capital letters, "HEY MARCH OF THE LIVING! COME INSIDE AND SEE SOME JEWISH LIFE." The word "life" was in larger letters, presumably to contrast with the March's focus on death.

43. A similar issue arises with antifascist graffiti depicting a swastika hanging from a gallows (indicating the attempt to execute fascism); for those not familiar with the common Polish graffiti convention, the swastika alone is eye-catching, suggesting the graffiti is pro- rather than anti-fascist. Another example of such overdetermination of symbols are the visible gouge marks left where *mezuzahs* were torn off by the Nazis (or later by Poles)—what Feldman calls "Jewish stigmata" (2008: xvii)—which are programmatically pointed out by guides and ritually photographed by visitors. But one building in Kazimierz, the former Kazimierz Biznes Klub at the corner of Izaak and Jakub Streets, already in 1998 had an interesting addition—in renovating the building, the owners included a new doorframe with a perfectly carved out empty space in the shape of a mezuzah. An apparent attempt to preserve the

memory of the building's Jewish inhabitants (or to prepare for the future return of Jews), this empty space is repeatedly read as an example of memory's erasure, as just another gap where a mezuzah had been torn away.

44. Schnitzer (1998). On Polish complicity in the Holocaust, see note 57 below.

45. Macdonald (2009:167, 178–82).

46. Polish Jewish American businessman, philanthropist, and founder of Warsaw's Beit Warszawa reform Jewish community Seweryn Aszkenazi. Ulman (2006).

47. Sheramy (2007: 308)

48. Zubrzycki (2006: 131). A recent study showed a positive correlation between antisemitic sentiments among Poles and their contact with Jewish tour groups. Bilewicz and Wójcik (2009).

49. Gruber (1994: 11).

50. Feldman (2008: 242).

51. These associations may be more likely among older generations; a younger Polish friend told me that her generation would likely associate flag waving with Polish neofascist groups such as Młodzież Wszechpolska or Narodowe Odrodzenie Polski, which occasionally walk the streets with Polish flags.

52. Szulc (2007). While the Polish ambassador to Israel indicated that the structure of the trips must change, Israeli ambassador David Peleg's concern was reportedly that "such articles portrayed Israel's youth in a negative light." Eichner (2007a) and Salama-Scheer (2007).

53. Kashti (2009). By 1990, after only two annual visits, the international Jewish press was registering criticisms of the trips (see Cashman [1990]), and particular attention was garnered in 1999 when students on one of the Israeli trips hired strippers for their hotel room in Poland. See Arnold (1999). Another incident occurred in 2007, when a group of thirty-five young Jewish men broke into the Majdanek death camp memorial site. See Eichner (2007b).

54. Bruner (2005b). Cited with permission.

55. Feldman (2005: 226).

56. Mission trips often bring pre-packaged food for participants, discourage them from spending money in Poland, and allow little or no time in itineraries for leisure activities like shopping.

57. Regarding Polish complicity in the persecution of Jews during the Nazi occupation, see Gross (2001) and (2006) and Gross and Grudzinska Gross (2012); on blackmail and denunciation, see Grabowski (2011) and (2003) and Engelking-Boni (2003), respectively.

58. The request was reported as honored in June 2007. The precise new name as listed on the UNESCO website is Auschwitz Birkenau: German Nazi Concentration and Extermination Camp (1940–1945) (whc.unesco.org/en /news/363). See also the Ministry of Foreign Affairs of the Republic of Poland website campaign "Against Polish Camps" (www.msz.gov.pl/Against,Polish ,camps,2076.html).

59. For President Obama's recent gaffe on this topic, and the resulting backlash from the Polish prime minister Donald Tusk, see Landler (2012).

60. Chancellery of the Prime Minister of the Republic of Poland, Policy Planning Department. (1999: 3).

61. This problem was brought to my attention by Andrzej Folwarczny, director of the Warsaw-based Forum for Dialogue among Nations, who organizes meetings between Jewish mission groups and Polish youth, as well as Jacek Olejnik, who has worked for both the Polish and Israeli embassies in both countries, and Eli Rubenstein, National Director of MOTL Canada. Folwarczny lamented the lack of partners on the American side for the Polish groups interested in Polish-Jewish dialogue.

62. Weinbaum (1988: 7).

63. See Gitelman (2003).

64. The guide does, however, include six pages about Rwanda and Darfur.

65. MOTL materials in 2007 included contemporary Polish Jewry in their curriculum materials only in a brief "postscript" based on outdated (1994) research that questions how welcome the local community is in Poland (www .motl.org/resource/curriculum/curriculum_11.htm).

66. Ulman (2006).

67. Konstanty Gebert, quoted in Zubrzycki (2006: 130). For other criticisms of the MOTL from a Polish Jewish perspective, see "Przyjeżdzają" [They are coming] (1999).

68. Critics include Yaron Karol Becker, director of the Forum for Polish-Jewish Dialogue at the Polish Institute in Tel Aviv (Szostkiewicz [2006: 82–83]); Haifa University law professor Fania Oz-Salzberger (2007); Israeli author and politician Avraham Burg (2008b); Israeli novelist Amos Oz (Eldar [2007]); Drew University professor and Orthodox rabbi Allan Nadler (1998: 7); former Israeli Minister of Education and Meretz Party leader Shulamit Aloni (see Halevi [1993: 28]); and late Israeli journalist Amos Elon (1993: 5).

69. For Polish criticisms see Gebert (1997b: 15) and Jutkiewicz (1997: 15–17).

70. Cited in Weinbaum (1998: 7–8).

71. John Karam's (2007) study of youth trips for diasporic Lebanese to sites of Lebanese martyrdom illustrates how some students deconstruct and resist the intended inculcation.

72. See Slutsky (2007); Ulman (2006); Schnitzer (1998: 20–36); Gruber (1994: 11).

73. The agreement was renewed in 2009 extending through 2011, with automatic two-year extensions unless terminated by one of the parties.

74. Jacek Olejnik, Polish Embassy in Israel, October 2010, telephone conversation with author. Alon Simhayoff (2010:182) notes that, while most Israeli youth do not meet their Polish cunterparts, between 2004 and 2009 around 13,000 Israeli students did have a chance to do so.

75. Individual efforts have also led to meetings between Polish and Israeli dancers, police officers, and soldiers.

76. I interviewed Eli Rubenstein at the Association for Jewish Studies meeting in Toronto in December 2007.

77. Kowalska (2009).

3. THE QUEST

The first epigraph is from Tuwim (1993: 43), originally written in April 1944 for the first anniversary of the Warsaw Ghetto uprising.
The second epigraph is from Rothenberg (1974).

1. Hirsch (2008: 107).

2. Feldman (2008).

3. Shapira (1998: 50).

4. Klingenstein (1993: 566)

5. The problem of such ideological templates as relates to recording and archiving Holocaust survivor testimony has been discussed by Diane Wolf (2007). Noah Shenker discusses the selection of "exemplary witness[es]" and "good testimony" in the use of such testimony (2009: 45, 48, respectively), and Monica Patterson (2013) similarly points to the emergence of "good stories" in the South African Truth and Reconciliation Commission.

6. Kugelmass (1996: 212).

7. Boyarin (1991: 11).

8. Epstein (1979); Hass (1990); Wardi (1992).

9. Two exceptions are Hirsch and Spitzer (2010) and Ronen (2007).

10. This methodological innovation complements the important question of "multi-sitedness" (Marcus 1995) and asks questions about the cultural ex-

perience of movement and transience itself (Fincham et al. 2010; Büscher et al. 2010).

11. Shapira (1998: 54–55).

12. Menachem Daum's film *Hiding and Seeking* (2004) is an excellent example of a "post-Polish" Jew using unresolved connections to Poland for both personal and cultural-political ends.

13. Huyssen (2003: 25).

14. On Jewish history as "lachrymose" see Baron (1964), as well as Cohen (1991) and Stillman (1991).

15. Basso (1996: 55).

16. Mendelsohn (2002: 26).

17. Feldman (2008: 269).

18. Grossman (1989: 109; my italics).

19. Hass (1990: 2; my italics).

20. Portelli (1997: 70).

21. The transfer of traumatic narrative and even affect among Jews is taking place not only through time, but across space. Former Knesset Speaker Avraham Burg offers a striking anecdote of an Israeli, whose parents were from Iraq, cutting short a business trip to Poland because it was too traumatic: "Everything came back to me," he said. Burg (2008a: 34).

22. Kugelmass (1992: 388).

23. Anthropologist Jasmin Habib (2004: 246) notes a similar "revoking" of her Jewish identity by other Jews because of her sympathetic opinions regarding Arabs in Israel.

24. Mendelsohn (2002: 27).

25. See Stein (2009).

26. See Kidron (2009).

27. Schama (1995: 27–28).

28. Hass (1990: 165).

29. Spielman (2000). Quoted with permission.

30. Jenkins (2002: 75).

31. Zerubavel (1995: xv).

32. Kleinman and Kleinman (1994: 716–17).

33. See Gilman (1991).

34. Kleinman and Kleinman (1994: 717), on Lawrence Langer's notion of "deep memory."

35. Kleinman and Kleinman (1994: 717).

36. On the ways Jews try to pick each other out, which she calls "Jew-Hooing," see Glenn (2002).

37. Bell (1997: xi).

38. Fishman (2002: 12).

39. Percy (1975: 54).

40. Mayer (2002); Cała (2005: 441).

41. The reference is to the August 1999 incident in which a member of the Aryan Nation fired at least seventy rounds into the North Valley Jewish Community Center in Los Angeles; the gunfire wounded five people, including three children.

42. For an excellent ethnographic article on the construction of trauma descendant identity, see Kidron (2008).

43. Rosenwald and Ochberg (1992: 5).

44. Rosenwald and Ochberg (1992: 8).

4. SHABBOS GOYIM

The epigraph is from Gay (1984).

1. Zdzisław told me this in 1994. He has since expanded, and other Jewish bookshops have opened as well: two in Kazimierz—at the Galicja Jewish Museum and in Klezmer Hois's affiliate shop on Józef Street—and at least one in Warsaw, inside the Jewish Historical Institute.

2. Their imprint is called Hagada.

3. Kugelmass (1995).

4. Gawron, "Społeczność żydowska w Krakówie w latach 1945–1995," 209, cited in Murzyn (2004: 394).

5. Cała (2005: 439).

6. Frank (1996).

7. Hoffman (1995: 276).

8. Irwin-Zarecka (1989: 5) coined the term "Jewish Memory Project."

9. Meng (2011); Irwin-Zarecka (1989); Steinlauf (1997).

10. See Gebert (1994a).

11. Irwin-Zarecka (1989: 90–91).

12. See for example Altfelix (2000); Embacher (2002); Bammer (1995: 49); Ochse (1994: 120); and Benz (2002). Regarding Polish engagements with Jewishness in the form of klezmer music, Waligórska (2008: 228) also offers an instrumental view—although a compelling and subtle one—noting how these engagements can function as "political correctness for all occasions,"

and are used as an apologetic rhetorical device by politicians to divert attention from unresolved Polish problems and conflicts, past and present, vis-à-vis Jews.

13. Kauders (2003: 112).

14. Roach (1996: 2).

15. Roach (1996: 36).

16. Goldman (2000: 187, 198–99, 201).

17. Gruber (2003: 363).

18. Makuch (1997: 9).

19. Irwin-Zarecka (1989: 135).

20. Kurin (1997: 19, 39).

21. In the late 2000s the Izaak synagogue was subsequently taken over by the Chabad-Lubavitch sect of Hasidim, and now houses a prayer space and small kosher shop.

22. See chapter 1 note 29 for information on the March of Remembrance. The photograph of Zdzisław is in the book *The Jews of Kazimierz*, written by local Jewish museum director Eugeniusz Duda (1999) and published by the Jarden Jewish Bookshop's own imprint, Hagada.

23. Makuch (1997: 9).

24. Bollag (1995: A29).

25. Howe (2001:52).

26. Gruber (2003: 365–66).

27. Gruber (2003: 365).

28. Hartman (2002: 769).

29. Jochnowitz (1998: 227).

30. Jochnowitz (1998: 226).

31. Today Ornat runs a single culinary/hostel establishment called Klezmer Hois, which includes guest rooms, a klezmer cabaret, and periodic literary salons. He also opened an affiliated bookshop in the High Synagogue building at 38 Józef Street in the late 2000s, and established the publishing house Austeria (www.austeria.pl)—a cutting-edge, bilingual (Polish/English) imprint for Jewish-themed works on history, culture, and religion—which includes works by local Jews and other participants in Jewish revival.

32. But Henryk, too, had his standards: Kugelmass and Orla-Bukowska (1998:327) contains a wonderful ethnographic moment illustrating Henryk's acknowledgment of an "invisible barrier" he would not cross encircling the "bad" Ariel, the locally (Jewishly) ostracized restaurant.

33. Pinto (2002: 251).

34. Gruber (2003: 364).

35. The Forum hotline was established in 1996, but was likely modeled on a similar, informal telephone service that cropped up in the 1980s, as discussed by Gebert (1999b).

36. Jochnowitz (1998: 227).

37. "Why is this night different from all other nights?"

38. Spielman (2000: 11–12).

39. Tencer et al., *And I Still See Their Faces* . . . www.shalom.org.pl/eng/index.php?mid=4.

40. Until mid-1943, all the prisoners at the Płaszów forced labor camp were Jews. In July 1943, a separate section was created for Polish prisoners. Except for "political prisoners," Poles served their sentences and were released. Jews remained in the camp indefinitely, or were sent on to nearby Auschwitz. For inmate population estimates see Offen and Jacobs (2008).

41. Dominguez (2000: 365–66).

42. Gebert (2001: n.p.). I translated Gebert's statement from German, "*In Polen kann man Antisemit sein und gleichzeitig fuer einen anstaendigen Mann gehalten werden.*"

43. Ingall (2003) describes his event in "Making a Tsimes, Distilling a Performance: Vodka and Jewish Culture in Poland Today." I was present at the event, having accidentally come across it during my daily errands.

44. Ingall (2003: 22).

45. Bakewell (1998: 22, 23). Genevieve Zubrzycki, for example, puts forth the useful notion of a "national sensorium," or the way that national mythology is "visually depicted, crystallized in material culture, and embodied in various practices and performances" (2011:22). She notes how the sensorium can "cue certain paradigmatic stories and sentiments, *or their subversion*" (24).

46. Choay (2001: 6).

47. In Polish the sign reads, "*Bajgle. Z Krakowskiego Kazimierza zawojowały cały świat. Najwyższy czas aby powróciły na nasze polskie stoły.*"

48. Thanks to Sławomir Kapralski for drawing this to my attention, as well as to the information about Rafael Scharf.

49. Kirshenblatt-Gimblett (1995: 374).

50. Schama (1995: 27).

51. Polonsky and Michilic (2004: 41).

52. Polonsky and Michilic (2004: 41).

53. Opalski and Bartal (1992: 20).

54. Steinlauf (2001: n.p.).

55. Kirshenblatt-Gimblett (1995: 375).

56. Until his death in 2009, Halkowski was advertised on the Klezmer Hois website as "the only Jewish tour guide in Krakow." In 2010 there was a memorial page for him on the site.

5. TRAVELING TSCHOTSCHKES AND "POST-JEWISH" CULTURE

The epigraph is from Bruner (1996: 300).

1. This particular effigy seems to represent an overlap with the tradition of burning and or drowning an effigy of Marzanna, a Slavic agrarian goddess associated with the cycles of death and rebirth, to celebrate the end of winter.

2. Bogdana Pilichowska (1989: 142) explains that wooden figures of the Jews were sold at three Krakow church fairs: At Emaus on Easter [sic] Monday, at Rękawka on the first Tuesday after Easter, and at Skałka on May 8 (the feast day of St. Stanislaus).

3. Goldberg-Mulkiewicz (1980).

4. Cała (2005: 102) notes, "Anti-Semitic as well as postwar propaganda did not touch people with a traditional philosophy of life," although she states that there were "indirect" effects on their attitudes, "strengthening mechanisms contained in folk culture."

5. Collection of the Seweryna Udziela Ethnographic Museum in Krakow. Another example of a figural beehive in the shape of a Jew circa 1900 is held at the Władysław Orkan Museum in Rabka-Zdroj.

6. Goldberg-Mulkiewicz (1980: 225).

7. Shenhav-Keller (1995: 151).

8. Schauss (1987: 27–28).

9. Gebert (1999a: 29).

10. Organized by Warsaw University professor Marian Pokropek at his private ethnographic museum in Podwarszawskie Otrębusy.

11. Goldberg-Mulkiewicz (1980: 221). Ironically, Czerwiński, who described carving while in a German POW camp "as an indictment of the Germans," noted how camp officers, enamored of his Jewish figurines, greatly improved his lot by trading him valuable commodities for them (Schauss 1987:128).

12. Schauss (1987: 198).

13. Riga (1992: G6).

14. Goldberg-Mulkiewicz (1980: 221).

15. Rogers worked for a foreign foundation to restore and preserve Jewish cemeteries in Poland.

16. Recent press articles debate the meaning of the new spate of figurines holding coins (Jędrzejewski 2012; Keff 2012; Tokarska-Bakir 2012). Shifra Epstein has suggested that this practice may be related to the tradition of rebbes handing out coins to followers in Hasidic courts. Personal communication, July 2008.

17. Some of the production is apparently outsourced to factories in China. Epstein (2009).

6. JEWISH LIKE AN ADJECTIVE

The epigraph is from Krog (2000: 385).

1. Borneman (1996: 132).

2. The last Polish national census in 2002, for example, listed Jewish as an exclusive ethnicity category, alongside but separate from Polish, forcing Polish Jews to check one or the other, but not both (Gebert and Datner 2011: 10).

3. The notion of a "universe of obligation" is from Fein (1979).

4. Borneman (2002: 286).

5. Borneman (2002: 286, 302) stresses that preconditions for reconciliation must include "an appreciation of the intersubjectivity of the present" with the uncomfortable encounters with difference this entails.

6. Kirshenblatt-Gimblett (2006: 40) makes this point in relation to heritage more broadly.

7. Gruber (2002: 11).

8. I thank Stephanie Rowden for this turn of phrase.

9. On the general phenomenon, see Baruma (1997).

10. Krajewski (2006: 164). Anthropologist Andrew Buckser, in his ethnography of the Jewish community of Denmark, notes that Polish Jewish immigrants "resented the [Danish] policies that insisted on a Halakhic definition of Jewishness" (2003: 113). He also mentions the differing responses of the "indigenous" Danish Jews and the Polish immigrant Jews to his own, mixed background—his father was Jewish, his mother not. "Most Danish Jews responded to this formulation by saying, 'So you're not Jewish.' At the [Polish Jewish social] Klub, by contrast, the immediate response was, 'Then you're Jewish!'" (2003: 246n4).

11. These observations are from the Israeli film The Secret, directed by Ronit Kertsner (2001).

12. Cohen (1999).

13. Claire Rosenson (1997) argued for such a definition of Jewishness in her doctoral dissertation on Warsaw's Jewish community.

14. Krajewski (2006: 163). The quote about fraud was made by the late Marek Edelman, last surviving member of the Warsaw Ghetto uprising. The full statement that community leader Konstanty Gebert recalls Edelman making is "You guys are a fraud, a literary fiction. The Jewish people is dead, and you simply thought yourselves up, looking for originality and exoticism. You are not for real" (Gebert 1994a: 165).

15. Tattooing of any kind is widely understood as being forbidden in halakha (Jewish law). See Leviticus 19:28: "You shall not scrape your flesh for a (dead) soul, and tattoos do not put upon you, I am the Lord." It has accrued a further, negative valence for Jews due to the Nazi practice of tattooing concentration camp inmates. None of this, of course, prevents many (especially young) American and Israeli Jews from getting tattoos, or even using tattoos to proclaim their Jewishness. (See for example Dora Apel's chapter "The Tattooed Jew" in her book Memory Effects: The Holocaust and Acts of Secondary Witnessing [2002].)

16. Traditional interpretations of halakha reckon Jewish descent matrilineally only. The Reform and Reconstructionist movements in the United States often accept children of Jewish fathers as Jewish, as does the State of Israel, in principle, under its Law of Return.

17. Ost (2005: 67).

18. www.midrasz.pl/en.php (accessed August 12, 2011).

19. Anna Gulinska, JCC Krakow Shiksa Club, www.facebook.com/group .php?gid=48176897376 (accessed August 15, 2011).

20. Seidman (1998: 266).

21. Butler (1997: 305).

22. "Żydokomuna" has a particular negative valence that makes Zdzisław's comment mocking and daring. The term refers to the widespread European notion that communism is a Jewish plot. While used already in the interwar years, the accusation gained force around the notion that Jews collaborated with Soviets to oppress Poles in Eastern Poland in the early war years (where Jews were said to have "welcomed the Soviets with bread and salt"), and in the harsh security forces (Urzad Bezpieczeństwo [UB]) in the early Polish postwar communist regime.

23. Pogranicze is an organization that uses the arts to support cultural intermingling and dialogue among cultural communities. See www.pogranicze

.sejny.pl. The conference was entitled "The Future of Jewish Heritage in Europe," Prague, Czech Republic, May 24–27, 2004.

24. Butler (1999: xxiii–xxiv).

25. For another example of "Jewish boundary-line redrawing" that illustrates intergroup identification as activism, see Shulamit Magnus's discussion of Jewish converts to Christianity in late nineteenth- and early twentieth-century Russia. These "Good Bad Jews . . . used their positions as both former Jews and current members of the majority religion to help Jews and Judaism in situations of extreme duress," and were thus deemed heroic by key members of the organized Jewish community despite more general theological condemnation of out-conversion (2010:133).

26. Jackson (1996: 179).

27. Gillis (1994: 3; my italics).

28. Michnik (2001: A17; my italics).

29. Błoński (1990: 44).

30. Porter (2002: 26).

31. Trigano (1997: 301).

32. Tokarska-Bakir (2003: n.p.).

33. Tokarska-Bakir (2003: n.p.).

34. Thanks to Butler's (1997: 310–11) discussion of Freud's "melancholic incorporation" for this idea.

35. Butler (1997:305).

36. LaCapra (2001: 215).

37. Boyarin (2003: 203).

38. hooks (1992: 36).

CONCLUSION

The epigraph is from Hannabuss (2000: 363–4).

1. *Cheder* is the name for the traditional Jewish elementary school, teaching basics of Judaism and Hebrew language. The Combatants' event took place on October 26, 2010.

2. Bennett (2009).

3. Burg (2011).

4. Spund (2006).

5. Michlic (2008: 11).

6. Gera (2010).

7. Vasagar and Borger (2011).

8. Lehrer and Waligórska (2013).

9. Klepczarek (2010); Tzur (2012).

10. Interestingly, a 2011 report on Jewish life in Poland based on survey and focus group data among Polish Jews notes that, exceptionally against the broader European scene, Israel is not a main reference point for contemporary Polish Jews, being generally absent from their reflections on a wide range of topics (Gebert and Datner 2011: 28).

11. Shryock (2004).

12. Pinto (2002).

13. Bey (1985). Thanks to Karen Underhill for the reference.

14. A September 2011 Institute for Jewish Policy Research report on Jewish life in Poland found that survey and focus group participants had indicated "marked deterioration of the entire concept of an open community," an inability to relate to established Jewish institutions, and complaints by younger Polish Jews that their project ideas (e.g., setting up a Jewish coffee shop) were turned down by potential sponsors as "not Jewish enough." Gebert and Datner (2011: 12–13).

15. The JCC statutes mandate that membership is open to people with at least one Jewish grandparent, like the Israeli Law of Return. Orenstein had it changed to also include people who make a contribution to Jewish life in Krakow, and those who check the "none" box for Jewish ancestry are judged on a case-by-case basis. Although most JCCs in the United States have an open membership policy, Orenstein's concern, particularly because the Krakow JCC's membership is largely subsidized from abroad, was that if they opened up membership to anyone in Krakow, they would have "10,000 members." His contention is that Krakow's new Jewish community will emerge from the JCC membership, which he thinks, at 300 people, is a good reflection of the contemporary state of Jewish life in Krakow.

16. Gruber (2014).

17. See Beliak (2011) and Liphshiz (2012) on the conflict between Orthodoxy and Progressivism in Poland.

18. Casey (2011).

19. Gądek was on a panel entitled "What is Jewish culture. The role of Jewish creators in our society. The boundaries. Which is the place for young artists and innovation?" European Association of Jewish Community Centers (2011).

20. The conflict was described in a widely read essay, "The Failure of the American Jewish Establishment," by journalist and political scientist Peter

Beinart (2010). The depth of the rift is also illustrated in literary scholar Alvin Rosenfeld's booklet *"Progressive" Jewish Thought and the New Anti-Semitism* (2006), published by the American Jewish Committee, which argues that "progressive" Jews are legitimizing antisemitism by critiquing Israeli policies, as well as the cancellation of prominent historian Tony Judt's speech at the Polish consulate in New York due to his criticisms of Israel. See also Powell (2006).

21. Frommer (2011).

22. This is historian David Engel's gloss of how to approach the attempt to "reconcile" Polish and Jewish views of their shared history (2009: 928).

23. See Lehrer (2010) and (2012).

24. In recent years this connection may have transcended its quasi-secret status, as the plight of homosexuals has become a public topic in Poland. A July 2009 weekend workshop in Krakow called "Antiphobia" (building on a 2005 campaign against homophobia co-sponsored by Krakow's *Czulent* Jewish youth club, *Szterndlech,* a Polish Jewish children's and family magazine, and Israeli Gay Youth) aimed to model coalition-building against acts of intolerance, antisemitism, and homophobia. Kampania Przeciw Homofobii (2009).

25. I mention these two because they stand out in Poland's homogenous (white) phenotypical landscape. Marysia helped with my own festival project in 2008, and I read about Witek in the *New York Times* (Smith [2007]).

26. Michael Meng critiques the way Germany has been the long-held norm of repair and reconciliation in *Shattered Spaces: Encountering Jewish Ruins in Postwar Germany and Poland* (2011: 14–15, 155–57, 208–11, and 254–55).

27. See Feldman (2001), Partridge (2010), Bunzl (2005) and Meng (forthcoming).

28. Pfeffer and Haaretz Service (2010). Other moments in which larger world politics have encroached in Kazimierz's Jewish cultural manifestations in particular include a 2002 call by a Polish veteran's association to cancel Krakow's Festival of Jewish Culture after the standoff between Fatah militants and the Israeli Defense Forces at the Church of the Nativity in Bethlehem, and a 2008 protest—prompted by the Festival's thematic focus that year on the sixtieth anniversary of the establishment of the State of Israel—by the radical nationalist group Narodowe Odrodzenie Polski (Polish National Renaissance), accusing Israel of genocide against the Palestinians. Both instances can be seen as appropriations of these foreign battles for more parochial Polish concerns, as described by Waligórska (2008).

REFERENCES

Aleksiun, Natalia. 2002. *Dokąd dalej? Ruch syjonistyczny w Polsce, 1944–1950*. Warsaw: Trio.

———. 2004. "Polish Historiography of the Holocaust—Between Silence and Public Debate." *German History* 3: 406–32.

Altfelix, Thomas. 2000. "The 'Post-Holocaust Jew' and the Instrumentalization of Philosemitism." *Patterns of Prejudice* 34.2: 41–56.

Apel, Dora. 2002. *Memory Effects: The Holocaust and Acts of Secondary Witnessing*. New Brunswick, N.J.: Rutgers University Press.

Arnold, Michael. 1999. "Israeli Teens Frolic with Strippers after Auschwitz Visit." *Forward*, November 26.

Auerbach, Karen. 2011. "Holocaust Memory in Polish Scholarship." *AJS Review* 35.1 (April): 137–50.

Aviv, Caryn, and David Shneer. 2005. *New Jews: The End of the Jewish Diaspora*. New York: New York University Press.

Avni, Ronit. 2006. "Mobilizing Hope: Beyond the Shame-Based Model in the Israeli-Palestinian Conflict." *American Anthropologist* 108.1 (March): 205–14.

Bahloul, Joelle. 1996. *The Architecture of Memory: A Jewish-Muslim Household in Colonial Algeria, 1937–1962*. Cambridge: Cambridge University Press.

Bakewell, Liza. 1998. "Image Acts." *American Anthropologist* 100.1 (March): 22–32.

Bakhtin, Mikhail. 1986. *Speech Genres and Other Late Essays*. Austin: University of Texas Press.

Bammer, Angelika. 1995. "Xenophobia, Xenophilia, and No Place to Rest." In *Encountering the Other(s): Studies in Literature, History, and Culture*, ed. Gisela Brinker-Gabler, 45–62. Albany: State University of New York Press.

Banac, Ivo, and Irena Grudzinska-Gross, eds. 2011. *East European Politics and Societies* 25.3 (August).

Baron, Salo. 1964. "Ghetto and Emancipation." In *The Menorah Treasury; Harvest a*

Half a Century, ed. Leo Schwartz, 50–63. Philadelphia: Jewish Publication Society of America.

Bartov, Omer. 2008. "Eastern Europe as the Site of Genocide." *Journal of Modern History* 80.3 (September): 557–93. www.jstor.org/stable/10.1086/589591.

Basso, Keith. 1996. *Wisdom Sits in Places: Landscape and Language among the Western Apache.* Albuquerque: University of New Mexico Press.

Bauman, Zygmunt. 2001. "The Holocaust's Life as a Ghost." In *Social Theory after the Holocaust,* ed. Robert Fine and Charles Turner, 7–18. Liverpool: Liverpool University Press.

Behar, Ruth. 1995. *Bridges to Cuba.* Ann Arbor: University of Michigan Press.

——. 1996. "The Story of Ruth, the Anthropologist." In *People of the Book: Thirty Scholars Reflect on Their Jewish Identity,* ed. Jeffrey Rubin-Dorsky and Shelley Fisher Fishkin, 261–79. Madison: University of Wisconsin Press.

——. 1997. *The Vulnerable Observer: Anthropology That Breaks Your Heart.* Boston: Beacon Press.

Beinart, Peter. 2010. "The Failure of the American Jewish Establishment." *New York Review of Books,* June 10. www.nybooks.com/articles/archives/2010/jun/10/failure -american-jewish-establishment (accessed October 23, 2011).

Beliak, Haim Dov. 2011. "Rabbi Haim Beliak comment to the Konstanty Gebert's article." Beit Warszawa, October 21. www.beit.org.pl/index.php?option=com _content&view=article&id=102%3Arabbi-haim-beliak-comment-to-the-konstanty -geberts-article&catid=39%3Acurrent-events&Itemid=77&lang=en (accessed August 20, 2011).

Bell, Catherine. 1997. *Ritual: Perspectives and Dimensions.* New York: Oxford University Press.

Bennett, Roger. 2009. "Letter from Krakow: At Annual Culture Festival, Jewishness Is Abundant; Jews, Scarce." *Tablet.* www.tabletmag.com/arts-and-culture/music/9994 /letter-from-krakow (accessed August 20, 2011).

Benz, Wolfgang. 2002. "Jewish Existence in Germany from the Perspective of the Non-Jewish Majority: Daily Life between Anti-Semitism and Philo-Semitism." In *Unlikely History: The Changing German-Jewish Symbiosis, 1945–2000,* ed. Leslie Morries and Jack Zipes, 101–18. New York: Palgrave.

Berendt, Grzegorz. 2006. *Życie żydowskie w Polsce w latach 1950–1956. Z dziejów Towarzystwa Społeczno-Kulturalnego Żydów w Polsce.* Gdańsk: Wydawnictwo Uniwersytetu Gdańskiego.

——, ed. 2009. *Społeczność żydowska w PRL przed kampanią antysemicką lat 1967–1968 i po niej.* Warsaw: IPN.

Bergman, Eleonora, and Jan Jagielski. 1996. *Zachowane synagogi i domy modlitwy w Polsce [Hidden Synagogues and Prayer Houses in Poland].* Warsaw: Jewish Historical Institute.

Bey, Hakim. 1985. *The Temporary Autonomous Zone, Ontological Anarchy, Poetic Terrorism.* New York: Autonomedia.

Bilewicz, Michal, and Ireneusz Krzeminski. 2010. "Anti-Semitism in Poland and Ukraine: The Belief in Jewish Control as a Mechanism of Scapegoating." *International Journal of Conflict and Violence* 4.2: 234–43.

Bilewicz, Michal, and Adrian Wójcik. 2009. "Antysemityzm na gruzach sztetł. Stosunek polskiej młodzieży do Żydów w miastach i miasteczkach południowej i wschodniej Polski." In *Etniczność, pamięć, asymilacja,* ed. Lech M. Nijakowski, 153–67. Warszawa: Wydawnictwo Sejmowe.

———. 2010. "Does Identification Predict Community Involvement? Exploring Consequences of Social Identification among the Jewish Minority in Poland." *Journal of Community and Applied Social Psychology* 20: 72–79.

Blobaum, Robert. 2005. "Introduction." In *Antisemitism and Its Opponents in Modern Poland,* ed. Robert Blobaum, 1–19. Ithaca, N.Y.: Cornell University Press.

Błoński, Jan. 1990. "The Poor Poles Look at the Ghetto." In *My Brother's Keeper? Recent Polish Debates on the Holocaust,* ed. Anthony Polonsky, 34–48. London: Routledge. Originally published in *Tygodnik Powszechny,* January 11, 1987.

Bollag, Burton. 1995. "Poland's Jewish Studies." *Chronicle of Higher Education* (August 3): A29, A31.

Borneman, John. 1996. "Identity, Exile, and Division: Disjunctures of Culture, Nationality, and Citizenship in German-Jewish Selfhood in East and West Berlin." In *Jews, Germans, Memory: Reconstructions of Jewish Life in Germany,* ed. Y. Michael Bodeman, 131–60. Ann Arbor: University of Michigan Press.

———. 2002. "Reconciliation after Ethnic Cleansing: Listening, Retribution, Affiliation." *Public Culture* 14.2: 281–304.

Borneman, John, and Jeffrey M. Peck. 1995. *Sojourners: The Return of German Jews and the Question of Identity.*Lincoln: University of Nebraska Press.

Boyarin, Daniel. 2003. "Interrogate My Love." In *Wrestling with Zion: Progressive Jewish-American Responses to the Israeli-Palestinian Conflict,* ed. Tony Kushner and Alisa Solomon, 198–204. New York: Grove Press.

Boyarin, Jonathan. 1991. *Polish Jews in Paris: The Ethnography of Memory.* Bloomington: Indiana University Press.

———. 1996. "Waiting for a Jew: Marginal Redemption at the Eighth Street Schul." In *Thinking in Jewish,* ed. Jonathan Boyarin, 8–33. Chicago: University of Chicago Press.

Breglia, Lisa C. 2006. *Monumental Ambivalence: The Politics of Heritage.* Austin: University of Texas Press.

Brown, Wendy. 2006. *Regulating Aversion: Tolerance in the Age of Identity and Empire.* Princeton, N.J.: Princeton University Press.

Bruner, Edward. 1996. "Tourism in Ghana: The Representation of Slavery and the Return of the Black Diaspora." *American Anthropologist* 98.2: 290–304.

———. 2005a. *Culture on Tour: Ethnographies of Travel.* Chicago: University of Chicago Press.

———. 2005b. "The Role of Narrative in Tourism." Unpublished manuscript. October.

University of Illinois, Urbana-Champaign, Department of Anthropology workshop series.

Buckser, Andrew. 2003. *After the Rescue: Jewish Identity and Community in Contemporary Denmark.* New York: Palgrave Macmillan.

Bunzl, Matti. 2005. "Between Anti-Semitism and Islamophobia: Some Thoughts on the New Europe." *American Ethnologist* 32.4 (November): 499–508.

Burg, Avraham. 2008a. *The Holocaust Is Over, We Must Rise from Its Ashes.* New York: Palgrave Macmillan.

———. 2008b. "One on One: Utiopian or Contrarian?" *Jpost.com*, August 20.

———. 2011. "When the Walls Come Tumbling Down." April 1. www.haaretz.com /weekend/magazine/when-the-walls-come-tumbling-down-1.353501 (accessed August 12, 2011).

Buruma, Ian. 1997. "Poland's New Jewish Question." *New York Times,* August 3.

Büscher, Monika, John Urry, and Katian Witchger, eds. 2010. *Mobile Methods.* New York: Routledge.

Butler, Judith. 1997. "Imitation and Gender Insubordination." In *The Second Wave: A Reader in Feminist Theory,* ed. Linda Nicholson, 300–316. New York: Routledge.

———. 1999. *Gender Trouble: Feminism and the Subversion of Identity.* New York: Routledge.

Cała, Alina. 2005. "Review of Larry Mayer 'Who Will Say Kaddish?'" *Polin: Studies in Polish Jewry* 18.

Cameron, D., and Z. Zuziak, eds. 1994. *Kazimierz Action Plan: A European Union ECOS Funded Project Carried out by the Cities of Cracow, Edinburgh and Berlin, 1993–94.* Cracow: Viator Co.

Casey, Anthony. 2011. "21st Jewish Culture Festival, Krakow." *Krakow Post,* June 19. www.krakowpost.com/article/2567 (accessed August 12, 2011).

Cashman, Greer Fay. 1990. "The March of the Living." *Jerusalem Post,* May 15.

"Chabad in Poland." January 24, 2008. www.crownheights.info/index.php?itemid =10252 (accessed December 30, 2011).

Chancellery of the Prime Minister of the Republic of Poland. 1999. *Poland: A Few Words about Its History, Culture and the Present.* Policy Planning Department.

Choay, Francoise. 2001. *The Invention of the Historic Monument.* Cambridge: Cambridge University Press.

Cichopek, Ania. 2003. "The Cracow Pogrom of August 1945: A Narrative Reconstruction." In *Contested Memories: Poles and Jews During the Holocaust and Its Aftermath,* ed. Joshua Zimmerman, 221–38. New Brunswick, N.J.: Rutgers University Press.

Clifford, James. 1986. "On Ethnographic Allegory." In *Writing Culture: The Poetics and Politics of Ethnography,* ed. James Clifford and George Marcus, 98–121. Berkeley: University of California Press.

———. 1988. *The Predicament of Culture: Twentieth-Century Ethnography, Literature, and Art.* Cambridge, Mass.: Harvard University Press.

———. 1989. "The Others: Beyond the 'Salvage' Paradigm." *Third Text* 3.6: 73–78.

Cohen, David William, and Michael D. Kennedy, eds. 2004. *Responsibility in Crisis: Knowledge Politics and Global Publics.* Ann Arbor: University of Michigan Press.

Cohen, Mark R. 1991. "The Neo-lachrymose Conception of Jewish-Arab History." *Tikkun* (May-June): 55–60.

Cohen, Robert. 1999. "For a Priest and for Poland, a Tangled Identity." *New York Times,* October 10.

Cordell, K., and A. Dybczynski. 2005. "Poland's Indigenous Minorities and the Census of 2002." *Perspectives on Politics on Society in Europe* 6.1: 103–28.

Czyżewski, Krzysztof. "Borderland." www.pogranicze.sejny.pl (accessed December 18, 2011).

Deloria, Philip J. 1998. *Playing Indian.* New Haven, Conn.: Yale University Press.

Dirks, Nicholas B. 2001. *Castes of Mind: Colonialism and the Making of Modern India.* Princeton, N.J.: Princeton University Press.

Dominguez, Virginia. 1993. "Questioning Jews." *American Ethnologist* 20.3: 618–24.

———. 2000. "For a Politics of Love and Rescue." *Cultural Anthropology* 15.3 (August): 361–93.

Drzewiecka, Jolanta A. 2010. "Public Memories in the Shadow of the Other: Divided Memories and National Identity." In *Handbook of Critical Intercultural Communication,* ed. T. K. Nakayama and R. T. Halua, 286–310. Malden, Mass.: Blackwell.

Duda, Eugeniusz. 1999. *The Jews of Cracow.* Krakow: Hagada and Argona.

Eichner, Itamer. 2007a. "Polish Weekly Slams Israeli Youth." *Ynet News,* May 21. www.ynetnews.com/articles/0,7340,L-3402765,00.html (accessed November 23, 2011).

———. 2007b. "Haredim Visiting Majdanek Vandalize Death Camp." *Ynet News,* August 2. www.ynetnews.com/articles/0,7340,L-3432851,00.html (accessed November 4, 2012).

Eldar, Akiva. 2007. "Amos Oz, in Spain, Says He Doubts the Government Is Brave Enough for Peace." *Haaretz,* October 28.

Ellison, Julie. 2009. "Keyword: Hope." *Imagining American News* 13 (Fall): 9, 11.

———. 2011. "The Humanities and the Public Soul." In *Practicing Public Scholarship: Experiences and Possibilities Beyond the Academy,* ed. Katharyne Mitchell. Malden, Mass.: Wiley-Blackwell.

———. 2012. "Lyric Citizenship in Post 9/11 Performance: Sekou Sundiata's *The 51st (dream) State.*" In *American Literature's Aesthetic Dimensions,* ed. Christopher Looby and Cindy Weinstein. New York: Columbia University Press.

Elon, Amos. 1993. "The Politics of Memory." *New York Review of Books* 40.16 (October 7). www.nybooks.com/articles/archives/1993/oct/07/the-politics-of-memory (accessed December 2, 2012).

Embacher, Helga. 2002. "Belated Reparations? Philosemitism in the Second Generation." Paper presented at the Fourth European Social Science History Conference, February 27–March 2, The Hague, Netherlands.

Engel, David. 2009. "On Reconciling the Histories of Two Chosen Peoples." *American Historical Review* 114.4 (October): 914–29.

Engelking-Boni, Barbara. 2003. *Szanowny panie gistapo. Donosy do władz niemieckich w Warszawie i okolicach w latach 1940–1941.* Warszawa: Wydawnictwo IFiS PAN (Institute of Sociology and Philosophy, Polish Academy of Sciences).

Epstein, Helen. 1979. *Children of the Holocaust: Conversations with Sons and Daughters of Survivors.* New York: Putnam.

Epstein, Shifra. 2009. "Imagining Hasidism in Wood and PVC: Hadisic Figurines Made Today in Poland, Ukraine and Israel." ZUTOT 6. Leiden: Koninklijke Brill NV.

European Association of Jewish Community Centers. 2011. "European Seminar on Creativity & Innovation in Jewish Culture." www.eajcc.eu/news.aspx?id=1163 (accessed August 20, 2011).

Farmer, Paul. 1992. *AIDS and Accusation: Haiti and the Geography of Blame.* Berkeley: University of California Press.

Fein, Ruth. 1979. *Accounting for Genocide.* New York: Free Press.

Feldman, Jackie. 2005. "In Search of the Beautiful Land of Israel: Israeli Youth Voyages to Poland." In *Israeli Backpackers: From Tourism to Rite of Passage,* ed. Chaim Noy and Erik Cohen, 217–50. Albany: State University of New York Press.

———. 2008. *Above the Death Pits, Beneath the Flag: Youth Voyages to Poland and the Performance of Israeli National Identity.* New York: Berghahn Books.

Feldman, Jeffrey. 2001. "Ghetto Association: Jewish Heritage, Heroin and Racism in Bologna." *Identities: Global Studies in Culture and Power* 8.2 (June): 247–82.

Fincham, Ben, Mark McGuinness, and Lesley Murray, eds. 2010. *Mobile Methodologies.* New York: Palgrave Macmillan.

Fishman, Sylvia Barak. 2002. "Relatively Speaking: Constructing Identity in Jewish and Mixed Married Families." David W. Belin Lecture in American Jewish Affairs. Ann Arbor: Jean & Samuel Frankel Center for Judaic Studies, University of Michigan.

Frank, Gelya. 1997. "Jews, Multiculturalism, and Boasian Anthropology." *American Anthropologist.* 99.4 (December): 731–45.

Frank, Jean. 1996. "I Went Back to Treblinka to Say Kaddish." In *Together,* ed. Alfred Lipson. New York: American Gathering of Jewish Holocaust Survivors.

Frommer, Benjamin. 2011. "Postscript: The Holocaust in Occupied Poland, Then and Now." *East European Politics and Societies* 25.3 (August): 575–80.

Gawron, Edyta. 2005. "Społeczność żydowska w Krakowie w latach 1945–1995." Ph.D diss., Jagiellonian University, Krakow.

Gay, Ruth. 1984. "Inventing the Shtetl." *American Scholar* 53 (Summer): 329–49.

Gebert, Konstanty. 1994a. "Jewish Identities in Poland: New, Old, Imaginary." In *Jewish Identities in the New Europe,* ed. John Webber. London: Littman Library of Jewish Civilization.

———. 1994b. "The Dialectics of Memory in Poland: Holocaust Memorials in Warsaw." In *The Art of Memory: Holocaust Memorials in History,* ed. James Young, 121–30. New York: Jewish Museum with Prestel-Verlag.

———. 1997a. "Divided by a Common Book." In *The Best of Midrasz: The Revival of Jewish Cultural Life in Poland.* New York: American Jewish Committee.

———. 1997b. "Marsz Żywych." *Midrasz* 1.2: 15.

———. 1999a. "Pamięc naiwna." *Midrasz* (September): 29–30.

———. 1999b. "Dial-a-Jew." *Blesok/Shine* 6 (January). M@P multimedia CD-ROM., ed. Igor Isakovski. Macedonia. www.cd-rom.com.mk/mapa/en/index.html.

———. 2001. "In Polen wird man zum Juden gemacht." *Die Welt,* March 15. www.welt .de/daten/2001/03/150315eu240528.htx?print=1.

———. 2002. "Nieautentyczność." *Midrasz* 6.62 (June): 45–46.

———. 2006. "Is It Dangerous to Be a Jew in Poland Today?" In *Difficult Questions in Polish-Jewish Dialogue,* ed. Maciej Kozłowski, Andrzej Folwarczny, Michał Bilewicz, 179–83. Warsaw: Jacek Santorski and Company.

———. 2008. *Living in the Land of Ashes.* Krakow: Austeria.

Gebert, Konstanty, and Helena Datner. 2011. *Jewish Life in Poland: Achievements, Challenges and Priorities since the Collapse of Communism.* September. JPR Report, Institute for Jewish Policy Research.

Gebert, Konstanty, Krzysztof Kobus, and Anna Olej-Kobus. 2009. *Polski Alef-Bet.* Warsaw: Carta Blanca.

Gera, Vanessa. 2010. "Poland Unveils Memorial to Warsaw Ghetto Fighters." *Guardian,* May 13, www.guardian.co.uk/world/feedarticle/9076631 (accessed October 23, 2010).

Gillis, John. 1994. "Memory and Identity: The History of a Relationship." In *Commemorations: The Politics of National Identity,* ed. John Gillis, 3–24. Princeton, N.J.: Princeton University Press.

Gilman, Sander. 1991. *The Jew's Body.* New York: Routledge.

Gitelman, Zvi. 2003. "Collective Memory and Contemporary Polish-Jewish Relations." In *Contested Memories: Poles and Jews During the Holocaust and Its Aftermath,* ed. Joshua D. Zimmerman, 271–90. New Brunswick, N.J.: Rutgers University Press.

Glenn, Susan A. 2002. "In the Blood? Consent, Descent, and the Ironies of Jewish Identity." *Jewish Social Studies* 8.2/3 (Winter/Spring): 139–52.

Glick, Leonard. 1982. "Types Distinct from Our Own: Franz Boas on Jewish Identity and Assimilation." *American Anthropologist* 84: 545–65.

Global Volunteers Poland. 1994. St. Paul, Minn.

Goldberg-Mulkiewicz, Olga. 1980. "Postać Żyda w polskiej rzezbie ludowej." *Polska Sztuka Ludowa* 34.3–4: 219–26.

Goldman, Ari. 1997. "Albright Finds Her Place among History's Victims." *New York Times,* February 9.

Goldman, Karla. 2000. "This Is the Gateway to the Lord: The Legacy of Synagogue Buildings for African American Churches on Cincinnati's Reading Road." In *Black Zion: African American Religious Encounters with Judaism,* ed. Yvonne Chireau and Nathaniel Deutsch, 187–202. New York: Oxford University Press.

Goluboff, Sascha L. 2003. *Jewish Russians: Upheavals in a Moscow Synagogue.* Philadelphia: University of Pennsylvania Press.

Grabowski, Jan. 2003. *"Ja tego Żyda znam!" Szantażowanie Żydów w Warszawie 1939–*

1943. Warsaw: Wydawnictwo IFiS PAN (Institute of Sociology and Philosophy, Polish Academy of Sciences).

———. 2008. "Rewriting the History of Polish-Jewish Relations from a Nationalist Perspective: The Recent Publications of the Institute of National Remembrance." *Yad Vashem Studies* 36.1: 253–70.

———. 2011. *Judenjagd: Hunting Down the Jews, 1942–1945. A Study of One County* [*Judenjagd.* Polowanie na Żydów, 1942–1945. Studium Dziejów Pewnego Powiatu]. Warsaw: Polish Center for Holocaust Research.

Green, James R. 2000. *Taking History to Heart: The Power of the Past in Building Social Movements.* Amherst: University of Massachusetts Press.

Green, Peter S. 2002. "Jewish Museum in Poland: More Than a Memorial." *New York Times,* January 9.

Gross, Jan. 2001. *Neighbors: The Destruction of the Jewish Community in Jedwabne, Poland.* Princeton, N.J.: Princeton University Press.

———. 2006. *Fear: Anti-Semitism in Poland after Auschwitz.* New York: Random House.

Gross, Jan T., and Irena Grudzinska Gross. 2012. *Golden Harvest.* Oxford: Oxford University Press.

Grossman, David. 1989. *See Under: Love.* New York: Picador.

Gruber, Jacob. 1970. "Ethnographic Salvage and the Shaping of Anthropology." *American Anthropologist* 72.6 (December): 1289–99.

Gruber, Ruth Ellen. 1994. "This Year's March of the Living Raises Some Troubling Questions." *Jewish Telegraphic Agency* (April 28): 11.

———. 2002. *Virtually Jewish: Reinventing Jewish Culture in Europe.* Berkeley: University of California Press.

———. 2003. "The Kraków Jewish Culture Festival." *Polin: Studies in Polish Jewry* 16: 357–67.

———. 2014. "Beyond Virtual Jewishness: Monuments to Jewish Experience in Eastern Europe." In *Jewish Cultural Studies IV,* ed. Simon Bronner. Oxford: Littman Library of Jewish Civilization.

Gulinska, Anna. JCC Krakow Shiksa Club. www.facebook.com/group.php?gid =48176897376 (accessed August 15, 2011).

Gupta, Akhil, and James Ferguson, eds. 1997. *Anthropological Locations: Boundaries and Grounds of a Field Science.* Berkeley: University of California Press.

Habib, Jasmin. 2004. *Israel, Diaspora, and the Routes of National Belonging.* Toronto: University of Toronto Press.

Halevi, Yossi Klein. 1993. "Who Owns the Memory?" *Jerusalem Report,* February 25.

Halkowski, Henryk. 2003. *Żydowskie Życie.* Kraków: Austeria.

Halpern, Jodi, and Harvey M. Weinstein. 2004. "Empathy and Rehumanization after Mass Violence." In *My Neighbor, My Enemy,* ed. Eric Stover and Harvey M. Weinstein, 303–22. Berkeley: University of California Press.

Harrison-Kahan, Lori. 2011. *The White Negress.* New Brunswick, N.J.: Rutgers University Press.

Hartman, Saidiya. 2002. "The Time of Slavery." *South Atlantic Quarterly* 101.4 (Fall): 757–76.

Hass, Aaron. 1990. *In the Shadow of the Holocaust: The Second Generation.* Ithaca, N.Y.: Cornell University Press.

Hayden, Delores. 2005. *The Power of Place: Urban Landscapes as Public History.* Cambridge, Mass.: MIT Press.

Hertz, Aleksander. 1988. *The Jews in Polish Culture.* Evanston, Ill.: Northwestern University Press.

Hirsch, Herbert. 1995. *Genocide and the Politics of Memory: Studying Death to Preserve Life.* Chapel Hill: University of North Carolina Press.

Hirsch, Marianne. 2008. "The Generation of Postmemory." *Poetics Today* 29.1 (Spring): 103–28.

Hirsch, Marianne, and Leo Spitzer. 2010. *Ghosts of Home: The Afterlife of Czernowitz in Jewish Memory.* Berkeley: University of California Press.

Hoffman, Charles. 1995. *Gray Dawn: The Jews of Eastern Europe in the Post-Communist Era.* New York: HarperCollins.

Holsey, Bayo. 2008. *Routes of Remembrance: Refashioning the Slave Trade in Ghana.* Chicago: University of Chicago Press.

hooks, bell. 1992. *Black Looks: Race and Representation.* Boston: South End Press.

Howe, Alyssa Cymene. 2001. "Queer Pilgrimage: The San Francisco Homeland and Identity Tourism." *Cultural Anthropology* 16.1 (February): 35–61.

Huener, Jonathan. 2004. *Auschwitz, Poland, and the Politics of Commemoration, 1945–1979.* Athens: Ohio University Press.

Huyssen, Andreas. 2003. *Present Pasts: Urban Palimpsests and the Politics of Memory.* Stanford: Stanford University Press.

InfoFeedback Survey Services Inc. 2010. *March of the Living Canada Long-Term Study 2000–2008 Final Report.* Montreal: InfoFeedback Survey Services Inc.

Ingall, Andrew. 2003. "Making a Tsimes, Distilling a Performance: Vodka and Jewish Culture in Poland Today." *Gastronomica: The Journal of Food and Culture* 4.1 (Winter): 22–27.

Irwin-Zarecka, Iwona. 1989. *Neutralizing Memory: The Jew in Contemporary Poland.* New Brunswick, N.J.: Transaction Publishers.

Jackson, John. 1996. "The Soles of Black Folk: These Reeboks Were Made for Runnin' from the White Man." In *Race Consciousness: African American Studies in the Next Century,* ed. Judith J. Fossett, 177–90. New York: New York University Press.

Jagielski, Jan. 1997. *Niezatarte ślady Getta Warszawskiego* [The Remnants of the Warsaw Ghetto]. Warsaw: Jewish Historical Institute.

Jagielski, Jan, and Robert Pasieczny. 1995. *A Guide to Jewish Warsaw.* Warsaw: Our Roots.

Jenkins, Richard. 2002. *Pierre Bourdieu.* New York: Routledge.

Jędrzejewski, Paweł. 2012. "Mam inny pogląd na "Żyda z pieniądzkiem." *Gazeta Wyborcza,* February 22.

Jochnowitz, Eve. 1998. "Flavors of Memory: Jewish Food as Culinary Tourism in Poland." *Southern Folklore* 55.3: 224–37.

Jutkiewicz, Katarzyna. 1997. "Nie zapomnimy, nie wybaczymy." *Midrasz* 1.2: 15–17.

Kampania Przeciw Homofobii. 2009. "Antyfobia 2009." www.kph.org.pl/pl/allnews/15 -kph/166-antyfobia-2009 (accessed October 23, 2011).

Kapralski, Sławomir. 2011. "(Mis)representations of the Jewish Past in Poland's Memoryscapes: Nationalism, Religion, and Political Economies of Commemoration." In *Curating Difficult Knowledge: Violent Pasts in Public Places,* ed. Erica Lehrer, Cynthia E. Milton, and Monica Eileen Patterson. New York: Palgrave Macmillan.

Karam, John Tofik. 2007. *Another Arabesque: Syrian-Lebanese Ethnicity in Neoliberal Brazil.* Philadelphia: Temple University Press.

Kashti, Or. 2009. "Education Ministry Seeks to Curb Unruly Behavior on Poland Trips." *Haaretz,* June 8. www.haaretz.com/hasen/spages/1090911.html (accessed November 23, 2011).

Kauders, Anthony. 2003. "History as Censure: 'Repression' and 'Philo-Semitism' in Postwar Germany." *History and Memory* 15.1: 49–84.

Keff, Bożena. 2012. "Żyd o imieniu Żyd." *Rzeczpospolita,* May 19.

Kelner, Shaul. 2010. *Tours That Bind: Diaspora, Pilgrimage and Israeli Birthright Tourism.* New York: New York University Press.

Kersten, Krystyna. 1992. *Polacy, Żydzi, komunizm: Anatomia półprawd 1939–1968.* Warsaw: Niezalezna Oficyna Wydawnicza.

Kichelewski, Audrey. 2008. "A Community under Pressure: Jews in Poland, 1957–1967." *Polin: Studies in Polish Jewry* 21: 178–81.

Kidron, Carol. 2003. "Surviving a Distant Past: A Case Study of the Cultural Construction of Trauma Descendant Identity." *Ethnos* 31.4: 513–44.

———. 2009. "Toward an Ethnography of Silence: The Lived Presence of the Past in the Everyday Life of Holocaust Trauma Survivors and Their Descendants in Israel." *Current Anthropology* 50.1 (February): 5–27.

Kirshenblatt-Gimblett, Barbara. 1995. "Introduction." In *Life Is with People: The Culture of the Shtetl,* ed. Mark Zborowski and Elizabeth Herzog, ix–xlviii. New York: Schocken.

———. 1998. *Destination Culture: Tourism, Museums, and Heritage.* Berkeley: University of California Press.

———. 2006. "Exhibitionary Complexes." In *Museum Frictions: Public Cultures/Global Transformations,* ed. Ivan Karp et al., 35–45. Durham, N.C.: Duke University Press.

Kleinman, Arthur, and Joan Kleinman. 1994. "How Bodies Remember: Social Memory and Bodily Experience of Criticism, Resistance and Delegitimation following China's Cultural Revolution." *New Literary History* 25.3 (Summer): 707–34.

Klepczarek, Rafał. 2010. "Skazani posprzątają żydowskie cmentarze." February 3. www .lodz.naszemiasto.pl/artykul/333562,skazani-posprzataja-zydowskie-cmentarze,id ,t.html (accessed August 8, 2011).

Klingenstein, Susanne. 1993. "Visits to Germany in Recent Jewish-American Writing." *Contemporary Literature* 34.3: 538–70.

Kosmin, Barry A., Sidney Goldstein, Joseph Waksberg, Nava Lerer, Ariela Keysar, and Jeffrey Scheckner. 1991. *Highlights of the CJF 1990 National Jewish Population Survey*. New York: Council of Jewish Federations.

Kowalska, Agnieszka. 2009. "Co zobacza młodzi Żydzi w Warszawie." *Gazeta Wyborcza*, April 17.

Kowalska, Beata. 1992. "A Receding World: The Jewish Religious Community in Cracow Today." In *The Jews in Poland*, ed. Andrzej K. Paluch, 369–75. Krakow: Jagiellonian University Research Center on Jewish History and Culture in Poland.

Krajewska, Monika. 1983. *A Time of Stones*. Warsaw: Interpress.

——. 1993. *A Tribe of Stones: Jewish Cemeteries in Poland*. Warsaw: Scientific Publishers.

Krajewski, Stanislaw. 1997. *Żydzi, Judaizm, Polska*. Warsaw: Vocatio.

——. 2006. *Poland and the Jews: Reflections of a Polish Polish Jew*. Krakow: Austeria.

Krog, Antjie. 2000. *Country of My Skull: Guilt, Sorrow, and the Limits of Forgiveness in the New South Africa*. New York: Broadway.

Kugelmass, Jack. 1992. "The Rites of the Tribe: American Jewish Tourism in Poland." In *Museums and Communities: The Politics of Public Culture*, ed. Ivan Karp, Christine Mullen Kreamer, and Steven D. Lavine, 382–427. Washington, D.C.: Smithsonian Institution Press.

——. 1995. "Bloody Memories: Encountering the Past in Contemporary Poland." *Cultural Anthropology* 10.3 (August): 279–301.

——. 1996. "Missions to the Past: Poland in Contemporary Jewish Thought and Deed." In *Tense Past: Cultural Essays in Trauma and Memory*, ed. Paul Antze and Michael Lambek, 199–214. New York: Routledge.

——. 1997. "Jewish Icons: Envisioning the Self in Images of the Other." In *Jews and Other Differences: The New Jewish Cultural Studies*, ed. Jonathan Boyarin and Daniel Boyarin, 30–53. Minneapolis: University of Minnesota Press.

Kugelmass, Jack, and Anna-Maria Orla-Bukowska. 1998. "If You Build It They Will Come: Recreating a Jewish District in Post-Communist Kraków." *City and Society Annual Review* 10.1 (June): 315–53.

Kurin, Richard. 1997. *Reflections of a Culture Broker: A View from the Smithsonian*. Washington, D.C.: Smithsonian Institution Press.

LaCapra, Dominick. 2001. *Writing History, Writing Trauma*. Baltimore: Johns Hopkins University Press.

Landler, Mark. 2012. "Polish Premier Denounces Obama for Referring to a 'Polish Death Camp.'" *New York Times*, May 30.

Lehrer, Erica. 2010. "Can There Be a Conciliatory Heritage?" *International Journal of Heritage Studies* 16.4–5 (July-September): 269–88.

——. 2012. "Relocating Auschwitz: Affective Relations in the Jewish-German-Polish Troika." In *Germany, Poland and Postmemorial Relations: In Search for a Livable*

Past, ed. Kristin Kopp and Joanna Niżyńska, 213–37. New York: Palgrave Macmillan.

———. 2013. "Virtual, Virtuous, Vicarious, Vacuous? Towards a Vigilant Use of Labels (A Response to Ruth Gruber)." In *Jewish Cultural Studies No. 4: Framing Jewish Culture: Boundaries, Representations, and Exhibitions of Ethnic Difference,* ed. Simon J. Bronner. Oxford: Littman Library.

Lehrer, Erica, and Magdalena Waligórska.2013. "Cur(at)ing History: New Genre Art Interventions and the Polish-Jewish Past." *East European Politics and Societies.* February 26.

Lerner, Michael. 2003. *Healing Israel/Palestine: A Path to Peace and Reconciliation.* Berkeley: Tikkun Books.

Lhamon, W. T. Jr. 1998. *Raising Cain: Blackface Performance from Jim Crow to Hip Hop.* Cambridge, Mass.: Harvard University Press.

Liphshiz, Cnaan. 2012. "In Poland, Orthodox and Reform Clash over Control of a Community." JTA.org, November 25, http://www.jta.org/news/article/2012/11/25/3110526/warsaw-sees-birth-of-contested-model-for-reform-orthodox-cooperation, accessed November 27, 2012.

Lott, Eric. 1995. *Love and Theft: Blackface Minstrelsy and the American Working Class.* New York: Oxford University Press.

Lungen, Paul. 2010. "Report Described Impact of March of Living." *Canadian Jewish News,* December 2.

Macdonald, Sharon. 2006. "Undesirable Heritage: Fascist Material Culture and Historical Consciousness in Nuremberg." *International Journal of Heritage Studies,* 12.1.1 (January): 9–28.

———. 2009. *Difficult Heritage: Negotiating the Nazi Past in Nuremberg and Beyond.* New York: Routledge.

Maddocks, Melvin. 1984. "A Most Famous Anthropologist." *Time,* August 27.

Magnus, Shulamit S. 2010. "Good Bad Jews: Converts, Conversion, and Boundary Redrawing in Modern Russian Jewry, Notes toward a New Category." In *Boundaries of Jewish Identity,* ed. Susan Glenn and Naomi Sokoloff, 132–60. Seattle: University of Washington Press.

Makuch, Janusz. 1997. "VII Jewish Cultural Festival in Kraków: To Knock on the Doors of Heaven." *Jidele* (November): 9. Reprinted in *The Best of Midrasz 1998.* New York: American Jewish Committee, Office of European Affairs, 1999.

Malecki, Jan M. 1997. "Cracow Jews in the 19th Century: Leaving the Ghetto." *Acta Poloniae Historica* 76: 85–96.

Malinowski, Bronisław. 1922. "Introduction: The Subject, Method and Scope of This Enquiry." In *Argonauts of the Western Pacific: An Account of Native Enterprise and Adventure in the Archipelagoes of Melanesian New Guinea,* 1–20. London: Routledge and Kegan Paul.

Malkii, Liisa H. 1995. *Purity and Exile: Violence, Memory, and National Cosmology among Hutu Refugees in Tanzania.* Chicago: University of Chicago Press.

March of the Living. 1994. *Guidelines and Handbook for Delegation Heads, Group Leaders, Madrichim, and Students.* Unpublished booklet.

Marcus, George E. 1995. "Ethnography in/of the World System: The Emergence of Multi-Sited Ethnography." *Annual Review of Anthropology* 24 (October): 95–117.

———. 1997. "The Uses of Complicity in the Changing Mise-en-Scene of Anthropological Fieldwork." *Representations* 59 (Summer): 85–108.

Marcus, George E., and Michael M.J. Fischer. 1986. *Anthropology as Cultural Critique: An Experimental Moment in the Human Sciences.* Chicago: University of Chicago Press.

Mayer, Larry. 2002. *Who Will Say Kaddish?: A Search for Jewish Identity in Contemporary Poland.* Syracuse: Syracuse University Press.

Mendelsohn, Daniel. 2002. "What Happened to Uncle Shmiel?" *New York Times,* July 14.

Meng, Michael. 2010. "From Destruction to Preservation: Jewish Sites in Germany and Poland after the Holocaust." *Bulletin of the GHI* (Spring): 45–59.

———. 2011. *Shattered Spaces: Encountering Jewish Ruins in Postwar Germany and Poland.* Cambridge, Mass.: Harvard University Press.

———. Forthcoming. *Silencing Racism in Contemporary Germany: Sarrazin's Deutschland schafft sich ab.*

Meskell, Lynn. 2002. "Negative Heritage and Past Mastering in Archaeology." *Anthropological Quarterly* 75.3 (Summer): 557–74.

Metzger, Deena. 1992. *Writing for Your Life: Discovering the Story of Your Life's Journey.* San Francisco: HarperCollins.

Meyerhoff, Barbara. 1979. *Number Our Days.* New York: Dutton.

Michlic, Joanna Beata. 2008. *Poland's Threatening Other: The Image of the Jew from 1880 to the Present.* Lincoln: University of Nebraska Press.

Michnik, Adam. 2001. "Poles and the Jews: How Deep the Guilt?" Trans. Ewa Zadrzynska. *New York Times,* March 17.

Milerski, Bogusław. 2010. "Holocaust Education in Polish Public Schools: Between Remembrance and Civic Education." *Prospects* 40: 115–132.

Minow, Martha L. 1998. *Between Vengeance and Forgiveness: Facing History after Genocide and Mass Violence.* Boston: Beacon Press.

Misak, Sonia. 1999. "The Jewish Communities of Vienna and Cracow: Communities against All Odds." In *Jewish Centers & Peripheries: Europe between America and Israel Fifty Years after World War II,* ed. S. Ilan Troen, 157–77. New Brunswick, N.J.: Transaction Publishers.

Miyazaki, Hirokazu. 2004. *The Method of Hope: Anthropology, Philosophy, and Fijian Knowledge.* Stanford, Calif.: Stanford University Press.

Murzyn, Monika. 2004. "From Neglected to Trendy: The Process of Urban Revitalization in the Kazimierz District in Cracow." In *Featuring the Quality of Urban Life in Contemporary Cities in Eastern and Western Europe,* ed. Iwona Sagan and Mariusz Czepczyński, 257–74. Gdańsk-Poznań, Poland: Bogucki Wydawnictwo Naukowe.

————. 2006. *Kazimierz: The Central European Experience of Urban Regeneration*. Krakow: International Cultural Centre.

Murzyn-Kupisz, Monika. 2012. "Cultural Quarters as Means of Enhancing the Creative Capacity of Polish Cities? Some Evidence from Krakow." *Quaestiones Geographicae*. Poznań: Adam Mickiewicz University Press.

Nadler, Allan. 1998. "Bibi's Misstep on the Grounds of Auschwitz." *Forward*, May 22.

Niezabitowska, Małgorzata, and Tomasz Tomaszewski. 1986. *Remnants: The Last Jews of Poland*. New York: Friendly Press.

Nora, Pierre. 1989. "Between Memory and History: Les Lieux de Mémoire." *Representations* 26 (Spring): 7–25.

Ochse, Katherina. 1994. "Representations of Jews in the German Media after 1989." In *Reemerging Jewish Culture in Germany: Life and Literature Since 1989*, ed. Sander L. Gilman and Karen Remmler, 113–29. New York: New York University Press.

Offen, Bernard, and Norman G. Jacobs. 2008. *My Hometown Concentration Camp: A Survivor's Account of Life in the Krakow Ghetto and Plaszów Concentration Camp*. London: Vallentine Mitchell and Company.

Opalski, Magdalena, and Israel Bartal. 1992. *Poles and Jews: A Failed Brotherhood*. Waltham, Mass.: Brandeis University Press.

Ost, David. 2005. *The Defeat of Solidarity: Anger and Politics in Postcommunist Europe*. Ithaca, N.Y.: Cornell University Press.

Oz-Salzberger, Fania. 2007. "Spain before Poland." *Haaretz*, April 16.

Partridge, Damani. 2010. "Holocaust Mahnmal (Memorial): Monumental Memory amidst Contemporary Race." *Comparative Studies in Society and History* 52: 820–50.

Passerini, Louisa. 1988. "Antagonisimi nella storia sociale." *Storia e soggettività, Le fonti orali, la memoria*. Firenze: La Nuova Italia.

Patterson, Monica Eileen. 2013. "Ethical Murk: On the Uses of Testimony in Oral Historical Research." In *Off the Record: Unspoken Negotiations in the Practice of Oral History*, ed. Anna Sheftel and Stacey Zembrzycki. New York: Palgrave Macmillan.

Peltz, Rakhmiel. 1998. *From Immigrant to Ethnic Culture: American Yiddish in South Philadelphia*. Stanford, Calif.: Stanford University Press.

Percy, Walker. 1975. "The Loss of the Creature." *The Message in the Bottle*. New York: Farrar, Strauss, and Giroux.

Pfeffer, Anshel. 2010. "IDF Objector Sprays 'Free Gaza' Graffiti on Warsaw Ghetto Wall." *Haaretz*, July 5, www.haaretz.com/jewish-world/news/idf-objector-sprays -free-gaza-graffiti-on-warsaw-ghetto-wall-1.300138 (accessed August 8, 2011).

Pilichowska, Bogdana. 1989. "Krakowskie Zabawki Odpustowe Przedstawiające Żydów." *Polska Sztuka Ludowa* 43.1–2: 129–33.

Pinto, Diana. 2002. "The Jewish Challenges in the New Europe." In *Challenging Ethnic Citizenship: Germany and Israel Perspectives on Immigration*, ed. Daniel Levy and Yfaat Weiss, 239–52. New York: Berghahn Books.

————. 2008. "Can One Reconcile the Jewish World and Europe?" In *The New German*

Jewry and the European Context: The Return of the European Jewish Diaspora, ed. Michal Y. Bodeman, 13–32. New York: Palgrave Macmillan.

Polonsky, Antony, and Joanna B. Michilic. 2004. "Introduction." In *The Neighbors Respond: the Controversy over the Jedwabne Massacre in Poland,* ed. Antony Polonsky and Joanna B. Michlic, 1–49. Princeton, N.J.: Princeton University Press.

Portelli, Alessandro. 1997. *The Battle of Valle Giulia: Oral History and the Art of Dialogue.* Madison: University of Wisconsin Press.

Porter, Brian. 2002. "Explaining Jedwabne: The Perils of Understanding." *Polish Review* 47.1: 23–26.

Powell, Michael. 2006. "In New York, Sparks Fly over Israel." *Washington Post,* October 9.

"Przyjeżdzają" [They are coming]. 1999. *Jidełe: Żydowskie pismo otwarte* 1.8 (June).

Riga, Andy. 1992. "'I'm Angry at What the World Can Do': Student Sobered by Visit to Concentration Camp in Poland." *Montreal Gazette,* June 4.

Roach, Joseph. 1996. *Cities of the Dead: Circum-Atlantic Performance.* New York: Colombia University Press.

Ronen, Shoshana. 1999. "Jak W Polsce Być Żydem." *Gazeta Wyborcza,* September 8.

———. 2007. *Polin—A Land of Forests and Rivers: Images of Poland and Poles in Contemporary Hebrew Literature in Israel.* Warszawa: Wolny Uniwersytet Warszawy.

Rosenfeld, Alvin. 2006. *"Progressive" Jewish Thought and the New Anti-Semitism.* New York: American Jewish Committee.

Rosenson, Claire Ann. 1996. "Jewish Identity Construction in Contemporary Poland: Dialogue Between Generations." *East European Jewish Affairs* 26.2: 67–78.

———. 1997. *Jewish Identity Construction in Contemporary Poland: Influences and Alternatives in Ethnic Renewal.* Ph.D. diss. Ann Arbor: University of Michigan.

Rosenwald, George C., and Richard L. Ochberg. 1992. *Storied Lives: The Cultural Politics of Self-Understanding.* New Haven, Conn.: Yale University Press.

Rothberg, Michael. 2008. *Multidirectional Memory: Remembering the Holocaust in the Age of Decolonization.* Stanford, Calif.: Stanford University Press.

Rothenberg, Jerome. 1974. "The Wedding." In *Poland/1931.* New York: New Directions.

Rudoren, Jodi. 2012. "Proudly Bearing Elders' Scars, Their Skin Says 'Never Forget.'" *New York Times,* September 30.

Salama-Scheer, Yaniv. 2007. "Poles Increasingly Put Off by Visiting Israeli Groups." *Jerusalem Post,* May 24.

Schama, Simon. 1995. *Landscape and Memory.* New York: Alfred A. Knopf.

Schauss, Hans-Joachim. 1987. *Contemporary Polish Folk Artists.* New York: Hippocrene Books.

Scheper-Hughes, Nancy, and Philippe I. Bourgois. 2004. *Violence in War and Peace: An Anthology.* Malden, Mass.: Blackwell.

Schnitzer, Shira. 1998. "The Mistakes of the March." *Jewish Student Press Service: New Voices* (October): 20–36. www.shmoozenet.com/jsps/stories/1098Shira.shtml (accessed February 16, 2011).

Seidman, Naomi. 1998. "Fag-Hags and Bu-Jews: Toward a (Jewish) Politics of Vicarious

Identity." In *Insider/Outsider: American Jews and Multiculturalism,* ed. David Biale, Michael Galchinsky, and Susannah Heschel, 254–68. Berkeley: University of California Press.

Serotta, Edward. 1991. *Out of the Shadows: A Photographic Portrait of Jewish Life in Central Europe Since the Holocaust.* Secaucus, N.J.: Carol Publishing Group.

Shapira, Anita. 1998. "The Holocaust: Private Memories, Public Memory." *Jewish Social Studies* 4.2: 40–58.

Shaw, Stephen, and Joanna Karmowska. 2003. "Conservation and Multiculturalism: Revitalization of Historic Neighborhoods in East London and Cracow." *Proceedings of the US/ICOMOS International Symposium Managing Conflict & Conservation in Historic Cities.* Annapolis, Maryland. www.scribd.com/doc/38101349/Conservation-and-Multiculturalism-Revitalization-of-Historic-Neighborhoods-in-East-London-and-Cracow (accessed December 2, 2011).

Shenhav-Keller, Shelley. 1995. "The Jewish Pilgrim and the Purchase of a Souvenir in Israel." In *International Tourism: Identity and Change,* ed. Marie-Francoise Lanfant, John B. Allcock, and Edward M. Bruner, 143–58. London: SAGE Studies in International Sociology.

Shenker, Noah. 2009. "Embodied Memory. The Institutional Mediation of Survivor Testimony in the United States Holocaust Memorial Museum." In *Documentary Testimonies: Global Archives of Suffering,* ed. Bhaskar Sarkar and Janet Walker, 35–58. New York: Routledge.

Sheramy, Rona. 2007. "From Auschwitz to Jerusalem: Re-enacting Jewish History on the March of the Living." *Polin: Studies in Polish Jewry* 19: 307–26.

Shore, Marci. 1998. "Język, pamięć i rewolucyjna awangarda. Kształtowanie historii powstania w Getcie Warszawskim w latach 1944–1950." *Biuletyn Żydowskiego Instytutu Historycznego* (December): 44–61.

Shryock, Andrew. 1997. *Nationalism and the Genealogical Imagination.* Berkeley: University of California Press.

———. 2004. "In the Double Remoteness of Arab Detroit: Reflections on Ethnography, Culture Work, and the Intimate Disciplines of Americanization." In *Off Stage/On Display: Intimacy and Ethnography in the Age of Public Culture,* ed. Andrew Shryock, 279–316. Stanford, Calif.: Stanford University Press.

Sieg, Katrin. 2002. *Ethnic Drag: Performing Race, Nation, Sexuality in West Germany.* Ann Arbor: University of Michigan Press.

Simhayoff, Alon. 2010. "Israeli Youth Delegations to Poland: Hidden Opportunities." In *Poland: A Jewish Matter,* ed. Kate Craddy, Mike Levy, and Jakub Nowakowski, 181–84. Warsaw: Adam Mickiewicz Institute.

Sinnreich, Helene. 2004. "Reading the Writing on the Wall: A Textual Analysis of Lodz Graffiti." *Religions, State & Society* 32.1 (March): 53–58.

Smith, Craig S. 2007. "In Poland, a Jewish Revival Thrives—Minus Jews." *New York Times,* July 12.

Slutsky, Carolyn. 2007. "March of the Living: Confronting Anti-Polish Stereotypes."

In *Rethinking Poles and Jews: Troubled Past, Brighter Future,* ed. Robert Cherry and Annamaria Orla-Bukowska, 189–96. Lanham, Md.: Rowman and Littlefield.

Snyder, Timothy. 2010. *Bloodlands: Europe Between Hitler and Stalin.* New York: Basic Books.

Sontag, Susan. 2003. *Regarding the Pain of Others.* New York: Picador.

Spielman, Barry. 2000. *The Streets of Kazimierz: A Personal Journey Back to Poland and Jewish Kraków—A Second Generation Perspective.* Unpublished manuscript.

Spund, Marc. 2006. "Reflections on Poland." www.heritageseminars.org/her_ABO _home.shtml (accessed June 20, 2007).

Statistical Yearbook of the Republic of Poland. 2011. Warsaw: Statistical Publishing Establishment. www.stat.gov.pl/gus/5840_2844_ENG_HTML.htm.

Stein, Arlene. 2009. "Trauma and Origins: Post-Holocaust Genealogists and the Work of Memory." *Qualitative Sociology* 32.3: 293–309.

Stein, Rebecca L. 2008. *Itineraries in Conflict: Israelis, Palestinians, and the Political Lives of Tourism.*Durham, N.C.: Duke University Press.

Steinlauf, Michael. 1997. *Bondage to the Dead: Poland and the Memory of the Holocaust.* Syracuse: Syracuse University Press.

———. 2001. "'Dreyfus' and 'Jedwabne.'" Paper delivered at the Association for Jewish Studies Conference Roundtable, "Jedwabne and Beyond." December. Washington, D.C.

Steinmetz, George. 2007. *The Devil's Handwriting: Precoloniality and the German Colonial State in Qingdao, Samoa, and Southwest Africa.* Chicago: University of Chicago Press.

Stier, Oren Baruch. 2003. "Performing Memory: Tourism, Pilgrimage, and the Ritual Appropriation of the Past." In *Committed to Memory: Cultural Mediations of the Holocaust,* 150–90. Amherst: University of Massachusetts Press.

Stillman, Norman. 1991. "Myth, Countermyth, Distortion." *Tikkun* (May–June): 61–64.

Stola, Dariusz. 2000. *Kampania antysojonistyczna w Polsce 1967–1968. (The Anti-Zionist Campaign in Poland, 1967–1968).* Warszawa: Instytut Studiów Politycznych Polskiej Akademii Nauk.

"Swastyka na museum." 2000. *Gazeta Wyborcza,* April 7.

Szaynok, Bozena. 1992. *Jewish Pogrom in Kielce, July 4, 1946.* Wrocław, Poland: Bellona.

Szostkiewicz, Adam. 2006. "Popatrzymy razem na Auschwitz." *Polityka.* August 5.

Szulc, Anna. 2007. "Młodzi Izraelczycy rozrabiają w Polsce." *Przekrój* 19, May 10.

Taglit-Birthright Israel. 2000–2011. "FAQs: What Is Taglit-Birthright Israel?" www .birthrightisrael.com/site/PageServer?pagename=about_faq (accessed June 9, 2011).

Taube, Tad. 2006. "Surprise! Poland Has Become One of Israel's Strongest Allies." Jweekly.com, February 10. www.jweekly.com/article/full/28383/surprise-poland -has-become-one-of-israel-s-strongest-allies (accessed December 19, 2011).

Tencer, Golda, et al. "Shalom Foundation: And I Still See Their Faces . . . " www.shalom .org.pl/eng/index.php?mid=4 (accessed November 23, 2011).

Tighe, Carl. 2001. "*Kazimuh*—Jewish Kraków." *Journal of European Studies* 31: 187–215.

Todorov, Tzvetan. 2001. "The Uses and Abuses of Memory." In *What Happens to History: The Renewal of Ethics in Contemporary Thought,* ed. Howard Marchitello, 11–22. New York: Routledge.

Tokarska-Bakir, Joanna. 2003. "Poland as the Sick Man of Europe? Jedwabne, 'Postmemory,' and Historians." *Eurozine.* www.eurozine.com/article/2003-05-30-tokarska-en.html (accessed December 19, 2011).

———. 2012. "Żyd z pieniądzkiem podbija Polskę." *Gazeta Wyborcza,* February 18.

Towarzystwo Społeczno-Kulturalne Żydów w Polsce. www.tskz.pl (accessed December 18, 2011).

Trigano, Shmuel, 1997. "The Jews and the Spirit of Europe: A Morphological Approach." In *Thinking about the Holocaust after Half a Century,* ed. Alvin Rosenfeld, 300–318. Bloomington: Indiana University Press.

Tzur, Nissan. "Reconstructing Attitudes to Judaism in Poland." *Krakow Post,* September 12, 2012. www.krakowpost.com/article/5840, accessed November 13, 2012.

Tunbridge, J. E., and G. J. Ashworth. 1996. *Dissonant Heritage: The Management of the Past as a Resource in Conflict.* Chichester: John Wiley.

Tuwim, Julian. 1993. *My, Żydzi Polscy . . . (We, Polish Jews . . .).* Warszawa: Fundacja Shalom.

Ulman, Jane. 2006. "Jews in Poland Speak of Shoah Remembrance as a Curse." *Jewish Journal* (April 26). www.jewishjournal.com/articles/item/jews_in_poland_speak_of_shoah_remembrance_as_a_curse_20060421 (accessed December 19, 2011).

———. 2007. "Poland and the Jews: Is It Time to Stop Hating the Country When Positive Changes Are Transforming It?" *Jewish Journal* (June 7). www.jewishjournal.com/articles/item/poland_and_the_jewsis_it_time_to_stop_hating_the_country_when_positive (accessed December 19, 2011).

United Nations Educational, Scientific and Cultural Organization. 2007. "World Heritage Committee Approves Auschwitz Name Change." whc.unesco.org/en/news/363 (accessed June 9, 2011).

United States Department of State. 2011. International Religious Freedom Report. Bureau of Democracy, Human Rights, and Labor. www.state.gov/j/drl/rls/irf/religiousfreedom/index.htm?dlid=192849.

Ury, Scott. 2000. "Who, What, When, Where and Why Is Polish Jewry? Envisioning, Constructing, and Possessing Polish Jewry." *Jewish Social Studies* 6.3: 205–28.

Vasagar, Jeevan, and Julian Borger. 2011. "A Jewish Renaissance in Poland." *The Guardian,* April 7. www.guardian.co.uk/world/2011/apr/07/jewish-renaissance-poland (accessed August 12, 2011).

Waligórska, Magdalena. 2008. "Fiddler as a Fig Leaf: The Politicization of Klezmer in Poland." *Osteuropa: Impulses for Europe,* 227–38.

Wardi, Dina. 1992. *Memorial Candles: Children of the Holocaust.* New York: Tavistock/Routledge.

Wasserstein, Bernard. 1996. *Vanishing Diaspora: The Jews in Europe since 1943.* Cambridge, Mass.: Harvard University Press.

Weinbaum, Laurence. 1998. *Polish Jews: A Postscript to the 'Final Chapter'?* Jerusalem: Institute of the World Jewish Congress, Policy Study no. 14.

Weissman, Gary. 2004. *Fantasies of Witnessing: Postwar Efforts to Experience the Holocaust.* Ithaca, N.Y.: Cornell University Press.

Wieviorka, Annette. 2006. *The Era of Witness.* Ithaca, N.Y.: Cornell University Press.

Wiśniewski, Tomasz, Ellen Elliott, and David Elliott. 1998. *Jewish Bialystok and Surroundings in Eastern Poland.* Ipswich: Ipswich Press.

Wodziński, Marcin. 2011. "Jewish Studies in Poland." *Journal of Modern Jewish Studies* 10.1: 101–18.

Wolf, Diane L. 2007. "Holocaust Testimony: Producing Post-memories, Producing Identities." In *Sociology Confronts the Holocaust: Memories and Identities in Jewish Diasporas,* ed. Judith M. Gerson and Diane L. Wolf, 154–75. Durham, N.C.: Duke University Press.

Zborowski, Marc, and Elizabeth Herzog. 1952. *Life Is with People: The Jewish Little-Town of Eastern Europe (The Culture of the Shtetl).* New York: International Universities Press.

Zerubavel, Yael. 1995. *Recovered Roots: Collective Memory and the Making of Israeli National Tradition.* Chicago: University of Chicago Press.

Zimmerman, Josh. 2003. "Introduction." In *Contested Memories: Poles and Jews during the Holocaust and Its Aftermath,* ed. Joshua D. Zimmerman, 1–18. New Brunswick, N.J.: Rutgers University Press.

Zubrzycki, Genevieve. 2006. *The Crosses of Auschwitz: Nationalism and Religion in Post-Communist Poland.* Chicago: University of Chicago Press.

———. 2011. "History and the National Sensorium: Making Sense of Polish Mythology." *Qualitative Sociology* 34: 21–57.

NEW ANTHROPOLOGIES OF EUROPE

MATTI BUNZL AND MICHAEL HERZFELD,
EDITORS

ERICA T. LEHRER

is Associate Professor in the History and Sociology-Anthropology Departments at Concordia University in Montreal, Canada, where she holds the Canada Research Chair in Post-Conflict Memory, Ethnography, and Museology. She is the founding director of Concordia's Center for Ethnographic Research and Exhibition in the aftermath of Violence (CEREV).

CPSIA information can be obtained at www.ICGtesting.com
Printed in the USA
LVOW060746180613

338965LV00003B/6/P